Shiva Rahbaran was born in Tehran. She was eight years old when the last Persian monarch, Mohammad Reza Shah Pahlavi, was forced to leave Iran giving way to the foundation of the Islamic Republic. Together with her family she left Iran for Germany in 1984, where she studied literature and political science at the Heinrich-Heine-University Düsseldorf. She continued her studies at Oxford University, where she obtained her doctoral degree (DPhil) in English literature. She has published several books on the relationship between art and freedom including *The Paradox of Freedom* and *Iranian Writers Uncensored: Democracy, Freedom, and the Word in Contemporary Iran*. She lives in London.

'Iranian cinema continues to twist, turn and fascinate. It now looks like a mighty river upon which every new generation of critics and scholars casts a new look. Shiva Rahbaran's *Iranian Cinema Uncensored* is an indispensable new addition to an already rich and diversified body of literature on Iranian cinema. Thorough, probing, insightful and fresh in her interpretative prowess, Shiva Rahbaran does not just update our understanding of Iranian cinema since the 1979 Revolution. Through her provocative interviews with some leading film-makers, she actually occasions a complete reassessment of what we have known about Iranian cinema. A beautiful read and full of joyous insights.'

Hamid Dabashi, Hagop Kevorkian Professor of Iranian Studies and Comparative Literature, Columbia University

'An informative book on post-revolutionary Iranian cinema and its development. Rahbaran provides engaging conversations with major figures in Iranian cinema such as Kiarostami, Bayzaie, Panahi, Bani-Etemad, Mehrjui, Farmanara and Majidi. Reflecting on film-makers' own work and the condition of film-making in Iran, they cover several issues, including the commercial cinema, the New Wave, the role of government and semi-government institutions and policy makers in shaping the contemporary cinema, the portrayal of women in film, and censorship.'

Mehrnaz Saeed-Vafa, Professor, Cinema Art and Science, Columbia College, Chicago

IRANIAN CINEMA UNCENSORED

CONTEMPORARY FILM-MAKERS
SINCE THE ISLAMIC REVOLUTION

SHIVA RAHBARAN

TRANSLATED BY
MARYAM MOHAJER AND SHIVA RAHBARAN

I.B. TAURIS
LONDON · NEW YORK

Published in 2016 by
I.B.Tauris & Co. Ltd
London • New York
www.ibtauris.com

Every attempt has been made to gain permission for the use of the
images in this book. Any omissions will be rectified in future editions.

References to websites were correct at the time of writing.

International Library of the Moving Image 36

ISBN (hardback): 978 1 78453 417 2
ISBN (paperback): 978 1 78453 418 9
eISBN: 978 0 85772 872 2

A full CIP record for this book is available from the British Library
A full CIP record is available from the Library of Congress

Library of Congress Catalog Card Number: available

Typeset in New Baskerville by A. & D. Worthington, Newmarket, Suffolk
Printed and bound in Great Britain by T.J. International Ltd,
Padstow, Cornwall

CONTENTS

INTRODUCTION

New Iranian Cinema in its Cultural, Historical and Political Context

'Dear Sirs,
We are staying right here!
Cinema will stay here because the people want it to.
Feel free to leave our cinema!'[1]

THE ISLAMIC REVOLUTION'S ATTITUDE TO THE ART OF CINEMA was thrown into sharp relief by the arson attack that destroyed Abadan's Cinema Rex on the eve of the uprisings in 1978, killing over 300 viewers.[2] For the Islamic reformers cinema was counter-revolutionary and thus its material embodiment deserved to be destroyed. This book will concentrate on the films that have been made in Iran since that tragic event and will examine, from the viewpoint of film-makers living and working in Iran, how cinema has been able to thrive in such a hostile environment.

In December 2011 the Ministry of Culture and Islamic Guidance (the Ershad) ordered the closure of the House of Cinema, an association to which 6,000 independent Iranian film-makers belonged. The institute had come under pressure after it condemned in an open letter the regime's punitive measures against some of its members who had allegedly cooperated with the BBC.[3] The House of Cinema was one of the oldest civil cultural societies to have been founded in Iran since the Islamic Revolution of 1979, which overthrew Mohammad Reza Shah Pahlavi and ended 2,500 years of monarchy in Iran. Under the leadership of Ayatollah Ruhollah Khomeini, Iran underwent a dramatic transition almost overnight, from a loosely pro-Western regional power to an Islamic state whose mission was, it seems, to eradicate all Western values from society.

The first decade after the revolution (during which the eight-year-long war with Saddam Hussein's Iraq took place) was one of the most brutal and bloody periods in the history of modern Iran. But with the end of the war and Khomeini's death in 1989, the rigidity of Islamic ideology began to soften a little. This created some room in which civil cultural institutions and associations were able to grow. The House of Cinema, founded in 1989, was one of them. It quickly became a place where film-makers could gather and exchange ideas, and thus provided a fertile ground for cultivating the art of cinema. Above all, it provided solidarity and support to film-makers living under a regime that was and still is intrinsically and demonstrably against independent artistic activity. Since the 2009 rebellion, the uprising that came to be known as the 'Green Movement',[4] which was triggered by the fraudulent elections that led to Mahmoud Ahmadinejad winning a second term, the censorship policies of the regime regarding cinema and all other arts have become more stringent and the climate for creativity has become increasingly difficult. The regime has openly declared war on cinema in the last few years, and its commonest tactics include refusing applications for making and screening films, withdrawing previously approved screening licences for films and abusing many film-makers publicly as 'counter-revolutionaries', 'agents of the decadent West', 'a danger to national security' and 'agitators of public opinion'. This has forced several film-makers – Bahram Beyzaie, Bahman Ghobadi and Mohsen Makhmalbaf among others – into exile or made it impossible for them to make films in Iran, as is the case with Abbas Kiarostami, while others, such as Mohammad Rasoulof and Jafar Panahi, have even been imprisoned.

Nevertheless, since the Iranian revolution and despite all past and recent pressures on film-makers, cinema – more than any other artform – has played a key role in manifesting and even shaping Iranian identity on the global platform. This is the main theme around which all the interviews and observations in this book revolve. An especially interesting aspect is that most Iranian film-makers conceive their role as a social one, in the sense that they see themselves as artists with a commitment to the society in which they live. The credo 'art for art's sake' does not work for them. Most of them see film-making as a form of resistance to the authorities in Iran – be it in the shape of a royal Shadow of God, as under the shah, or of the Prophet's *locum tenens*, as under the regime of the mullahs. Especially after the revolution, and as harsh censorship policies proliferated, these film-makers started to make films that tried to convey the reality in which they lived. Whereas under the shah this resistance manifested itself in escapist and surrealist films, such as those of Ebrahim Golestan and Sohrab Shahid Saless (both of whom went into self-imposed exile in Europe before the revolution took place), after the revolution realism became the main subject of the cineastes. In a way, the revolution broke down the barriers between artists and the society in which they lived. Whether reality was shown 'poetically', as in the works of Dariush Mehrjui and Barham Beyzaie, or realistically, as in the films of Rakhshan Bani-Etemad and Jafar Panahi, the subject matter of post-revolutionary film-makers has been Iran and its people from the viewpoint of artists who see themselves as part of that reality.

One important outcome of this intense artistic preoccupation with society, despite harsh censorship under the Islamic regime, has been the transformation of the *engagé* artist into a political and intellectual figure, in the sense that artistic commitment inevitably becomes social and political commitment. This has always been the case in Iran: the imprisoned film-maker Panahi embodies the artist as a freedom fighter, while writers, such as the *grande dame* of poetry in Iran, Simin Behbahani, or the novelist Amir Hassan Cheheltan, are sources of intellectual and moral resistance under the repressive regime.[5] This politicization of the arts is not confined to contemporary Iran but is encountered in all totalitarian regimes where the project of a modern democratic state has failed. The imprisoned Chinese poet and writer and former head of the Independent Chinese PEN, Liu Xiaobo, is a good example of this. Under censorship, the artist is forced into resistance in order to make a truthful work of art; resistance in turn morphs the artist into a voice of the repressed and ultimately into a political figure. This kind of politicization increased immensely after the Islamic Revolution as censorship criteria became much stricter and their scope became wider, especially in cinema – a medium that could reach many more people, both in and outside Iran, than could other forms of art. Every aspect of film-making – from the seeding of a subject to production, filming and distribution – is permeated by politics. Financing and distribution are especially sensitive issues in Iran today, as international fame has made quite a few film-makers of interest to Western and multinational companies but at the same time vulnerable to the punitive policies of the Ministry of Culture and Islamic Guidance, which condemns such collaborations as 'anti-revolutionary'. On the other hand, the Islamic Republic of Iran benefits internationally from the success of these film-makers and can use them as a means of propaganda and self-promotion. At international festivals the regime attempts to 'sell' its Islamic ideology – primarily to the suspicious West – as a promoter of free artistic expression and high culture. Thus many successful domestic film-makers are seen simultaneously as 'instruments of the decadent West' *and* 'exporters of the values of the Islamic Republic' by the regime. For these film-makers, preserving their independence and their proximity to the people of Iran and to viewers worldwide is a Herculean task that many master resourcefully.

The success story of Iranian film-makers in this most adverse environment brings us to the main concern of this book, namely, how New Iranian Cinema has succeeded in acquiring such world-wide acclaim.

After the revolution, Iranian cinema had to grapple not only with official censorship but also with a decrease in the number of film theatres, many of which were closed down or converted into shopping malls and offices after the fanatic mullahs began to see them as breeding grounds for decadence and Western influence. Despite all this, Iranian cinema, especially the auteur variety, has been able to establish a strong reputation and achieve success both nationally and internationally.

One of the reasons for this considerable success – especially compared to the meagre success of Iranian writers and painters internationally – is the medium in which film-makers work. It is much easier, faster and – in the age of internet downloads in a country that does not abide by international copyright laws – cheaper to 'consume' films. In comparison, works of literature that attempt to break into European and English-speaking markets face manifold difficulties. For a Persian book to be 'consumed' in the West, the manuscript has to be translated, published and promoted in a foreign book market, where, unless it achieves substantial publicity, it is unlikely to reach a wide readership. Furthermore, film has a particular immediacy and, in a culture of instant gratification, is much more accessible to a broad audience. However, what is especially interesting about post-revolutionary Iranian cinema is not the success of commercial 'entertainment' films but the popularity of auteur cinema.

However, the majority of the interviewees who have contributed to this book point out that the 1979 revolution should not be seen as the beginning of Iranian art cinema, as regime-friendly scholars and critics would have the world believe, in an attempt to obliterate the artistic endeavour of film-makers before the revolution. Renowned film-makers such as Golestan, Shahid Saless, Beyzaie, Kimiavi, Ghaffari, Mehrjui, Kiarostami, Naderi, Farmanara and Ovanessian, most of whom represent the backbone of New Iranian Cinema today, started their careers in the 1960s and 1970s, some 20 years before the revolution took place. These film-makers wanted to stand up to the commercially successful but aesthetically and morally risible 'Film Farsi'. This term refers to cheap Iranian reproductions of popular Egyptian, Turkish or Bollywood romantic films that feature scantily dressed young female dancers, blood, kitsch music and excessive alcohol consumption in seedy cafés.

Most young intellectual film-makers felt that such productions blunted the senses of the viewer and were just as serious an obstacle to art cinema as official censorship. Whereas the aim of Film Farsi was to offer viewers an escape from reality through fast and cheap entertainment, the primary concern of the new film-makers was to depict reality. Many of their films were experimental. They used both a realistic, almost journalistic language, as well as a surreal, almost poetic one. Shahid Saless portrayed reality in strongly minimalist films with little or no plot, while Kiarostami tried to convey the everyday lives of deprived children. The majority of such experiments employed a symbolic – almost coded – language both because of censorship, which did not allow film-makers to project a critical view of social reality as they saw it, and also because of the influence of contemporary European experimentalist cinema. Indeed, in the two decades before the revolution, many Iranian film-makers looked to European (mostly French) experimentalism, which had little to do with the Iranian reality.

After the revolution of 1979 Iranian cinema managed not only to survive the Islamization of cultural institutions, the hostility of Islamic fanatics and fundamentalists, and harsh censorship measures, but to shine on the international scene. As Rakhshan Bani-Etemad points out in her interview, the clash between 'Islamic intellectuals' and 'Islamic fundamentalists' was a matter 'of life and death' for Iranian cinema. Islamic intellectuals believed that cinema, despite being associated with the decadent West, could be used to propagate Islamic values, whereas fundamentalists categorically rejected any artform that used images, since, in their eyes, the making and showing of images went against the Islamic understanding of art itself, which forbids the reproduction of images of God's creatures. Bani-Etemad believes that it was in the fissure caused by the clash between these two groups that New Iranian Cinema found fertile ground on which to grow.

This growth came about mainly because of certain views that intellectual film-makers and their adversaries, namely, Islamic ideologues, happened to share. Both groups were vehemently against Film Farsi and Hollywood movies. Most interviewees mention this shared view as the key to understanding the success of New Iranian Cinema after the revolution. Mohammad Beheshti, the former head of the Farabi Cinema Foundation,[6] for example, sees the revolution as a 'cleansing agent' that cleared out the shallow, decadent, sex-obsessed Iranian and foreign productions and gave intellectual Iranian films the opportunity to grow. He believes that, at that time, this could only have come about through a cultural revolution in Iran, especially with regard to the dominance of American and multinational production and distribution companies. He goes on to point out that, above all, the revolution made way for the liberation of women, in that it freed them from being seen as 'sex objects'. Without Islamic censorship the chances of Iranian actresses portraying strong characters, instead of sex objects reduced to dancing on tables in sordid cabarets or crying while men fought over them, would have been infinitesimal. Another important outcome, Beheshti goes on to say, was the ban on Hollywood and European films. This made it difficult for Iranian film-makers to emulate foreign schools and modes of filmmaking and forced them to concentrate on the reality of the society in which they lived and to try to use whatever means time and place put at their disposal. Thus the revolution provided the right conditions for the 're-education' of already established and active directors, and for the emergence of new autodidacts. Iranian filmmakers, he argues, now saw that it was possible to acquire success nationally and internationally without having to follow the lead of the capitalist entertainment market, which more often than not forces film-makers to compromise their aesthetic and moral values for the sake of profitability.

Significantly, however, for the majority of the film-makers interviewed here this view is nothing but a sham. Most of them – especially those who had been active before the revolution, such as Kiarostami and Beyzaie – dismiss Beheshti's view as no more than a justification of censorship and an attempt to erase and rewrite the rich past of Iranian film-making, which goes way back before the revolution. Beyzaie goes so far as to consider this view a trick by which the mullahs and those who profit from them try to portray the revolution as the source of all cultural and moral virtue. He and others vehemently reject the idea that the revolution was essential for the progress of auteur films in Iran; on the contrary, they see the revolution as an obstacle that threw back the cinema movement – which had already been flourishing more than a decade before – by at least ten years. Moreover, they draw attention to the fact that film-makers had to wait at least seven or eight years after the revolution before internationally acclaimed films, such as Beyzaie's *Bashu, the Little Stranger* (produced in 1986 and released in 1989) or Kiarostami's *Where is the Friend's Home?* (1987), could be made and screened. From their viewpoint the revolution has actually succeeded in what they always feared, namely, erasing the pre-revolutionary history of the arts in Iran (and to some extent its cultural history) from the world's memory. They are aware that this kind of obliteration is a characteristic of all revolutions. Nevertheless, what disappoints them greatly is that many renowned film critics and scholars in the West contribute unwittingly to this process by supporting the view that the revolution was pivotal in the development of Iranian cinema. In the meantime, the regime continues to suppress film-makers in Iran while posing as the patron of Iranian cinema in the eyes of the world. Despite all this, the observer of the cinema scene in Iran cannot overlook the common grounds on which both auteur films and the aesthetics of Islamic intellectualism thrive, namely, the vehement rejection of Hollywood and Film Farsi, which were dominant before the revolution. It should be noted that over the past two decades both Hollywood and Film Farsi have reinvaded the living rooms of the Iranian viewers in an unprecedented way via satellite dishes and underground pirate copies. There is hardly any stopping them, although the Revolutionary Guards impose periodic bans on these dishes and dismantle them by force.[7]

What is striking about Iranian auteur cinema is its success both amongst 'common viewers' and intellectual reviewers not only in Iran but internationally. Dariush Mehrjui's *The Cow* (produced in 1969 and released in 1971; also known by its original title *Gaav*),[8] the first Iranian film to win the International Critics' Award at the 1971 Venice Biennale, put Iranian film on the fast track to success at international festivals. Likewise Beyzaie's *Bashu, the Little Stranger* and Kiarostami's *Where is the Friend's Home?* marked the beginning of a golden age in post-revolutionary Iranian cinema, which was to reach a high point first at the 1997 Cannes Film Festival, where Kiarostami's *Taste of Cherry* (1997) won the *Palme d'Or*, and later on at the 2012 Academy Awards, where Farhadi's *A Separation* (2011) won the Oscar for best foreign film. These success stories show a continuity in the development of Iranian cinema up to the present day, four decades after Mehrjui shone at the Venice Biennale. The new generation of film-makers such as Bahman Ghobadi, Mani Haghighi, Sadaf Foroughi, Mona Zand Haghighi, Asghar Farhadi and Babak Payami, among others, are, given their age, children of the revolution in the truest sense and are still carrying the torch of the older generation, which laid the foundations of New Iranian Cinema over five decades ago.

The interviews in this book present many arguments on the advantages and disadvantages of the revolution for New Iranian Cinema. One thing on which all film-makers are agreed is the idea of the revolution as a useful and sensationalist means of propaganda for Iranian cinema. The Western media, they argue, lives off sensation. Both the revolution and its consequences – from the hostage-taking at the American embassy in Tehran[9] to the bloody eight-year war with Iraq under Saddam Hussein – delivered nourishment to newspapers and television. The images of women wrapped in black *chadors* punching their fists into the air and chanting 'Down with America!' alongside angry bearded men outside Western embassies brought the revolution into the living rooms and cinemas of the West. No matter how negative its perception in the West, the revolution provided great marketing potential for Iranian cinema, and Iranian film-makers have been able to use this to good effect. On the one hand, they have delivered beautiful images of a utopian, peaceful countryside, hardly touched by modern urbanization (as in Kiarostami's *Koker Trilogy* made between 1987 and 1994), thus nullifying the negative image of Iran in the Western media. On the other hand, however, they continuously confirm the West's idea of post-revolutionary Iran by making highly realistic films that depict the harsh life of city dwellers and their struggle to survive corruption, exploitation, repression, poverty and drugs, as in the films of Bani-Etemad (*Mainline,*

2006) or Panahi (*The Circle*, 2000; *Crimson Gold*, 2003). In this manner, these film-makers show that, in contrast to their government and its backward policies, they are extremely well acquainted with the rules of modern cinema: through their beautiful images of a 'demonized' Iran they force viewers to *doubt* the image of the country in the general media. Whereas religion and other pre-Enlightenment concepts were based on certainties, enlightened, modern concepts rest on doubt. Modern man constantly falsifies, re-evaluates and reinvents his or her conception of (relative) reality. Through critical films that show the backwardness and repression of contemporary Iran, Iranian film-makers signal that they are committed to the values of modernity and are thus on the side of (largely Western) democracies. In that way, once they have sown doubt in their domestic and international viewers' minds, Iranian film-makers immediately confirm the advantages of Western values and way of life.

Some film-makers interviewed in this book are, however, not pleased with this perception of Iranian cinema in the West. Directors such as Tahmineh Milani and Majid Majidi believe that the way in which such films criticize Iran does not create solidarity with – and consequently respect for – Iranian film-makers amongst international viewers. They believe that by watching images of backwardness, repression and poverty in Iran, the West confirms its feeling of superiority towards the East and welcomes such films only for that reason. As a result, they argue, Iranian film-makers have been receiving – probably involuntarily – the admiration of the 'enemies of the Islamic East' in the West. This preoccupation with Islam and its philosophy of aesthetics is perhaps the key to understanding the degree of attention given to the post-revolutionary Iranian cinema in the West and the rest of the world.[10] Considering that in Islamic philosophy reproducing the images of living things is forbidden or only allowed in exceptional circumstances, films coming out of the Islamic Republic are a conundrum in the eyes of Western viewers and this makes them especially interesting. This of course is a plausible view, considering that in the early days of the revolution many film prints – especially those that portrayed the anti-Islamic, decadent way of life – were destroyed by fanatical

Islamists. However, the Leader of the Islamic Revolution, Ayatollah Khomeini, realized the huge potential of this medium for the propagation of the revolution's ideology and, as a result, from the very early days of the republic, the state never forbade in practice the reproduction of moving images. The Iranian revolution was primarily inspired by Shi'a ideology, which reflects the progressive changes in the interpretation of the Qur'an that have been made over time. Islamic thought and way of life are reinterpreted constantly by clerical scholars and jurists who can derive new legal norms from the Qur'an and Mohammad's teachings according to their personal understanding of daily life, political developments and culture.[11] Khomeini's interpretations and guidance were criticized by many other clerical scholars as too modern. However, because of his position as Leader of the revolution, images as a medium, and the cinema in particular, were very soon accepted as ways of propagating Islamic values and furthering the revolution.[12]

After his victorious return to Tehran in January 1979, Khomeini gave a historic speech at the Behesht-e Zahra Cemetery, in which he declared that the revolution was not opposed to cinema, as cinema can facilitate the Islamic enlightenment of the people and especially the youth, but he was vehemently opposed to the corrupting influence of pre-revolutionary cinema, particularly the influence it exerted on the young.[13] From now on the clergy would ensure that cinema would be used as an educational medium. In his interview in this book, Mehrjui confirms Khomeini's position towards the cinema, recalling that the Ayatollah on more than one occasion pointed to Mehrjui's internationally acclaimed film *The Cow* as an example of an educational film.[14] This suggests that, paradoxically, through its Islamization, Iranian cinema was rescued from the slaughter that awaited it at the hands of Muslim fundamentalists.

In fact, a number of cultural institutions for the promotion of films that complied with Islamic guidelines were founded during the early turbulent years after the revolution. Almost all the interviewees in this book agree that the most important of these was the Farabi Cinema Foundation, which was highly influential, especially under Mohammad Beheshti's leadership (1986–93), and played a key role in the promotion and distribution of Iranian cinema domestically and worldwide. All interviewed directors mention the Farabi's influence on their careers after the revolution; however, they evaluate it in quite different ways. Some, such as Majidi and Hatamikia, see the Farabi (especially during the Beheshti years) as an indispensable broker between the Ministry of Culture and Islamic Guidance and the film-makers; the Farabi, they argue, shielded them from the censors' attempts to butcher their films. Others, such as Bani-Etemad, believe that the golden days of the foundation under Beheshti, who tirelessly supported and promoted Iranian cinema worldwide, are long gone. Yet others, such as Kiarostami and Beyzaie, see the Farabi Cinema Foundation as the 'respectable face' of the Ministry of Culture and Islamic Guidance, as an instrument that constantly justifies the censorship policies of the regime and at the same time exploits films to promote the image of the regime as a patron of culture. From the viewpoint of this latter group, the Farabi has obstructed rather than promoted the progress of Iranian cinema, which had already begun to make its mark in the world more than 15 years before the revolution. All film-makers, however, see the Farabi as influential, whether positively or negatively, in the development of Iran's post-revolutionary cinema. That is why it was important for me to give the controversial former head of the Farabi, Mohammad Beheshti, the opportunity to have his say on the foundation's role in the development of Iranian cinema after the revolution.

What is important for the reader to bear in mind when reading these interviews is that they were carried out in contemporary Iran, whose development as a modern, democratic country has been arrested over the last 30-odd years as a result of the 1979 revolution. In a way Iran has existed 'outside' global time in the last three and a half decades, whether under Khomeini, or Rafsanjani, or Khatami and his 'dialogue of the civilizations' or under the fraudulently re-elected Ahmadinejad or in Rouhani's post-nuclear talks era. This sense of frozen time is a direct consequence of the Islamic Revolution that brought a totalitarian regime to power instead of the promised democratic one. Thus those who have been interviewed in this book, like the interviewees of my last book, *Iranian*

Writers Uncensored, point out that their situation, despite a succession of different administrations, has not changed at all. Some feel imprisoned in a bubble of time that froze over three decades ago or that, within Iran, time ticks to a different clock from that on the outside.[15] Most of them point out that the ideology of the Islamic Revolution, which was unmasked as an instrument of repression quite early on and has long lost whatever moral values it had in its early days, has been stifling their artistic expression since the birth of the Islamic Republic. That is why it would not have mattered whether they were asked their opinions yesterday or 30 years ago.

The interviews in this book were conducted during Mahmoud Ahmadinejad's two presidential terms and in the course of many trips to Iran. The first one was conducted in 2007 with Jafar Panahi, less than 18 months before the Green Movement uprising, and the last one some four years later with Bahram Beyzaie, just a few months before he reluctantly left his homeland for Berkeley. In the interim, Khatami's attempts to introduce a 'dialogue of the civilizations' clashed dramatically against the ideology of the guardians of the Islamic Revolution, while Ahmadinejad was re-elected in one of the most dubious elections of the last 30 years (even by the standards of the Islamic regime and its famous election engineering practices). It was that election that led to the Green Movement, the largest uprising in Iran since the 1979 revolution.[16] Once again, the ugly images of bearded men treading on the hopes of the Iranian people and the footage of protesters bleeding to death invaded living rooms around the world; once again Iran was the topic of the day and its negative image provided publicity for New Iranian Cinema at international festivals. At the same time, the lives of those film-makers who openly condemned repression in Iran on these international platforms were endangered. The imprisonment of film-maker Jafar Panahi is the most prominent example of the risks that speaking out can entail.

The election of Hassan Rouhani in 2013 led to high hopes not only amongst ordinary people but also artists, writers and intellectuals. The historic agreement made in Vienna in July 2015 between Iran and the 5+1 powers (US, UK, Russia, China, France and Germany) to curtail Iran's nuclear ambitions and as a 'reward' end the stifling sanctions against Iran marked the beginning of a new chapter in the post-revolutionary relations of this country with the West.[17] Many intellectuals and ordinary people already see the beginning of an opening towards the West that will not only put an end to the country's – not always voluntary – isolation from the world community but possibly modify the political and ideological line of the regime and thus gradually change its oppressive policies towards the population.

For many the rapprochement between Iran and the West and the country's return to the world community above all meant that Iran was on the way to a liberalization of life an art. However, up to this day none of these hopes has materialized. The leaders of the Green Movement, Mir-Hossein Mousavi, his wife Zahra Rahnavard and Mehdi Karroubi, are still under house arrest. Two months before the international sanctions against Iran were lifted, the director Keyvan Karimi was sentenced to six years in prison and 223 lashes for 'anti-regime activities'. Panahi's 20-year ban from artistic activity has yet to be lifted (although this has not deterred him from making films under cover in Iran which are shown at foreign film festivals)[18] and great masters such as Kiarostami and Beyzaie have either stopped making films in Iran or left the country. Iran thus continues to be one of the most restrictive countries regarding freedom of the arts.

At this point it should be noted that these interviews are neither a critique nor an evaluation of the works of the film-makers who took part in them. The interviewees were chosen solely on the basis of their public prominence in Iran and on the international scene. All interviewees were asked similar questions that form a thematic framework and provide the reader with points of comparison. Their answers serve to outline their role in portraying and creating the post-revolutionary Iranian identity.

Shiva Rahbaran
London

MOHAMMAD BEHESHTI

The Role of Post-Revolutionary Institutions in the Development of Iranian Cinema

AMONG THOSE INTERVIEWED IN THIS BOOK, Mohammad Beheshti is the only one who is not a film-maker. However, an interview with him seemed appropriate, as Beheshti was head of the Farabi Cinema Foundation for over a decade during the most fruitful years of New Iranian Cinema. Films that became the vanguard of post-revolutionary Iranian cinema were made under his administration in the 1980s and 1990s – such as Beyzaie's *Bashu, the Little Stranger* (1989), Kiarostami's *Where is the Friend's Home?* (1987), Mehrjui's *Hamoun* (1990), Bani-Etemad's *Nargess* (1992) and Makhmalbaf's *Salaam Cinema* (1995), to name but a few. From his point of view, the revolution proved highly conducive to the success of Iranian films worldwide, as it forced art film-makers to distance themselves from pre-revolutionary intellectual symbolism on the one hand, and quelled the vulgar cinema of commercial film-makers on the other. Thus the revolution brought Iranian cinema back to reality and compelled film-makers to focus on everyday life.

In the following interview, Beheshti talks above all about censorship. In his eyes, censorship in general – and Islamic censorship in particular – is one of the most important topics of discussion on Iranian cinema among Western critics and scholars. Beheshti observes that while these scholars turn a blind eye to the history of

censorship in the West and its sundry official and unofficial mechanisms, they see film-making (in fact, all art and literature) in Iran
solely through the prism of Islamic censorship. As far as censorship
is concerned, Beheshti believes that, especially in the late 1980s
and early 1990s, the Farabi was the only institution that was able to
mediate between film-makers and the (sometimes nonsensically)
restrictive policies of the Ministry of Culture and Islamic Guidance
(the Ershad). He believes that, as a mediator, the Farabi was able to
turn the destructive powers of censorship into creative mechanisms
that enabled Iranian art film-makers to work. In his view, the
Farabi both managed to loosen the rigidity of the Ershad's policies
and to curb the influence of foreign (mainly Hollywood-based)
producers and of pre-revolutionary Film Farsi[1] in Iran. Thus, in
Beheshti's eyes, New Iranian Cinema owes a lot to the Farabi for its
commercial success at both the national and international level.

Shiva Rahbaran: Mr Beheshti, the aim of this project is to explore
the influence of New Iranian Cinema and its makers on the evolution of Iranian society after the Islamic Revolution, as well as the
influence of society on the development of New Iranian Cinema.
This project is solely concerned with the role of those film-makers
who live and work in Iran today. The reason why I chose to include
you in this project as the only interviewee who is not a film-maker
is that you were the head of the Farabi Cinema Foundation in the
most fruitful years of New Iranian Cinema. Under your management post-revolutionary Iranian films became key participants in
international festivals. This resulted in opening up – however little
– the world's attitude towards us. Whereas the international media
were filled with images of violence and brutality in Iran, Iranian
films offered an alternative picture of the country. To what extent
has New Iranian Cinema – or the Iranian New Wave – played a role
in the making of revolutionary Iran?

Mohammad Beheshti: I do not think that cinema or any other art,
in fact, is an identity maker! Cinema may *introduce* the identity of a
society, but it cannot *produce* that identity. The identity of a walnut

tree lies in its being a walnut tree – there is nothing that you could do to make it an orange tree, for example. The only thing you could do is to employ various ways to make me understand that this tree is a walnut tree and not an orange tree. In fact, the main relationship between New Iranian Cinema and Iranian identity is that it is a window for the world to look through. Our cinema gives the world an opportunity to get to know Iran and Iranians. It does not forge our identity but it can make it possible for a relatively closed international community to go beyond its biased views and look at our society from a new angle, to free itself from its preconceptions and misconceptions because it is not restricted by politics and diplomacy. At some time our president will give one of his famous speeches at the UN assembly; at another point, some cinema will be screening *Where is the Friend's Home?* Anybody who is interested in Iran can watch and listen to both and try to make up his or her own mind freely and independently.

SR: The window that you are talking about originates in an artform imported from the West. In comparison to the art of poetry, which has ancient roots in this country, Iranian cinema is very young. How have the Iranians been able to make this artform their own and harvest such great success worldwide?

MB: I daresay that cinema was re-invented in Iran. Cinema is not a stranger to us. Iranians became familiar with film only two years after it was invented in Europe. We are one of the few countries in the world to own a prestigious film museum.[2] Most of the things that are on show there are almost as old as their Western counterparts. We celebrated the centenary of our cinema only two years after the Americans and Europeans celebrated theirs. In other words, cinema is native to this country. In all artforms, especially cinema, the technical aspect is very important. Film-making is a complicated business. These complexities have been tackled in Iran even when Western know-how was lacking. For example, in the early days, film strips were 'washed' and processed in the same buckets in which the artists washed their clothes! If you go to the Film Museum of Iran you will find apparatus and techniques that are Iranian inventions and re-inventions. In other words, Iranians did not merely copy Western technology; we never had to import technical experts of cinema into our country. So, cinema in its technical sense is native to this country, just as it is native to France and Germany. Cinema as an art, as a subject, has been taught in this country for at least 50 years. So, I have no idea why we should consider cinema an 'imported good' or a 'foreign art'.

Here cinema is like a plant whose seed has been blown onto the earth and is now thriving and bearing fruit because of the conditions of the soil. So, it is native to us. But it is important to bear in mind that the success of our film-makers is not only due to the 'Iranization' of cinematic techniques. They draw the greatest part of their sustenance from their cultural heritage – a heritage that is much more active in their subconscious than in their consciousness. Let me give you an example of this. Imagine someone rowing a boat on a river. He can definitely influence the movements of his boat to some extent by using his oars, but the boat is moving fast because of the strong current of the river. The boat, no matter in what direction you move your oars, will always move according to the strength and direction of the current. It is the current that determines the direction and speed of the journey – whatever the boatman does is inevitably overpowered by the force of the river. In that kind of way, Iranian film-making is the result of the movements of the culture and mentality in which it is embedded. Just as all Hollywood films – no matter how good or bad – are part of the Hollywood culture, so are all Iranian films part of New Iranian Cinema. When we speak of Hollywood films, everybody knows what we are talking about. It's the same with Iranian films. The common denominator between all Iranian film-makers, from Kiarostami to Mehrjui and so many others who are relatively unknown internationally, is their 'Iranianness' – their being here and working here. What I am trying to say is that they make good films *here* – no matter what the socio-political situation is like. It's the same in our literature: just as Hafez and Ferdowsi and Attar and Saadi are all radically different, yet typically Iranian in their sensitivities and their poetry, so are our film-makers. What makes Iranian cinema what it is today is that these film-makers consciously and unconsciously sail the same river – the river that is Iranian culture and its several thousand years of history.

SR: This brings me to the question of contemporary Persian literature in Iran. Although the history of Persian language and literature goes back at least 1,000 years, contemporary Persian novels and poetry exist in isolation, so to speak, whereas Persian cinema is known worldwide. Except for a few contemporary writers and poets, such as Sadegh Hedayat and Forough Farrokhzad, the world is hardly acquainted with modern Persian literature.[3]

MB: Let me answer you with a question: are Forough, Nima and Shamlu[4] 'on the same train' as Saadi, Ferdowsi, Rumi, Attar and Sohrevardi? I think the reason why these modern poets did not become world renowned is that they left the train or, if you will, the boat, that the masters of Persian literature were on.

SR: In my book *Iranian Writers Uncensored* I interviewed authors and poets living in Iran and most of them saw the real reason for their isolation – compared to film-makers – in their choice of artistic tools. Whereas film-makers are not dependent on language and work with images (whose consumption is much easier), Persian writers write in a language that cannot match English or French in terms of worldwide usage. They are thus dependent on translators, which presents serious probems. So they need much longer to make their voices heard – if at all – on the international stage.

MB: I wonder why they say such a thing! May I draw your attention to the fact that Hafez, Khayyam and Rumi also wrote in the same language as the twentieth- and twenty-first-century writers and poets in Iran. They are known as great poets all over the world and never needed translators over the past centuries to make them great. The people who told you this are wrong. Translation does not make poets great – if anything, good poetry loses a lot of its quality in the course of translation. For example, let's look at the English translations of Rumi's poems. All Persian speakers find such translations, if not unsatisfactory, at best amusing. It

makes you think that the translators have just skimmed the surface
of Rumi's poetry and re-written it in English. However, even this
thin superficial translation has preoccupied many in the English-
speaking world for hundreds of years. Why are these people so
much into Rumi? Why is Rumi always fashionable, whether in Old
Europe or among Madonna's fans? You could say the same thing
about Khayyam, Hafez and Ferdowsi. What I am trying to get at, of
course, is that there is a technical issue when it comes to writing in
a language whose compass is not the same as, say, that of English.
However, our problem – the problem of our writers and poets –
is not only the choice of language. What we have to ask here is:
does our modern novel ride on the same train as Khayyam, Rumi
and Ferdowsi? Our novelists suddenly decided to follow Borges, for
example – the funny part of that is that Borges was inspired by
our old masters of poetry – instead of following the way of their
forefathers. You have to look at the curriculum of the departments
of drama and performing arts in Iran's universities in order to
understand what I'm trying to get at. Here, our students have to
read Shakespeare and Molière as part of their curriculum, but they
do not have to read Ferdowsi's *Book of Kings* or Nizami's *Khamseh*.
Anyone who decides to read those is seen as backward, reeking of
opium! All students want to be a new Shakespeare. What they don't
realize is that we cannot produce a small Shakespeare in our country when the English have produced a great one in theirs.

When you look at the literary scene in Iran in the past 100 years
you'll see that all that our poets and writers have been preoccupied
with was how to get off the train that their forefathers had ridden
for more than 1,000 years. All that our modern men and women
of letters have been doing is to get rid of rhyme and rhythm, and
they've yet to make successfully a train that functions well and can
move as fast and as steadily as the old one. Which passenger in his
or her right mind would take this modern rickety train instead of
the one that belongs to Khayyam, Ferdowsi, Attar, Nizami, Saadi,
Hafez and the rest? Give the modernists 2,000 years; maybe they
will succeed as well, who knows? Pray, tell me, when you lose your
way in a city whom do you ask for assistance? Those who have just
started on their way, or the expert guides who are acquainted with

all the streets and alleyways? Would you ask Rumi for directions or a youngster?

SR: We started our interview with a discussion of Iranian identity. You compared this to a flowing river with strong currents. What is the nature of this river? What is 'being Iranian' like?

MB: What makes Iranians a people is not their race. It's not even their geography. It's not even their language. It's something intangible and indescribable called 'culture'. Race, language and geography are all parts of being Iranian, but they do not define our identity as a whole. You see, Iranian identity is like water. If you pour water into a cup it will take the shape of that cup; if you pour it into a bottle it will take the shape of that bottle. But it remains water. It only takes on the shape of the container. When you look at the large minorities that live in Britain or the USA, you will realize quickly what I'm trying to get at. You realize from miles away that you are entering the territory of the Chinese or the Italians, but when walking in an Iranian neighbourhood you will never notice their presence as a minority, even if you know that area intimately.

SR: Unless you are Iranian yourself!

MB: Of course. What I'm saying is that in order to be Iranian you don't need to keep your appearance or traditions or even language. Why? Because this identity is not transferred from generation to generation through race or language or geography.

SR: I disagree. I find that the Iranians of the diaspora, despite their distance from the Persian language, still identify with that language.

MB: Of course, Persian is a very precious fruit of Iranian culture, but it does not define that culture, and that culture is not dependent on this fruit for its survival. If you plucked that fruit, the tree would not die. It has a thousand and one other fruits. For example, many people think that our writing is one of the key elements in which our culture manifests itself. But we all know that, in this land, we have never had our own, exclusively Iranian writing. Cuneiform script, for example, has Sumerian roots. Greek script was used in this country for centuries under the Parthians, Pahlavi script has Aramaic roots, and modern Persian, as it has been written over the past 1,200 years, has Arabic roots. So we never had our own script, although we had our own language, which we wrote in borrowed scripts. There are quite a few similar phenomena in our culture. Our traditions, our beliefs, our religions, all are our own Iranian versions of the originals. Our interpretations of these borrowed cultural artefacts make us what we are, make us Iranian as a whole. This is the strong river that carries us with it – a river of learning. We have been at a crossroads of cultures for thousands of years. We had to learn from all passers-by in order to survive. We were never an isolated culture or people as, say, the Japanese were. We are a meeting point of cultures and that is our strength. Persepolis was made by artisans from 28 nations, but Persepolis is still a uniquely Iranian phenomenon. We cannot live in cultural or racial isolation. It is not in our nature. We are cosmopolitans, world citizens, as soon as we are born. No government can take that away from us. No government will succeed in fighting this openness, which is central to 'Iranianness'. Those who try to stop the river or try to get off the boat that is carried by the river are doomed to fail. You see, history is not like journalism. History is ruthless. We know that if you cut off connections with your past, you might make it as a hero in a comic strip, but three volumes later nobody knows your name. You will see that history will remember the contemporary poet Mr Shafiei Kadkani, because he is still on the boat sailing the river of Iranian culture, but it will forget most of the poets that are known as great poets and writers today and are present in the fashionable literary magazines. It's a matter of the survival of the fittest!

SR: Let us get back to cinema.

MB: Yes. Cinema is the only artform whose exact date of birth we know. There are artforms whose date of decease is known, but the only date of birth we know is that of cinema. The advantage that our film-makers have is exactly this newness. In contrast to our poets, architects, musicians and painters, they do not have great 'ancestors' in whose presence they can hardly breathe. You can profit from the vast, massive roofs that past masters have built above your head only if you know how – otherwise you suffocate. That is the advantage of our film-makers – the lack of history in their métier.

SR: What is especially unique about Iranian cinema is that it became a global phenomenon within such a short time after the 1979 revolution – and that despite the regime's opposition.

MB: Iranian cinema was very lucky to enjoy good management in the first couple of decades after the revolution. Management is a vital factor in the arts and yet it is, and should be, a hidden – almost secret – activity. If we look at the history of arts and letters, we will see that management has always been vitally important to cultural activities and productions. When you read the hymns that Hafez wrote for his patrons, you will see that he is thanking guardians of Iranian culture. Today the 'job' of these guardians would be similar to culture managers or arts managers. So the question is, what is arts management or management in general? Management consists in making possibilities available and accessible so that new (and hopefully valuable) products can thrive. From my point of view there are two sorts of management: one is the 'carpenter-style' and the other the 'gardener-style'. A carpenter takes tools in his hands and hopes to make a familiar product, such as a chair or a table, according to certain guidelines. The things at his disposal, though, are lifeless, will-less. They do not have an independent identity. They are totally at the disposal of the carpenter. That's why a carpenter can say, 'I'm the one who makes the table.' A gardener, on the other hand, would never say that he created the trees and the flowers. He would take you to his garden and show you every single plant lovingly, as if it were a son or a daughter. Your child is not a piece of wood. It is a tree that has its own will and special qualities. What you do as a parent is to help the child find out and cultivate his or her hidden talents. When your child comes home with an 'A' in the school report, usually you don't think that this grade is for you, even if you have helped your child get it. As a parent you must go unnoticed. You must try to reveal all of your child's talents without being seen yourself. You work behind the scenes. This is the fortunate thing that happened to cinema after 1979.

SR: I believe that you are talking about the role of the Farabi Cinema Foundation, of which you were head in the 1980s and 1990s. But as you are well aware yourself, the new wave of Iranian cinema started in the 1950s and 1960s – decades before the Islamic Revolution – with film-makers such as Shahid Saless, Golestan, Beyzaie, Mehrjui, Kiarostami, Naderi, Farmanara, Kimiai, Ovanessian, and so on. Quite a few of these are still living and working in Iran. However, there is the impression that their work – as a wave, as a globalized Iranian phenomenon – came into its own only after the 1979 revolution. In what way was the Farabi an important factor in the realization of this phenomenon?

MB: I was the head of the Farabi for 11 years, but nobody ever knew my views on the films that were made under my auspices. For 11 years I kept myself to myself. I always said that I had not seen the finished version of any of the films made under my supervision. So, why did I have to do that? You see, if somebody asked you, 'What do you think about each of your children?', you'd try to evade the subject instead of saying, well, my daughter is much more intelligent than my son! But the film-makers themselves knew exactly what I thought about each of them. It was like calling your children to come to you and whispering praise or criticism in their ears without anybody else hearing you. You should never praise or criticize your child in public. And that is what I did as head of the Farabi. Our management was of the gardener's sort rather than of the carpenter's.

SR: Bearing in mind the countless restrictions and censorship policies that made and make life hard for Iranian film-makers, did you ever feel that you were the executive arm of the Ministry of

Culture and Islamic Guidance [the Ershad]? Did you ever feel that you were the one who held the scissors of censorship?

MB: First, you must make clear what you mean by censorship. Censorship means that you take your film to the Ershad and they tell you that you cannot show it. Self-censorship, on the other hand, means that you act from the beginning as the authorities would want you to. Like Mr Panahi, who says that he avoids making films in the interior of houses because he would not be able to show women as they really are. Mr Panahi always told me, 'I undertake self-censorship in order to be able to show a part of reality as it is. I won't go near subjects where I would have to lie – like showing women in bed with the full Islamic *hijab* on!' You know what, you should show me a place in the world where there is no censorship. It is true that censorship is quite strong in Iran, especially where eroticism is concerned. But we have to define censorship first in order to be able to speak about it. The most basic characterization of censorship is that a film-maker wants to shoot a certain scene but is forbidden to do so by the higher authorities. These authorities are sometimes governments, sometimes the law and sometimes private persons. The question, 'Where do the boundaries of censorship lie?' is asked all over the world. You cannot do whatever you want in France or the USA either, although, admittedly, they don't have a Ministry of Culture and Islamic Guidance! They, too, have guidelines and organizations and institutions, all of which have the right to object to a scene or a whole film. There are organizations that classify films as being suitable for viewers of certain ages – that in itself is a form of censorship.

SR: But that is for the protection of younger people. The films get made anyway, as long as they do not violate anyone's rights. Adults can decide for themselves what they want to see or not see.

MB: Do be patient. We will get to that as well. We have agreed that all over the world there are institutions that regulate the activities of film-makers and censor their films if they feel that they potentially endanger their society's moral welfare. In most parts of the modern world, this task is carried out by civil and non-governmental institutions, but in our country, because the civil institutions are not well developed, this task is inevitably allocated to the government and its dependent bodies. I, for my part, find rational censorship useful for the welfare of society. They do it in the West as well. But when censorship is placed in unqualified hands or performed according to some warped political ideology or misconception, then it endangers society's welfare. In this case, censorship prevents film-makers from benefiting society. That is very bad, no matter in which part of the world it occurs.

Now I want to draw your attention to the mechanisms of censorship in the West. Have you not noticed that in the West – in the so-called cradle of freedom – out of mere political calculation, things that are good for society are also censored? One tangible illustration of this is how Iran is portrayed. You witness our reality often enough during your trips to this country. Do you not agree that the difference between what you witness in the everyday life of this country and the way in which this country is depicted in the Western media is a form of censorship? Is it not funny how the West censors us and then accuses us of censorship? Censorship is much more effective when it means showing things instead of forbidding them. When, by showing a few hundred people shouting angrily and burning some flag or other in front of an embassy, you try to imply that the whole Iranian population of about 75 million is like that, you are censoring a whole nation in the most primitive way. In the course of the worldwide controversy surrounding the Danish cartoons of Mohammad,[5] there were perhaps 200 Iranians in front of the Danish embassy shouting and burning flags, but the Western media presented these people as representative of the whole Iranian population! This is censorship in its worst form. Now I would like to reverse the situation. If in the West insulting sacred things and breaking taboos is supposed to contribute to a culture of healthy self-criticism and thus enlightenment, why can't we make fun of the Shoah?[6] It distresses me to say this. I think the Shoah is one of the greatest crimes against humanity. What I'm trying to say is that the Shoah is just as sacred to the modern world – perhaps it is one of the very few sacred things that still exist in the modern world, as all religions and all values have lost their meaning in the course of enlightenment and modernity – as the Prophet Mohammad is to the Muslim world. You cannot touch the sacred values upon which the historical, political and social structures of the modern world rest. You will definitely end up in jail if you ever attempt it. Now, going back to our discussion about censorship in Iranian cinema, yes, it is true that we had to forbid some things and introduce certain measures. But we had to do this in order to be able to have cinema at all. What we had to do was to try to create an environment in which the nightmare of Film Farsi would not be repeated, chomping on the tender buds of our intellectual art films.

SR: When did Film Farsi morph into Iranian New Wave or New Iranian Cinema?

MB: Film Farsi had its own identity before the revolution, but after 1979 we tried with all our might to stop anything that might help the resurrection of that genre of film. We wanted New Iranian Cinema to be able to breathe and grow and that is why we treated Film Farsi as a nasty weed. In your garden you too would tear out such weeds so that your flowers could breathe, wouldn't you? For us, anything that smelled of Film Farsi was a nasty weed. We even had to put a ban on popular Film Farsi actors such as Mohammad Ali Fardin[7] because they symbolized the putrid and vulgar pre-revolution cinema. Fardin was a fine, respectable man, but he had two identities: one was that of a real-life person who was a good and likeable man, and the other was a screen persona, which was characteristic of the base heroes of Film Farsi – the 'carefree Ali', eating kebabs in second-rate cabarets, pouring arak[8] down his throat and falling in love with cheap dancers. His face in any film, no matter how artistic, would have brought back memories of the dark days of Film Farsi.

Another problem that we had to tackle was the appearance of women in films. We had to enforce the *hijab* on screen.

SR: Yes, that is a central issue in any discussion of modern Iranian cinema.

MB: You see, there are several points of departure here. There is the traditional standpoint of *Feqh* – of Islamic theology – according to which there is no problem in looking at a woman who covers herself properly, as long as the person who looks at her is not satisfying his base instincts. So, if looking at a Muslim woman in that way is not a sin, why should it be a problem to show female actors wearing a proper *hijab* in films? You are only watching their image, anyway. The image is not the person, is it? So, from the viewpoint of *Feqh*, women in films did not have to cover themselves completely, as a pious Muslim woman is supposed to do. In addition, not even the most pious and devout Muslim women cover themselves completely at home in front of their close male relatives. So, from the theological point of view, you could theoretically show women without a *hijab*. You see, these are the fine lines in theological discussions that became of vital importance to the existence of Iranian cinema after the revolution. However, it was not really a theological issue we grappled with; we had to confront another problem, that of authority. Those in authority just dictated that if we wanted to have a cinema at all, we would be obliged to show women wearing the *hijab*. We did want to have a cinema, so we had to play by their rules. We live in a country where everybody knows that women don't go to bed with their scarves on! But being in such a situation, we had to and still have to compromise and at times even show women in strange apparel. Putting the *hijab* issue to one side, we should not ignore the fact that Iranian films are highly critical when it comes to social issues. And this in spite of the restrictions and censorship that they face in this country.

SR: Of course, but a great proportion of such films cannot be seen in this country. They are censored and are not granted permission to be screened. Some of them are allowed to be shown only outside Iran.

MB: That is not true as such. A lot of them have not been shown for a long time because of the downright stupidity and mismanagement of those in charge and not because of censorship. Most of the films that take a critical stance on the Islamic Republic are screened, albeit sometimes after a long wait. Films are put on hold, but not banned. I bet even Panahi's *Offside* will soon obtain permission to be screened in Iran, after it has been shown at so many foreign festivals.[9]

SR: In a few years? Would you not call that censorship?

MB: I completely agree that this is censorship. I am not responsible for censorship in cinema and do not defend it. I'm just saying that, because of downright stupidity, some film-makers cannot show their films. But when we look at the report card of Iranian cinema, we see that almost all films made in Iran have been shown at some point – even after several years. Panahi's *The Circle*, for example, was highly critical of the state, but it was eventually shown. And so were other critical films.

You see, those in the West are always surprised by our cinema. I remember a French journalist at the Fajr Festival asking me, 'You also make comedies?!' Yes, sir! We know how to laugh! You must bear in mind that cinema in Iran started to take shape at a time when there was a brutal war going on. There is no country in the world that develops such a cinema in the middle of a nasty, costly and seemingly unending war. Even in countries such as Germany and France the cinema had to be completely at the service of war propaganda as soon as these countries became engaged in conflict. But in Iran, at the height of the war, we were able to make a film like Kiarostami's *Where is the Friend's Home?*

SR: That was in 1986, two years before the war ended.

MB: Exactly. That is an astounding achievement. I remember that, in those years, when Iranian films were sent to festivals, the first reaction we got was one of surprise. It was an almost impossible task. The key years for our cinema – our auteur cinema – were the years 1983 to 1988, that is, at the height of the war with Iraq. The most surprising thing about our cinema is its critical and contemporary character. It tackles social and political issues. It is very close to our reality despite all those restrictive measures. Again, we must remember that it succeeds exactly because it travels on the boat that sails along the current of this country's culture and history.

The West reacts to our cinema with surprise. They are not surprised when they see good films coming out of other Asian or African countries. They are only surprised at us! Why? They see themselves as the centre of the world and anything that opposes them or follows a different trajectory is considered surprising!

You see, our cinema, as I mentioned earlier, has been so successful because the revolution forced it to stay close to our reality. Before the revolution, both our art cinema and our Film Farsi were completely divorced from Iranian reality. Our art cinema was concerned with symbolism and the rest was preoccupied with second-rate cafés and cabarets. The imagination of the filmmakers, in both cases, was not inspired by Iranian reality. Our intellectuals mainly looked towards Third World cinema, such as that of South America and Asia, and our 'cheap' films took their inspiration from Turkish, Egyptian, Hollywood and Bollywood productions. To be fair, one could say that Film Farsi had more to do with life in Iran – or at least a part of life in Iran – than our wholly symbolic, abstract art movies did. Now, after the revolution we had a totally different story. We started to discover our reality. What you notice most pointedly in post-revolutionary films is the setting: the films take place mostly on the street. When you see a taxi driver in an Iranian film, you think of him as a real taxi driver on the streets of Tehran.

I remember right after the revolution we had, if you like, something similar to 're-education' sessions with famous film-makers and producers. The old producers and film-makers accused us of forbidding everything that made cinema attractive. They said, 'With your guidelines and dos and don'ts we're all going to go bankrupt!' We told them to write a list of things upon which they thought the commercial success of cinema is based. They listed 27 things. The first thing on the list was the image of women.

SR: Yes, obviously!

MB: What I told them was that we did not have a problem with showing women – it was *they* who had a problem with it. They protested and said that it was nonsense! After all, it was they who thought that the female sex is the main attraction for cinema goers. Then I asked, 'Is that all that you can think of when you depict women? Is sexuality the only special feature of a woman?' We had long discussions and the producers could not understand how you could look at a woman without considering her sex. I said, 'Listen, when you look at your mother or your sister or your daughter, do you think of their sex? Are you aware of their sexuality?' This was hard for them to digest. We had a lot of films made in the first years after the revolution – early 1980s – in which there were no female actors, not because the actresses were banned from playing but because film-makers could not show women as characters to which sexuality was not central. There was a film called *The Emissary* [directed by Fariborz Saleh, 1982], set in Kufa, in the first century AH [seventh century CE]; all the women walking in the bazaar were men wearing the *chador*! They could have used women for these roles but were unable to do so, as they had no idea how to view women beyond their sexuality. What we were trying to tell them was to accept that everything that they showed in their films should have a *parallel* in the reality outside the film. In the beginning this was hard for them to understand and for us to convey. I'll give you another example. When the war broke out, only a year and a half after the revolution, the film-makers found it difficult to make war films because they all wanted to make Hollywood-style films or Yugoslav partisan-style films or Japanese World War II films. They could not 'see' the war as it was. It took quite a few years for somebody like Hatamikia to make a good war film.

The years between 1982 and 1986 were the most difficult yet decisive for our cinema. We had to go through a lot of hardship in order to have a cinema that was ours, that showed our own reality – our day-to-day life. I must also add that by now this style has become a bit of a handicap to us. Our young film-makers have become such realists that they forget that a good film is not merely reportage. The pendulum is swinging towards journalistic style. You know, a film like Kiarostami's *Where is the Friend's Home?* will always remain a masterpiece because it also shows the poetic dimension of our Iranian reality. It will not age and die. It will always be fresh. Our young generation must be careful not to fall into the trap of a journalistic hyperrealism that only documents and reacts to daily events.

SR: The other form of censorship in Iran concerns the restrictions on importing foreign – especially Hollywood and European – films.

MB: Now we can no longer take such measures. We are living in a globalized world where everything is available on the World Wide Web, and films – banned or not – are found everywhere and can be viewed legally and illegally. Today it would be wrong to try to ban international films from being shown. We were able to impose restrictions on the screening of European and American films only in the first decade or so after the revolution. In those years we could put our cinema in a sort of quarantine, which was necessary. We mainly restricted Hollywood films from being shown in Iran because Hollywood dictated and still dictates what films can or cannot be shown worldwide. In Turkey, for example, Hollywood dictates what films can be shown on the big screen. We did not want that sort of tyranny. We wanted to show that the world of cinema is diverse, that Poland, the Soviet Union, Japan and India also make good films. In most countries in the world, non-Hollywood films can only be shown in small cinemas. Hollywood does not give them much space. Even in France, where the government hugely subsidizes the film industry, it is Hollywood that determines what is shown and for how long. We were against that. We knew that in those years Iranian cinema was a sapling. We had to be protective so that it could grow and become native to our country. Only then would we be able to export it as our product. That's why we became successful. We found ourselves. The revolution and our restrictive measures gave us the opportunity to find ourselves, and our filmmakers were intelligent enough to take that opportunity. There is no point in making Hollywoodesque Iranian films when the best of them are made in Hollywood! You can only become global if you remain native.

SR: Do you believe that art in general and the art of cinema in particular must be socially engaged? I mean, do you believe that art has any social or moral obligations?

MB: An artist must be committed to himself and his art in the first place. Of course, cinema is very important for educating society. Rumi was committed to his society and so must our cinema be committed. Saadi's *Bostan* and *Gulistan*[10] have survived not because of their beauty but because of their commitment to society – to humanity at large.

SR: So, do you believe that films can create pockets of freedom in a closed society?

MB: Of course.

SR: But then, is not a film that is concerned with creating pockets of freedom in danger of becoming politicized? Is not such a film a victim of ideology?

MB: One of the important tasks of a film-maker is to teach the viewer how to see better, more clearly. If he or she can do that, then the viewers can conceive of different truths; they can understand things differently. When a society is armed with different ways of seeing, then that society can change; it can evolve. That's when an individual can move himself or herself, as well as society as a whole, in the right direction.

SR: My next question concerns the relationship between literature and film in Iran. When we look at the West, we see a deep and intricate exchange between literature – especially the novel – and film. In Iran, though, with a few exceptions such as Farmanara's *Prince Ehtejab* or Kimiai's *Brother Akol*,[11] there are not many novels that have been made into films.

MB: I wish our contemporary literature, our novel, was strong enough to inspire our film-makers. Our cinema moves at a much faster pace than our novels and short stories. It overtook our contemporary literature in showing experienced reality – also because it had the quicker impact. Our cinema had to confront challenges that were vital to its growth – such as being forced to face the audience and being critically and publicly appraised. Our contemporary literature was not put in such a situation. It remained in the mind of the writer and could not find its interlocutor. So, it could not grow and mature. The issue is not so much that we don't have enough stories for film-makers to turn into films. The main problem of our literature is that it has not produced a story like, say, Kiarostami's *Taste of Cherry*.

SR: Considering that Kiarostami made some of his masterpieces, such as *The Wind Will Carry Us* or *Where is the Friend's Home?*, by leaning strongly on Forough's or Sohrab Sepehri's poems,[12] we cannot say that our cinema is indifferent to our literature.

MB: I am not saying that. What I am trying to say is that there were things that should have developed in our literature before they developed in our films. For example, the historical conception of our country should have first materialized in our novels. We do not have worthwhile historical novels such as the Europeans and Americans do. We do not have a living picture of the Safavid or Qajar periods[13] in our novels. When such things don't develop in literature – when our contemporary literature cannot relate to our history – obviously our cinema starts to fill the gap. Our cinema takes on the task of telling us our stories, stories that should have been told in modern literature. European film-makers can lean on at least six or seven centuries of stories, novellas and novels. They have myriad opportunities to use these stories for their film-making purposes. The novels *Les Misérables* and *Jane Eyre* have been adapted so many times, from so many different perspectives. We could never do that! Not even our most famous contemporary novel, Hedayat's *The Blind Owl*, has been 'experienced' as a film. And that's because *The Blind Owl* is only a spark in our literature – a very bright spark to be sure, but it could not generate a movement; it could not become the source of a strong stream that could carry our modern literature.

SR: Many of our contemporary writers and poets complain that such a stream or movement could not come into being because the despotic regimes that have ruled our country over the past centuries have continuously stifled literary progress. Yet we see that New Iranian Cinema has celebrated and continues to celebrate its worldwide successes under a regime that is not exactly keen on freedom, human rights and democracy.

MB: That is exactly my point. I want to say that even the worst regimes in the world cannot stop literature and art from thriving. Some of the best works of art in the West were produced in the first half of the twentieth century – an age of great wars, unimaginable bloodshed, brutality and genocide. Was not Bertolt Brecht living in Hitler's Germany? Was not Ignazio Silone a victim of Mussolini's fascism? So, what happened there? Why did the West produce world-class literature then? Why is it only in this country that the writer's source of creativity dries up under the undemocratic sun? The reason is that the European writer did not get off the train upon which Goethe and Dante travelled, whereas our modern writers left the 1,000-year-old caravan.

SR: I do not think that the reason for the success of the European writer is his or her connection to Goethe or Dante only. The train upon which the writers and artists of the West travel is called 'modernity'. The discussion concerning modernity is a long and difficult one, and I won't get into it. However, I'll just mention the two main pillars upon which modernity is built: one is the separation of religion from the state, and the other is the focus on man (women, as you know, had to fight for a couple of centuries after the dawn of the Enlightenment before being considered full human beings) as the centre of the universe. The despotic regimes in Europe, such as Nazi Germany and the Stalinist Soviet Union, were the rotten fruit of such thought – in other words, they were the dark side of the Enlightenment. Modern writers, film-makers and artists in the West deal with these two sides of modernity in their works. Now, judging by the historical, political and social development in Iran today, we could say that we have a long way to go in order to understand and achieve modernity, and as a result produce universal, modern works of art and literature.

Let us go back to our Iranian intellectual cinema. You've just mentioned that, in contrast to literature, our film was able to travel on the 'right' train and to show Iranian reality as it is. My question is, why has such a medium been unable to produce at least a few good films about the Iran–Iraq War – a war that went on for eight years and almost broke the back of the Iranian nation? Why is such an important historical event so under-represented in Iranian films?

MB: First, it's not the case that we have made hardly any films about the war. We were actually able to find our cinematic language during the conflict, so I do not agree with you. We have even made some comedies about the war – and that in a country where the Iran–Iraq War was considered 'holy' by the government. For example, Kamal Tabrizi's *Leily is with Me* [1996] is an extremely popular comedy. But why did it not have the same international success as other films? It's because we can be present at a festival only if we are allowed to. Only films that are chosen by the jury of foreign festivals can be shown there and not necessarily films that sell well in Iran.

SR: So, are you trying to say that the choices for those festivals are a form of censorship?

MB: Definitely. I remember that when we sent films to international festivals in the early years after the revolution, they were kept at customs for an awfully long time. There were times when the films were sent to the Iraqi embassy instead of the Iranian embassy because of the similar ways that the two countries are spelled in the Latin alphabet. So, the films did not reach the festivals in time. Sometimes the juries just turned down our films without even watching them. These were all ways of censoring us. We had to force our way into the international community. We were always dependent on the goodwill of independent and committed festival organizers in Cannes, Locarno, Venice, etc., who thought beyond political borders and pushed our case through. And thus we forced our way into the international festivals, which gradually became a tribune for us. All of a sudden it became fashionable to be a fan of Iranian films!

SR: You were talking about war films.

MB: Yes, I digress. Our war cinema was not, as was the case in Europe or America in the first half of the twentieth century, born after the war. It was born right in the middle of it. Hatamikia's films were made while our heroes were fighting for our country. Then, during the war and the West's hostile depiction of Iran in the media, there was no way that we could send our war films to important overseas festivals. The West was completely against Iran in those days.

SR: But my impression is that it is not the West but the Iranian audience that has no inclination to watch these war films.

MB: That is not true. They loved *Leily is with Me.*

SR: Well, that was a comedy.

MB: But if a film is good, people watch it – whether it is a war film or not. But I do agree with you that there are only a few blockbuster war films in Iran. The problem was that as soon as war films started to mature and attract attention they became the victim of a political tug of war. All of a sudden, the government and the Ministry of Culture and Islamic Guidance started to take care that the 'right' image of the war was projected. These people were not qualified. They were ideologues who had no idea about film and just annexed the war films' terrain. That was when war films started to become boring propaganda films and nobody wanted to watch them. Nevertheless, here and there good films were made; the war-film genre, however, became something that a lot of film-makers avoided.

SR: Now, at the end of our interview, I want to talk about one of the most important subjects in cinema, namely, love. How are love stories made in Iran, if at all? It's very difficult for Iranian actors and actresses to portray love on the screen. You said earlier that women have found a new and better role in post-revolutionary Iranian cinema; they are no longer sex objects but mothers, sisters, daughters, who are respected for what they are. I wonder how these actresses can portray lovers and loved ones when their sexuality is taboo? You said that New Iranian Cinema owes its success to its realistic style. Do not men and women fall in love and have erotic relationships in the Iranian reality?

MB: Most films made in Iran after 1986 are love stories.

SR: But in none of them are erotic scenes shown – not even a kiss or a handshake between lovers is tolerated.

MB: As I said before, because of the restrictions that we have, the setting of our realist movies is the street and not the house.

SR: Indeed! But does Iran's reality exist only in the streets?

MB: Let me elaborate. Many things are forbidden in our cinema and it was good to put a ban on them. But, as I mentioned earlier, forbidding some things was unfortunately the price we had to pay in order to have a cinema under a government that was not exactly cinema friendly! We are not necessarily for all these restrictions, such as those concerning the depiction of erotic love between men and women, but we have no other choice than to follow them. On the other hand, these restrictions have offered us the possibility of depicting love in a very subtle and tender way that has become a characteristic feature of Iranian cinema.

SR: I am not so sure. Most relationships between men and women that are depicted in Iranian cinema concern either forbidden love or divorce, since in such situations you don't have a lot of physical contact anyway!

MB: That is not true. Those films show the difficult social issues that the protagonists have to cope with. They are not about love. We have real love stories. Maybe they are not widely shown outside Iran, but they are very popular in Iran. Actually, most films shown in Iran are love stories because that's what the audience wants! People want to see romance. If Iranian cinema did not produce love films, it would be bankrupt by now. Our love stories do not concentrate on the physical and erotic parts of love. We have to deal with love relationships in the same way that we deal with the woman's *hijab*. We try to turn these restrictions into funny situations. For example, a boy and a girl run towards each other and leap as if to embrace, but miss and end up hugging themselves! Or the boy takes a leap to kiss his sweetheart, but the Islamic Moral Police[14] come in between them and he ends up kissing the officer! Humour is the film-maker's tool for dealing with restrictions and showing what is forbidden despite its being forbidden. Anyway, in our culture we have a long tradition of having a thousand and one ways of saying things without uttering them. That is subtlety. When we are among friends we might say, 'I have to go for a piss', but in front of others we say, 'I have to go to the restroom.' Both say the same thing but in different ways. So, in a sense, censorship just makes us talk about things more subtly – in a less in-your-face way.

SR: So, if one of the by-products of censorship is subtlety and a more imaginative language, do you conclude that censorship is good for creativity?

MB: I'm not saying that. I said at the beginning that censorship is a very complex issue. We can easily say that we want freedom. Saying things and not saying things are both a form of censorship. As I

said before, not showing or not saying things does not always have
to do with formal censorship; sometimes it's a matter of politeness
or morality. If somebody starts talking about his father to me and
the first thing he mentions is his father's haemorrhoids, in a way he
is censoring his father! He is reducing his father!

On the other hand, beauty is also a form of censorship. A few
years before the revolution, Ali Hatami made a TV series about
Amir Kabir, the famous vizier of Nasser al-Din Shah Qajar in the
nineteenth century. The series, *Soltan-e Sahebgharan* [1974], was
very popular. In an early episode there is a close-up shot of his
wife, played by Zari Khoshkam, who tells the story of her husband's
assassination to camera. The problem is that Zari Khoshkam is so
beautiful that the viewer doesn't take in any of her words! You see,
censorship is a very complex issue.

2

BAHRAM BEYZAIE
The Myth of Revolutionary Cinema

BAHRAM BEYZAIE FOUND IT DIFFICULT TO TALK about Iranian cinema after the revolution because he believed that that event had played a destructive role in the development of cinema, and of the other arts for that matter. From his point of view, the revolutionaries and their Islamic government were initially preoccupied with excluding good film-makers from the market and securing a place for 'Islamic' directors. Only a few pre-revolutionary avant-garde directors were able remain in Iran and they tried to pass on their knowledge to the younger generation of film-makers. On the whole, Beyzaie is more concerned about the absence of good pre-revolutionary film-makers rather than the presence of post-revolutionary prize-winners in New Iranian Cinema today. If we ignore this, he argues, we inevitably become collaborators in a regime that attempts to re-write and 'cleanse' the history of Iranian culture and 'sell' the revolution as the very source of New Iranian Cinema to the world.

For Beyzaie, the issue is not simply that the revolution was *not* the source of New Iranian Cinema but that it actually stopped the Iranian film industry from growing – more so than the shah's regime ever did. However, Iranian cinema grew despite these restrictions. Beyzaie believes that censorship in the classical sense

27

of the word was not the only obstruction put in the way of Iranian cinema. The greatest calamity that the Islamic Revolution brought upon Iranian cinema was the expropriation of 'great' subjects for the purposes of promoting Islamic ideology. The Iran–Iraq War is the most telling example of this policy.

Beyzaie believes that the only thing that saved Iranian cinema from dying under the dogma of fanatics and fundamentalists was the regime's sense of 'market-oriented business'. Business and the desire to have 'fun' and go to 'beautiful places' were the main drivers of the authorities' tolerance towards the desire of film-makers to attend international film festivals. However, he also adds that while the desire to do business freed film from the fangs of fundamentalist Islamists, at the same time it limited the territory in which art film-makers and their ideas could thrive. Business is a double-edged sword as far as the expansion of New Iranian Cinema is concerned, and that is why Beyzaie is not very hopeful about the future of Iranian film. His despair manifests itself especially in his decision to leave Iran – a country which, as he insisted in our talk, was crucial to his creativity – for the United States only a few months after the completion of this interview. Once in the US, he embarked on a series of talks and symposia about Iranian literature, theatre and cinema. However, since his departure, he has yet to make any films or publish any plays.

––––––––––––

Shiva Rahbaran: Mr Beyzaie, the aim of this project is to examine the influence of Iranian film-makers on the development of post-revolutionary Iranian society. I want to look at this development through the eyes of those film-makers who live and work in Iran today.

Bahram Beyzaie: In that case, the picture of Iranian cinema after the revolution that you're going to paint will be incomplete. If you don't take into account those who left Iran because of extreme pressure or those who live in Iran and cannot make their films because of the regime's censorship policies, then your picture will be quite misleading.

SR: Obviously I cannot talk to everyone who is part of the scene. That's why I chose people like yourself, whose works are recognized as great both inside and outside Iran. I want to look at the development of post-revolutionary Iranian cinema and the environment in which it is made, from your point of view and from the point of view of those who stayed in Iran.

BB: But where are those film-makers who did not leave and yet do not have permission to make films or, if they do, have to make films that are not *theirs*? If our enchantment with post-revolutionary Iranian cinema makes us turn a blind eye to the background in which films are made, the cost will be great.

SR: The enchantment that you mention is actually the result of the contradictions between the tender and beautiful images in Iranian films and the violent and brutal ones of contemporary Iran that are shown in the international media. The Western viewer finds Iranian films moving but at the same time is alarmed by images of angry, intolerant women in black *chadors*. The question is which one is the reality of Iran?

BB: Have the Western media fabricated the images of angry women in black *chadors*? You see, the image of the heroine in my film *Bashu, the Little Stranger* [1989] does not reflect Iran as a whole; violent, angry women trained to exercise brutality exist side by side with the woman-protagonist in *Bashu*.[1] However, I do not have permission to show these! Those who dictate what can and cannot be shown are just as much a part of this universally admired New Iranian Cinema as film-makers like me! So not only those who *are* allowed to make their films but also those who are *not* allowed are part of New Iranian Cinema. Those who stayed behind and are allowed to make a film only once in a while and those who left because they were not allowed to make any films at all are both part of the picture. If we were to look at Iranian cinema only from the viewpoint of those who stayed behind, then you probably would cut me out of your book – in case I decided to leave the country because of the unbearable pressure from the regime on people

like me![2] This is just another way of expropriating the image of our
country: the re-writing of the history of Iranian art, in which the
Islamic Republic has shown such prowess in the last three and a
half decades.

We have to bear in mind that those who have been forced to
leave the country and take their image of reality with them have,
despite their absence, left an imprint on Iran – the imprint of
their exile, of their diaspora. This imprint is what the regime has
been trying to hide all these years, and people doing 'projects' on
Iranian cinema must be careful not to add grist to the regime's
mill.

SR: So, let us look at the films that exist in Iran and those that
could have existed. Perhaps this awareness of the 'hidden half' will
offer us a better perspective from which we can view the visible
part.

BB: I can only speak for myself. I stayed in Iran because I would
hate the psychological consequences of being forced to leave. I'm
not a good traveller and cannot adapt easily. I have neither the
financial means nor the ability to start from zero. Nobody awaits
me; I don't have attractive goods to sell; I cannot be thrown into
some corner of the world and then decide to become part of it –
because the culture and history of *my* country takes up most of
the space in my head. And the thought of leaving this culture to
those who expropriate and sell it for a farthing makes me sad. My
cultural home is not cinema alone; it is *every* domain of human-
ist common sense and reason. You cannot expropriate a domain
entirely, but you can damage it greatly and that's what's being done
here. If I were to make films *only* and do nothing else – remember
that the conditions under which I work force great delays upon me
and mean that I can screen a new film only once every eight years
or so and, even then, it is not the film I wanted to make! – then I
would not cling on to this culture so readily.

SR: But the films that you have made – especially the ones after
the revolution – are highly admired worldwide and have made

Iranians proud. Especially in the West, which is generally seen as the enemy of the Islamic Revolution, your films and those of your colleagues are much praised. What is the secret of New Iranian Cinema's success? I am asking this question with the current isolation of Iranian literature in mind, despite its 1,000-year history.

BB: Literature needs translation. It needs agents and publishers who want to make money. This is what the market wants and literature is increasingly becoming a consumer product which must obey the rules of the market. Considering the cost and trouble of translation, contemporary Persian literature does not make for good business.

SR: But films also have to obey market rules and we see that even in Iran itself, where translation is not needed, people are more into films than into poetry – and this despite Iran's reputation of being the land of poets.

BB: So, does this make Iranian cinema better than contemporary Iranian literature? Not even Shakespeare and Dostoyevsky could compete with Film Farsi! Even before the birth of Edison and the Lumière brothers, Iranians did not read much. Reading is a burden that doesn't suit our self-centredness, our addiction to 'just hanging around' and the happy-go-lucky way of life of the majority of our people. In this country, the intellectual, the reader, the scholar has traditionally been mocked and avoided. Both religious and ruling elites have always scared the masses that they'll become corrupt and be damned if they read too much. Watching films, however, is an easy task; you don't have to take any responsibility but simply take a bowl of nuts and sit comfortably with your friends. You joke, shout insults at the film-maker or compliment him. In all backward countries cinema is much more successful than literature. But who says that cinema is better than literature?

SR: I take your point, but I want to know why Iranian film is so esteemed both among world-class connoisseurs and the public? Was it not the revolution that made our cinema what it is today?

BB: Oh, what would we do if there weren't all those respectable Western critics to assure us of our prowess?! Now that our cinema has been given the seal of approval of Western connoisseurs, maybe it's time to inform them that the Iranian New Wave came into being quite some time before the 1979 revolution.

SR: So it was not thanks to the revolution that it became popular and accessible worldwide?

BB: The truth is that the revolution could not hold back the popularity and growth of our art cinema. Our intellectual and artistic cinema had already emerged in the 1960s *despite* the hostile conditions. Mehrjui's *Gaav* [*The Cow*]³ is seen as a paragon of this kind of cinema and was made and won prestigious international prizes about a decade before the revolution took place. Golestan, Faroughi, Farrokhzad, Shirdel, Shahid Saless, Kimiavi, Farmanara, Mehrjui, Sayyad, etc. had all been praised in the West and the East long before the revolution took place. So it was not the revolution that gave birth to New Iranian Cinema. Quite the opposite. Fanatical administrators could not stop our cinema, so in the end they came to the conclusion that they could expropriate it and promote it as their own creation. That was much more profitable for them.

SR: Many believe nevertheless that the revolution cleansed the Iranian 'filmscape' of the vulgar Film Farsi and Hollywood productions and thus created a good climate in which New Iranian Cinema could flourish.

BB: Those who like to believe such nonsense are free to do so. There is no stopping them anyway. We won't forget, however, that these 'revolutionaries' tried everything in their power to stop the fruit of two decades of pre-revolutionary auteur cinema from being screened: the pre-revolutionary films of Mehrjui, Kimiavi, Taghvai, Naderi, Ovanessian, Shahid Saless, Farmanara, Hatami, Kiarostami, Aslani, and even those of a generation before, i.e., the films of Golestan, Ghaffari and Rahnama, were all prohibited from being shown. Was it them or the 'vulgar' Film Farsi that banned my pre-revolutionary films from seeing the post-revolutionary light of day – films such as *Safar* [*The Journey*, 1972], *Ragbār* [*Downpour*, 1972], *Qaribé va Meh* [*Stranger and the Fog*, 1976], *Kalāq* [*The Crow*, also known as *The Raven*, 1976], *Cherikeh-ye Tara* [*Ballad of Tara*, 1979], *Marg-e Yazdgerd* [*Death of Yazdgerd*, 1982]? My post-revolutionary films – even the popular ones such as *Bashu, the Little Stranger* [1989] – were all banned for years. I had to wait almost five years in order to be able to screen *Bashu*, which was celebrated internationally as *the* post-revolutionary Iranian film. If only the world knew! Even the majority of my scripts, such as *Eshghal* [*Occupation*], *Aynehhaye Rou-beh-rou* [*Facing Mirrors*], *Ghessehay-e Mir-e Kafanpoush* [*The Tales of Mir-e Kafanpoush*], *Dibachehye Novin-e Shahnameh* [*A New Prologue to Shahnameh*], *Toumar-e Sheikh Sharzin* [*The Scrolls of Sheikh Sharzin*], *Ayarnameh*, *Safar beh Shab* [*A Jounrney into the Night*],[4] were banned from being made. What do you call this? Is this what the authorities mean by 'cleansing Iranian Cinema of the vulgarities of Film Farsi'? Those who ride the wave of New Iranian Cinema's worldwide success can praise themselves as the guardians of this cinema. But in the eyes of a person like me, who looks at the outside from the very inside of cinema, I can assure you that those responsible for the 1979 revolution did not want to see this cinema remain alive!

In the beginning the revolutionaries conceived of our cinema as an obscenity, as corruption. First they branded unveiled women as corrupt in order to be able to ban films that showed them. That became an instrument for banning art films as well as Film Farsi. Mehrjui's *Gaav* by necessity only showed provincial veiled women, so it became a sort of 'model film' for post-revolutionary cinema. You see, after the revolution New Iranian Cinema was stuck in a state of confusion for a very long time – faced with contradictory guidelines and ideologies and a myriad of dos and don'ts. The regime would brutally do away with anybody who criticized them, even if it was only a misunderstanding! A number of film-makers were jailed and sometimes tortured both psychologically and physically so that they could no longer work or had to make farcical films complying with the most absurd Islamic guidelines, which in the end finished them off as good, serious film-makers. In short, what the revolutionaries wanted in the beginning was to use cinema as a propaganda tool that would produce a new generation of obedient people ready to give up their lives for the Islamic Republic. Particularly during the war with Iraq the camera was used for such ends. On the other hand, organizers of foreign festivals were immensely interested in intellectual film-makers from Iran, whom they were already acquainted with from pre-revolutionary times. Thankfully, they knew that artists and people don't just disappear because a revolution wills it to happen. This was not at all to the liking of the regime and the Ministry of Culture and Islamic Guidance. However, they had to give in, even if only minimally, in order to save face to some extent on the world scene. Slowly they came to like the trappings of international festivals: the travelling, the shopping, the proximity to beautiful unveiled women and important people. All of a sudden, these Islamic revolutionaries discovered the fun and decadence of the West and they liked it!

SR: You're saying, then, that had the revolution not happened, the Iranian New Wave would still have been successful?

BB: Even if the revolution had not happened, art cinema – despite the success of Film Farsi – would have kept expanding and progressing day by day. Although we were all young and inexperienced then and stood on the threshold of our careers, festivals in the West and the East were very enthusiastic about our work and it was obvious that our young movement was going to play an important role in world cinema. We were gaining a lot of attention not only because of our critical outlook but also because of our ability to produce films that shed their provincial skin and were ready to take their place alongside world-class films. I repeat: it is a shameless lie to say that New Iranian Cinema is a product of the revolution.

SR: Mohammad Beheshti, who was the head of the Farabi Cinema Foundation in the 1980s and 1990s, believes that one of the greatest achievements of his institute was, on the one hand, to weed out Film Farsi from the landscape of Iranian cinema, and, on the other, to ban Hollywood and multinational productions. In that way, the Farabi was able to open up the necessary space in which art films could grow. From his point of view, the power that big foreign – mainly American – production and distribution companies had in Iran was far more detrimental to Iran's art films than post-revolutionary Islamic censorship ever was.

BB: I truly hope that we will see the day on which people such as Mr Beheshti, who surely does not personally agree with much of the censorship for which he had to take responsibility, will give their honest opinion about these matters rather than churn out the official version of 'the truth'.

The Farabi Cinema Foundation already existed a couple of years before the revolution. Its head was Noreddin Ashtiani, a man of the world who spoke a number of foreign languages and was very well read in the art of cinema. He ran the first Tehran International Film Festival in 1972. With the advent of the revolution, the Farabi was taken over by the government and became – in the government's own words – 'the executive arm of the Ministry of Culture and Islamic Guidance'.

The heads of the Farabi tried to keep cinema going after the revolution and some of them, after they'd given up their post, even said in private that they had had to abide by several policies against their will. I have tried to believe them. However, none of them has been able to give me a satisfactory explanation for the 28-year-long ban on *Death of Yazdgerd*, or the 30-year ban on *Ballad of Tara* or even the four-and-a-half-year ban on *Bashu, the Little Stranger*. Was banning me also part of their battle against Film Farsi and imperialist Hollywood? You know, I actually believe that Film Farsi is alive and well in Iran today – the only difference is that now heroines don't wear miniskirts and don't dance on tables in second-rate casinos. The Film Farsi directors only have to abide by the *hijab* regulations and continue what they did before the revolution. And anyway, vulgar films do not justify censorship as it is carried out in Iran today. Those who suffer censorship are still, as in the days before the revolution, the intellectual and critical film-makers. To

me Mr Beheshti is really a respectable man – despite our differences – and I truly believe that he did his job without wishing to
gain materially from it. From my point of view, among all the heads
of the Farabi after the revolution, he was the only one whose ratio-
nale was clear, even if we did not agree with him. Today I believe
that what he really wanted was to let Iranian cinema live and go on
living. That was his aim and it was a hard task to achieve in a climate
where revolutionaries wanted to ban film altogether as un-Islamic.
I would like to believe that he wanted to protect me from myself,
so that I could survive as a film-maker. Yes, I want to think favourably of him. Years later I heard that Beheshti's advice to the jury at
the Tehran Fajr Festival was, if you really like Beyzaie's work, don't
vote for him! Maybe he knew that what the Ministry of Culture and
Islamic Guidance wanted was to destroy my popularity among critics and the public. However, I don't know whether my film-making
career after the revolution is worth being seen as a career at all.
In the past 30-odd years my films have been so badly sabotaged,
banned, censored and mutilated that you cannot really speak of a
career. Even my name was banned in the first few years after the
revolution and there were young, hot-headed revolutionaries (one
of whom later became a film-maker himself) who demanded my
execution! And I assure you that I was neither a proponent of Film
Farsi nor of Hollywood's hegemony.

SR: Despite all this, it was your *Bashu, the Little Stranger* that was
hailed in the West as one of the first post-revolutionary Iranian art
films. How do you evaluate the Farabi's role in this matter?

BB: *Bashu*'s screening was completely accidental. The film was a
great success in Iran after only five shows. That was reason enough
for the authorities to ban it. It remained banned for about five
years, during which the director and crew suffered depression.
Then somehow the new men in charge realized that they could
make money and travel to nice places by allowing this film and
others to be screened at international festivals. But the maker of
Bashu was banned from working in his own country and was not
even informed that his film was being shown abroad.

SR: Your films do not aim at commercial success. How is it, then, that they are so popular with the public? *Sag Koshi* [*Killing Mad Dogs*, 2001] won the Audience Award at the Tehran Fajr Festival after it was released.

BB: Do you give the authorities or the film itself credit for its popularity? As for the authorities, they banned me from working for about ten years after I made *Mosaferan* [*Travellers*, 1991]. After I finally got permission to work on *Sag Koshi*, I suffered yet another eight-year ban before I was able to screen my most recent film, *Vaghti Hameh Khaabim* [*When We Are All Sleeping*, 2009]. The list of my banned scripts, films and plays is miles longer than the one of those I've been able to make.

SR: So why don't you emigrate like many of your colleagues?

BB: My staying here does not mean that I agree with everything that goes on here. Many would love to get rid of people like me, who love and care for this country and its culture. Iran is my home.

SR: That's what's very interesting about your work. Your cinema has flourished in a country that treats you pretty badly.

BB: But this does not mean that this country was a garden full of weeds that became a rose garden through the efforts of the Islamic Republic's authorities! You see, the authorities thought from the beginning of the revolution that our cinema belonged to them. It was something they could ride on. Thanks to cinema many people are employed by the government and so can propagate their views! The Iranian authorities can do magic! They managed to show Tarkovsky's *Sacrifice* without showing the film! [They showed a heavily censored version.] They even managed to make edited copies of the films they banned, such as my *Stranger and the Fog*, which they renamed *The Other Side of Fog*! In it they showed God behind the fog! I tell you one thing: the only aim of the authorities in all these years has been to cut off the independent, critical, intellectual artist from his or her audience. Many left, many became silent, but a number of us stayed behind and tried to resist. So, if you ever happen to observe that New Iranian Cinema is still growing and producing good films, you should never conclude that this is thanks to censorship policies. It is happening *despite* censorship policies. To believe otherwise would be to justify not only the policies of this regime but also those of the shah!

SR: Do you feel you're in exile in your own society? I'm asking this question with great Iranian artists and poets in mind, such as Sadegh Hedayat, who committed suicide in Paris in the early 1950s, and Forough Farrokhzad, who was ostracized because of her poetry and lifestyle and who died very young in a car accident – some say it was suicide – in the 1960s. I'm also thinking of film-makers such as Golestan and Shahid Saless and Naderi, who felt that they had to leave Iran either before or after the revolution. We must bear in mind that these artists could no longer work in Iran and were forced into exile – whether internal or external – not necessarily as a result of political persecution but because they were very modern, very much ahead of their time. On the other hand, when I speak with poets, writers and film-makers, the majority assure me that they don't feel at all exiled in their own country but are at one with the people. They feel that together with the people they form a front against a regime that tries to open a rift between artist and audience.

BB: In the spiritual realm of poetry, in the old days in Iran, our poets always complained that they were in exile; that they did not deserve the shackles of this earthly life. In that sense they felt in exile. In our modern world we have three types of exile. The first group are those who physically have to leave their country although they don't want to. The second group are those who are physically in their country but feel that within it they are misunderstood – they feel that they're yelling in a vacuum. And then there's the third group which plays the role of the exile in order to get some attention and make some money.

SR: You seem to belong to the second group.

BB: In the beginning we all think that we're going to change the world through our art. We see our own and society's progress mirrored in our work. After a few years, we realize that we've been running for many decades without moving even one step ahead.

SR: Why do you feel that way? It's not just the cinephiles inside and outside Iran who find your films remarkable. Even housewives and taxi drivers in Iran know about your latest films; they realize that you are not only a first-class film-maker but also a disobedient resistance fighter!

BB: That is so very kind of them! I am not the only one who keeps running and shouting without achieving anything. I am only one of a huge group of artists who have lost their hope and their life in the struggle for even minimal progress, for freedom of speech, for living without fear. We're like mice on a treadmill and that's why it has taken so long for us to understand that we have not progressed. The worst thing is that most of us have got used to this and are like hypnotized creatures who believe that this is reality. We are actually getting further and further away from our aims, and unfortunately there are people here who make huge amounts of money from our meaningless activities.

SR: I should like to go back to the role of the regime in pushing people like you into exile. Many believe that the government tries to sever the ties between artists, writers and film-makers and their audience or readers. Others believe that a lot of artists like to spread such rumours because in this country it is always good for those who create art and poetry to be in some sort of confrontation with the government and thus be celebrated as *engagé* artists. What are your views on this?

BB: Well, this question is so naive that I feel that, if I answered it, I would be one of those people who tell you what you want to hear instead of the truth. I do not want to become such a person, so I refuse to answer directly. I do not have any expectations, nor do I prefer one political group to another, nor do I consider one form of censorship better than another. I believe that any government – be it religious, left, right, capitalist, communist – that sees itself as the centre of the universe and believes its values to be the very foundation of society, and on the strength of which forcibly curtails thought, art, speech and progress, is in the wrong. And when the government starts to create fake artists and fake audiences who celebrate the system and poses as a lover of freedom that supports the arts, then we have a Kafkaesque situation: we have a system that is engaged in creating conspiracy theories within conspiracy theories in order to prolong its existence! The trouble is that there are artists who play the role of the exile in order to attract attention but at the same time are fed by the system and in turn feed the conspiracy of the system. The problem arises when the borders that separate real, independent artists from con artists become fuzzy. Then we have a situation where official censorship gives way to a sick, underground, informal form of censorship that's very difficult to eradicate, because it grows its roots into the deepest part of the soil of religiosity and traditionalism in societies such as ours. Those who really feel lonely and cut off in this society have realized the depth of the catastrophe, and the worst thing is that they cannot uproot the weed – at least not now!

SR: In societies where people lag behind the caravan of modernity and where despotic regimes reign, artists and poets are almost forced to become political thinkers. But the paradox is that the more the regime tries to oppress political thought and intellectuality, the more political the society becomes. As a result, art also becomes highly political; the artist is thus bound to become *engagé* and committed. Are you a committed artist? Are you trying to educate and change your audience and thus your society? Does your art have a message?

BB: I am a committed artist – I am committed to myself. This means that first and foremost I will not lie to myself. Only in this way will I not lie to others. I do hope to change my society, but not as a man of politics; and, anyway, society can only change if the majority is willing to change. In contrast to businessmen and merchants, who are unwilling to share their gains, people of culture are willing to share their ideas. This is not a 'message' or indeed a solution to problems. No, this is a sort of invitation to see the unseen and to participate intellectually. It is not actively giving a message; the message is inevitably passed on through this way of thinking. As soon as we deliberately choose a message in order to achieve some end, we become merchants and men of politics.

SR: Many acclaimed Iranian films feature beautiful pastoral scenery and offer a flight into the rural calm of the country; there is a lot of rural nostalgia in many Iranian films. On the other hand, when films are made in urban settings, they tend to show poverty and crime. The city is depicted as the source of all evil. Few films are preoccupied with showing the complex, multilayered reality of city life, but your films are an exception in this respect. They depict modern cities as places where the people are not all poor and unhappy or all rich and happy. Except in *Bashu, the Little Stranger*, most of your post-revolutionary films are preoccupied with the conflicts between old and modern Tehran, its urban structures and the features that both free and imprison its inhabitants, such as its chaotic and claustrophobic traffic.

BB: I have made three pastoral films set in villages. Like my urban films, my rural films are not documentaries. They are ethnographic, with a lyrical language. In *Stranger and the Fog*, a wounded and amnesiac stranger disturbs the calm of the village that lies across the river. In *Ballad of Tara* the return of a centuries-old historical figure in search of his lost sword ties the village to his forgotten sense of identity. In *Bashu, the Little Stranger* the war in faraway cities 'gives' a homeless boy to a village, but at the same time takes the arm of a villager. None of these films is a typical pastoral Iranian film – especially if one considers that women are at the centre of the villages and indeed the films themselves. You could say the same thing about my historical films. None of them is typically historical. In *Death of Yazdgerd*, the king flees from the capital – Ctesiphon – to a dark, miniature Asia, followed by only a few of his courtiers; the cast is made up of only seven characters.

The film examines the contradictions of an ancient monarchy that, from our viewpoint, seems to be a distant illusion.

The rest of my films have urban settings. In *Downpour*, the arrival of a new teacher in a poor quarter of the city leads the inhabitants to turn the teacher into a plaything whom they can fight and make fun of, thereby changing both themselves and the teacher. In *Crow*, a TV presenter and his wife, who is a teacher of people with hearing and speech disabilities, look for a lost young girl in Tehran. The mother of the TV presenter – who embodies the lost girl's old age – is looking for a lost Tehran or maybe a lost past or her lost youth. In *Perhaps Some Other Time* [1987] a woman pregnant with her first child is troubled by the fact that she doesn't know her origins – and there's also her distrustful husband who, while following her around in his car, leads her to find her lost self. In *Travellers* [1991] the inhabitants of a house that is being renovated are waiting for travellers from the other side of the sea to bring a recently married couple a mirror. Even the accident that befalls these travellers and their consequent deaths, which turns the wedding celebrations into a wake, does not free them from the responsibility of delivering the mirror! In *Killing Mad Dogs* [2001] a female writer who is trying to save her husband from going to prison in postwar Tehran is forced to travel to every corner of the city and thereby gain important insights into the nature of the society around her and of herself. In *When We Are All Sleeping* [2009] the meeting between a suicidal woman and a man recently released from prison is the subject of a film that's being shot in Tehran. In the meantime, another group tries to sabotage the film. I think that the image of the place, the city and the society as the source of all events is present not only in my films but also in my plays – even those that are set in times past.

SR: You are both a writer and a film-maker. Your writing draws on a thousand years of (New) Persian literature – even when you break away from that tradition. As a film-maker, though, you don't have as rich a background. Film has a very short history in Iran, not only in comparison with poetry but also in comparison with cinema in other countries. In other words, cinema is a Western, imported art. My question is, who were your major influences? Did you learn your craft from foreign film-makers only or did you have Iranian role models as well?

BB: My generation learned to make films by watching them, without the luxury of role models. This way of learning – by watching without having the means to make things – opens up interesting paths to every individual film-maker. Iranian culture has unintentionally given us some guidelines. Saadi is the best teacher in our literature and in his poetry he enjoins us to learn manners from those who don't have any, to learn perseverance from ants and to be daring and aim for the best, even if that means taking risks. We learned from great masters of the cinema but we did our own thing.

SR: That means that your role models were mostly foreign rather than Iranian?

BB: What I am trying to say is that we did not learn so much by studying the works of masters as by trying to distance ourselves from what we saw as the perversion of cinema, as bad taste, commerciality. There were few art films made in the 1920s and 1930s; we had *Haji Agha, the Cinema Actor* [1933] made by the Iranian-Armenian film-maker Avanes Ohanian, and later the first Iranian film with sound, *The Lor Girl* [written by Abdolhossein Sepenta and directed by Ardeshir Irani, 1933], which was made in Bombay in the Persian language. After a few experimental films, Iranian art cinema started to become more robust in the 1950s and 1960s by trying to follow the opposite course to that of commercial films – which wrongly became known as Film Farsi. At the same time, some of the techniques used in these films served as important guidelines for us. There weren't many Persian films that we could use as exemplars. There were some good short films and feature films, but you could count them on your fingers. We had to learn by doing, by trial and error.

For me, personally, an important source of inspiration is Persian carpets, which feature in my short, eight-minute film about Iranian rugs called *The Speaking Carpet*. You know, a lot of Persian, Indian and Central Asian carpets depict a talking tree. The 'Talking Tree' is a Persian myth that is mentioned in Ferdowsi's *Book of Kings.*[5] I refer to this theme and compare film-making to carpet-weaving. You weave a carpet on a loom, which allows you to combine images and patterns – like an ancient computer, in a way – until you end up with a whole picture. As well as Persian poetry and Persian carpets, I have been much influenced by Persian illuminations and *Ta'zieh* [Shi'i religious passion plays], which I view not only in a religious light but also in an ancient Persian light and in which the epic story of tragic heroes is celebrated. I have also been influenced by Western painting and drama. I'm just saying this in order to give you an idea of my cultural background – into which I've been thrown and which I'm trying to make sense of through my film-making and other artistic activities.

SR: By grappling artistically with this cultural package you have become a celebrated film-maker worldwide and a very influential one in your own country.

BB: The meagre result of four decades of work, because of endless censorship, does not satisfy me. Independent Iranian film-makers have to pay heavily for that small reward. I just try to remain as honest as possible by refusing to become a salesman.

SR: This takes us back to our discussion about censorship. If you lived under different conditions – in a place where censorship did not exist – would you make different films?

BB: I'm one of those lucky film-makers who have a list of all the films and scripts that would have made it to the screen had the regime not forbidden them. Thank God we have an underground culture here where my forbidden scripts are circulated! All our foreign neighbours have made films about Ferdowsi – we are the only country that, despite claiming Ferdowsi as our greatest poet, has not made a film about him. My *Dibachehye Novin-e Shahnameh* [*A New Prologue to Shahnameh*][6] was forbidden for fear of causing trouble with the conservative clergy. In the case of my film about a woman looking for her lost husband during World War II in Tehran, I hope the Farabi has not forgotten how much pressure they put on me to change the female part and have another man look for her husband instead! They think a film-maker's imagination is a blank paper upon which they can write whatever script they want!

SR: You are one of the few film-makers who almost always show very strong heroines around whom the story revolves – and that, despite the fact that women-related issues are the foremost concern of censorship in this country. Would you have concentrated on women in that way had it not been for that form of censorship against which you fight in your films?

BB: I was asked this question many years ago in a press conference outside Iran. I was at a festival showing my *Perhaps Some Other Time* [1987] and was asked whether I would have made the same film in a free country. I answered, 'I do not know – I have no idea what freedom is!' I was asked why I go in for unrealistic and seemingly irrational scenes, such as the one of the woman who wears a scarf in bed even though no man is present in the house. I explained that the Farabi and the Ministry of Culture and Islamic Guidance believe that the viewer should not set eyes on a woman's uncovered hair! There was a loud exclamation of surprise in the audience. I explained to them that the main reason why my films *Ballad of Tara* and *The Death of Yazdgerd* were forbidden was that the heroines did not wear scarves! So my choice was between giving up making films altogether and making them with such 'unrealistic' scenes, which will surely be seen as historical evidence of the regime's backwardness and denial of the reality of Iran. Of course, I could have given up making films and done the regime a favour. I did not want to do that and so chose to make films in such unfavourable conditions. That's why I answered the question about freedom and film-making with: 'I do not know – I have no idea what freedom is!'

SR: Was it not easier for you to make films under the shah, where censorship was not concerned with women's appearance?

BB: Hold your horses! We had very strict censorship in those days too. It is true that we did not have to clothe women in scarves and *chadors*, but in all films, all good women – or those who atoned and became good – ended up wearing scarves or *chadors*! In fact, the covered woman has always been a traditional moral value hidden under the surface of our society. The revolution did away with that layer and revealed the morality that became the dominant morality among all people. Even in those days it was forbidden to examine the psychological issues and contradictions that arose between people and society. Anything that might be problematic from the aspect of politics, religion, tradition, class or society was forbidden. You see, a conservative society mainly gives rise to conservative intellectuals. You might be surprised, but a fortnight before the revolution all that our intellectuals were concerned about was how to preserve the morality of society, which has its roots deep in tradition.

SR: But, as I asked earlier, does not censorship based on such values make you use subtle techniques in order to criticize those values? Does it not make the viewer, who has to use his imagination in order to get your message, your 'partner in crime'? Does not censorship make you more creative?

BB: I beg the authorities to stop trying to fertilize art and give us some freedom of action! If we don't give the patient the right to speak, we will never know what ails him! We cannot prescribe boracic for all illnesses! If I'm thirsty, don't stop me from drinking water by pretending to fear that I might choke! If you give me freedom, as a grown-up I can use my faculties and decide how much water I need to drink without choking. If the West thinks censorship is good for your creativity, we are more than happy to export despotism, which we have in abundance, alongside gas and oil.

SR: Well, among my interviewees, those who do not find censorship a bad thing per se remind me that in the West there are mechanisms of censorship as well. Restrictions on what can and cannot be said also apply there.

BB: You cannot apply the same name both to the regulations that block all paths of negotiation and to those regulations that give you space for dialogue and freedom of movement. If you call both sets of regulations 'law', then you are insulting lawfulness. In Iran large sums of money are spent trying to prove that other countries have censorship as well. Despite the fact that the regime calls regulation in other countries 'censorship', in order to justify its own doings, we have to ask ourselves one question: do the wrongdoings of other countries justify the wrongdoings of our country? And, anyway, in our country, censorship is not regulated. It's a matter of taste. One minister of guidance may forbid your film and a few months later, when the post is occupied by someone new, you may get permission to screen that very same film! This has happened to me quite a few times: the fate of my film *Travellers* is especially illuminating. The Ministry of Culture and Islamic Guidance had forbidden it, but the Farabi Cinema Foundation took the responsibility for its production and the film was screened. Then, however, the Farabi pretended not to know anything about it and the Ministry of Culture and Islamic Guidance pulled all the copies from the movie theatres, took the film out of the programme and cut out all the 'corrupt' parts. The film was ruined and everybody's face – except that of the film-maker – was saved. So there you go. Censorship is often a matter of rivalry between the people in charge. It is a means of exercising power. Perhaps it is an Iranian trait. We are a people that will stick a knife in each other's backs if we find it convenient.

SR: I don't agree with that. Most Iranians who live in the diaspora share a feeling of solidarity that is necessary for leading happy and successful lives. Most Iranians don't have the problems of other large immigrant groups – such as the Turks in Germany or the North Africans in France – and have very good reputations as academics, doctors, lawyers, entrepreneurs and other types of professional. So, should we not conclude that if Iranians could live at home in a modern, healthy political system, they too would act in the same way?

BB: I think we are both getting at the same thing. I did not mean to accuse any group. I just wanted to point out the behaviour of people who live in despotic systems and are not even aware of such traits in themselves. As you've noted yourself, their environment has made them so.

However, at the very hearts of those very modern and success-ful people in the diaspora, you will very often find old-fashioned, traditional ways of thinking that feed on religious prejudice, racism, ethnic background, misogyny – in short, an authoritar-ian and inveterate culture that will always stop progress towards true modernity. Most Iranians deny this fact when confronted with it. And in that respect, the Iranians in the diaspora are not much different from their countrymen living in Iran. I guess we are just starting to become aware of these traits that obstruct our path towards a truly modern way of living. However, the road is long and we cannot yet accomplish the big leap together as a nation.

SR: Let us talk about unofficial social censorship that goes hand in hand with official censorship from above.

BB: Inevitably, New Iranian Cinema could only grow by comply-ing with the regulations and simultaneously finding ways to evade them. This was the case both before and after the revolution.

SR: Well, you cannot deny that the majority of films before the revolution were cheap and superficial Film Farsi.

BB: I am not defending that genre. I hope you are aware of the fact that a considerable percentage of people in this country are still watching illegal copies of those cheap and superficial films. Or worse, they are consuming legal, Islamic copies of them. Anyway, we are repeating ourselves. As I said before, we always had art films and commercial films. It was the art films that were labelled 'New Iranian Cinema' in later years.

SR: So the revolution had nothing to do with the progress of art films?

BB: You seem to be ignoring the time factor. More than 30 years have passed since those days. Do you honestly believe that art films or New Iranian Cinema would have stayed at the point where they started in the 1950s and 1960s if the revolution hadn't taken place? Do you honestly believe that without a revolution we would not have attained the highly esteemed position that we have in the world today? On the contrary, we'll never know how our cinema would have developed had its progress not been slowed by the revolution. I must say that I can't think of any film that could only have been made in a revolution! In each phase of our film-making, whether before or after the revolution, a considerable amount of time and energy was spent on forbidding films and silencing intellectual and independent movements. What we must constantly bear in mind is the fact that our world did not start with the revolution! We are the product of a culture that gave rise to works such as the *Avesta*, *Khodaynameh* [*Khwaday-Namag*] and *Hezar Afsan*,[7] and poets such as Rudaki, Ferdowsi, Rumi, Saadi and Hafez.[8] The museums of this world are filled with our art and history. I do not understand how our rulers, who never fail to notice a single uncovered hair, completely disregard this vast cultural and geographical entity out of which we grew. We are not the product of the revolution alone but also of our vast history and culture.

SR: One of the reasons why people in the West are amazed by post-revolutionary Iranian films has to do with their understanding of Islamic aesthetics. The large-scale 'Islamization' of all spheres of art, culture and private life has greatly overshadowed the identity of this country worldwide. So, the people in the West ask themselves, how is it possible that films from the Islamic Republic are so successful when showing images is forbidden in Islam?

BB: That the West is 'amazed' does not surprise me. They will always be patronizingly amazed by our achievements, so enthralled by themselves. However, what disturbs me is the fact that the Iranian government on the one hand presents itself as the great avenger of the Third World against the West, and on the other profits from the attention the West gives to the films coming out of

Iran, which in fact have nothing to do with the regime! This shows
the extent of the identity crisis that reigns in this country! Iran's
taking pleasure in the attention of the West shows that both the
regime and the people measure themselves according to Western
standards and in that way confirm the status of the hegemonic
West as being 'the world'!

Since the revolution all we've been doing is giving our entire
attention to the West and at the same time – to the satisfaction of
our Arab neighbours in particular – obliterating our whole culture
and all our achievements that predate the dawn of Islam in general
and the Islamic Revolution in particular.

Talking of Islam at this point, I would like to know whether
people in the West always refer to Christian aesthetics when they
talk about their various cultures and achievements? Do their
museums put all Western art and culture and identity in the one
pot of Christianity and thus 'erase' the nations of Europe? Why do
they do it to us, then? By looking through the filter of Islam at
the peoples of our part of the world, they 'erase' our cultures, our
diversity, our histories. If that's the way to do it, why don't they do it
to themselves? The Iranians happened to exist before Islam, before
Christianity and before Alexander the Great. In the West, Iranian
art from pre-Islamic times – from the Achaemenid, Arsacid and
Sassanid periods – is often not even labelled correctly. The West,
from the time of the ancient Greeks, very often relies on the stories
of the enemies of Iran for getting to know Iran. This leads them
to feel confused about us and amazed at our artistic achievements. And look at us: we're so in awe of the compliments of these
confused people!

Perhaps in order for the West to understand the relationship
between Islam and Iranian art it is useful to recall an event from
the time of the Arab invasion of Iran in the seventh century CE.
When the Muslim troops reached the Sassanid palace in Ctesiphon
[which lies in Iraq today], they saw a wonderful carpet called
Baharestan ['the spring garden'] which, like a garden of gems,
stunned them. What did they do? They cut it into a hundred pieces
and took it as loot! They did not cut the carpet into pieces because
their religion forbade the image but because they could sell each

bit for a lot of money. From this anecdote the West can learn that, depending on the circumstances, depiction is not forbidden in Islam if it brings a profit to merchants. That is the very reason why cinema became successful in a country like Iran, where the Islamic regime was, in fact, against it.

SR: So it was business and commerce that helped our New Iranian Cinema rather than our art?

BB: It's a mistake to think that the government was uniformly agreed on matters of art. There were those who wanted to make a public toilet out of the Theatre-e Shahr [City Theatre] and those who wanted to abuse theatre and cinema as a means of propaganda for their political and ideological ends. They somehow reached an agreement and did not completely burn and ruin everything. We don't know why. But what we certainly do know is that business considerations accounted for at least half the grounds on which they reached their agreement. They realized that they could use national television for their ideological propaganda and the Iranian cinema as a platform for self-promotion on an international level and even make quite a bit of money out of it!

SR: That means that, eventually, good came out of evil.

BB: Yes, especially for the middlemen and those brokers and wheeler-dealers who got a commission.

SR: The festivals to which your films were sent gave you an important platform. How do you view them?

BB: Do I really have to answer this question? I've always felt ill at ease at festivals.

SR: But you cannot deny that they served as a marketplace where new products could be introduced.

BB: I am not a merchant. I'm supposed to be a film-maker!

SR: Some connoisseurs of Iranian film, such as the former head of the Farabi Cinema Foundation, Mohammad Beheshti, are of the opinion that these film festivals were initially not a platform for Iranian film but more of an obstacle. In the beginning Iranian films were boycotted or sabotaged precisely because they came out of the Islamic Republic. It was only thanks to the Farabi's persistence and to the attention of some lovers of independent European film that our cinema was able to secure a place for itself, and the festival organizers realized how useful that was for them.

BB: I respect Mr Beheshti greatly for his intelligence and for having helped film-makers as much as he could. But my experience of the government's attempts to introduce Iranian cinema to the world is a different one. It was first and foremost the regime and the Ministry of Culture and Islamic Guidance that put a myriad of obstacles in our way with regard to foreign film festivals. The West was not necessarily an enemy of the Iranian revolution when it came to allowing Iranian films to be shown at their festivals. The Islamic Republic, on the other hand, was very active both at home and abroad in denouncing as decadent and corrupt the art and culture of the West. Anyway, what I learnt from my years of exile in the West was that its cultural institutions treated me just as the Farabi and the Ministry of Culture and Islamic Guidance wanted them to treat me: they very politely refused to offer me help or an opportunity to realize my projects – as if they had been schooled by the government in Tehran.

You see, we don't need any enemies when we have a government that denies our identity, our culture, our literature and our history and thus pleases our arch enemies in the outside world. Not only that, we have the highest brain-drain in the world, thus aiding the prosperity of the West and the East, without them having invested a penny in the training and education of the Iranians who go over to them. Nobody can top us in wounding ourselves. There is no difference between assassinating our intellectuals and flooding our centuries-old archaeological sites through new dam projects; no difference between forcing our best brains out of the country and banning our films from being shown in Iran until they crumble to dust in their boxes. Why did they stop Naderi's film *Water, Wind, Dust* [1989] from going to the Cannes Film Festival even though the festival organizers had requested it?[9] Why did they always find excuses to stop me from being present at the festivals where my films were being shown?

During the Toronto Film Festival, where my film *Travellers* was being screened, the festival organizers phoned me in Tehran and asked why the Farabi kept telling them that either they didn't know me or that I am not in Iran or that I refuse to go to the festival for personal reasons. So I complained to the Farabi which swiftly apologized for the confusion and sent someone to get my passport so that they could arrange a visa for my trip to Canada. A few days before the festival, they said the visa had been issued but that they had no access to my passport because the person in charge at the Farabi had locked it in the drawer of his desk and had taken the key away with him! Some days later they called me excitedly and said that they had succeeded in breaking the lock and could now send me to Toronto. However, the festival was almost over by then and all the critics were in the process of leaving. The list of the festivals where I was sabotaged by the government is long. I could either not be present when my films were shown or else my films were chopped and shown as abridged versions.

SR: So, it wasn't the West that sabotaged and censored you?

BB: Madam, I've just given you an account of my personal experience!

SR: One of the most important historical events in post-revolutionary Iran was the war with Iraq. Why do we see so few worthy films about this? You yourself have only made *Bashu, the Little Stranger* about the war.

BB: What they did to me after that film was made was enough for me to realize that it is futile to go anywhere near that war. They can't begin to understand an independent person. They believe that if you don't think like them, then you are their enemy. They thought the war belonged to them and nobody had the right to make a film about it from a different point of view. I could have made more films about the war – but not about celebrating death and destruction. I have written two scripts about the Iran–Iraq War: *Hura in the Mirror* and *The Evidence*. I was not allowed to make either of them. I have given up on my most important war-film projects.

SR: Earlier on we discussed the importance of business for the survival of Iranian cinema after the revolution. We concluded that it was saved partly because of the inclination of the men in positions of power to do business – otherwise our cinema would have been sacrificed on the altar of dogmatic Islam.

BB: I repeat again and again that New Iranian Cinema started in the 1950s and 1960s, before the Islamic Revolution. It was halted for a while after the revolution. In the beginning, those who were fanatically against the cinema seemed to have the upper hand. They tried everything in order to distance themselves from the pre-revolutionary film-makers and to use the medium of film only as a means of ideological propaganda. These propaganda films were repeatedly denied access to world festivals and the regime saw this not as a comment on the quality of the films but as a manifestation of the hostility of the West towards the Islamic Republic. Gradually more rational minds managed to convince the fanatics that famous pre-revolutionary film-makers could be used as door openers in the West. In that way the Islamic Republic would gain a worldwide presence. The authorities also came to understand that the many films that reflected human values, without being explicitly political or critical, could be sold as films with Islamic values! So, after a while, Iranians were seen as living in a peaceful society whose problems, however trivial, could be solved with a little self-sacrifice! The West and the East received the message as an offer of peace and reconciliation and, in their simplicity, conceived of Iranian films as a pleasant alternative or supplement to their own highly technical and complex offerings. Little by little everybody forgot about the storm of the Islamic Revolution that almost ruined our cinema. They closed their eyes to the violence behind the pastoral scenes of New Iranian Cinema. Everybody was having fun! However, the new Iranian film-makers, who had initially tried to operate on the same wavelength as the authorities, soon realized that real film-making requires independence. Some of them even started to openly criticize and confront the government and its institutions.

SR: What was the role of foreign producers here? Did you ever have any fruitful encounters with them?

BB: Opportunities did arise. There were very kind producers with whom I would liked to have worked had they not relied so much on their Iranian consultants. A couple of times I was promised financial help by foreign producers, but somehow the money ended up going elsewhere.

SR: By foreign producers do you mean MK2, Sony and Miramax, who have a reputation for being supporters of art movies and independent cinema?

BB: I am not going to name names. But I understood − a little too late − that a lot of Western producers approached me and others in order to find out which film-makers passed muster with our government and which were too risky to invest any money in! I mean, they are businessmen and do not want to take risks. However, the world's view of Iran and its cinema is always changing. Maybe nowadays you make money by investing in films that are critical of the regime − I don't know!

SR: Many people believe that investing in an Iranian film − regardless of its stance in relation to the regime − is never that risky for European or multinational producers. The cost of producing an Iranian film is perhaps one tenth or one hundredth of the cost of a French or American film. So the chances that a company could profit from being active in a Third World country are not negligible.

BB: And of course their Iranian partners profit even more from such collaborations because they get the money in foreign currency, which, in view of our worthless money and high inflation, could quadruple in a short while. In the meantime, they spend only a fraction of that money on the actual film and in the end the film doesn't get screened anyway. So you see how much we could profit from film-production companies that love art and moral values?

SR: Why did you not participate in such projects? As you mentioned earlier, what saved our cinema was to a large extent the love of business.

BB: And the other thing that saved it was the intellectual and moral independence of those who had ideas to realize. *Ballad of Tara* sold very well at the beginning of the revolution. At the time, it was made with great difficulty amid quarrels between the pro- and anti-cinema groups. The contracts for foreign release were automatically cancelled after the regime decided to ban the film and so I just stood there with empty hands, barely able to pay the actors and technicians. However, they couldn't destroy me even though I was unable to make many of my planned films. Still, I don't believe that those who banned my films lead a happy life today.

Anyway, I am not a businessman. Many years ago I took one of my scripts to an amenable, so-called independent producer in Paris. The film I wanted to make was about the last two hours of Hedayat's life before he committed suicide. The producers had already read the summary, paid me many compliments and told me how honoured they were to meet such an important international figure! Well, at the very end of our meeting they said that they were very keen on producing the film but on condition that 51 per cent of the budget would come from Iran. After all, the subject of the film would be of greatest interest to Iranians! I knew right there and then that they must have been advised by a very clever Iranian consultant, knowing full well that no one in Iran would agree to such an undertaking. In that way the French could be let off the hook without offending me. I told them that if I were able to make this film in Iran, I would not have troubled them in the first place. Hedayat had to put up with so much hardship in order to get to Paris and kill himself. He could not choose his place of birth, but at least he had the freedom to choose his place of death in a city that's supposed to be the cradle of freedom. I told them that they had good reason to produce my film without the partici-pation of any Iranian producer. They said that their hands were tied, that they were sorry, but that they had to accept the advice of their Iranian consultants who were well aware of the value of the great Beyzaie to Iranian cinema. Well, there you go! The Iranian consultants are brokers and keepers of good relations with the authorities. They knew that a film about Hedayat does not smell of money!

(ﺩ ﺱ ﺍﻥ)

3

ABBAS KIAROSTAMI

Where is the Revolution?

ABBAS KIAROSTAMI AGREED TO GIVE AN INTERVIEW only reluctantly. I reminded him insistently that the absence of a film-maker with whom film is supposed to end (see below), would be catastrophic for a project whose subject is post-revolutionary New Iranian Cinema. Eventually he agreed. Sitting across from me, he grins ironically and says that ever since Alberto Elena decided to quote Jean-Luc Godard ('Film begins with D.W. Griffith and ends with Abbas Kiarostami') on the cover of his monograph *The Cinema of Abbas Kiarostami*,[1] that remark is mentioned every time someone says or publishes anything about Kiarostami. He is at pains to point out that Godard made this statement only in relation to *Life, and Nothing More* (also known as *And Life Goes On*, 1992), the second part of Kiarostami's *Earthquake Trilogy*, which is also known as the *Koker Trilogy* (the other two parts being *Where is the Friend's Home?* and *Through the Olive Trees*, released in 1987 and 1994 respectively), which was made in the early 1990s. However, Kiarostami explains, the statements that Godard has made about him in the last ten or 15 years clearly show that he no longer believes that film ends with Kiarostami!

I ask him what he means by that. He just smiles, waves his hand and says, joking aside, that talking about New Iranian Cinema is

59

quite difficult for him. First and foremost he has a problem with discussing the idea of a New Iranian Cinema 'after the Islamic Revolution', because this is tantamount to accepting the (from his point of view) wrong thesis that the revolution played a crucial role in the development of Iranian cinema. From his point of view, this theory is a falsification of history. The Iranian New Wave had already arisen before the revolution. He is convinced that those who earn their daily bread in government and quasi-governmental film institutes spread rumours about the benefits of the revolution for fear that they might lose their jobs if they didn't. For Kiarostami, the revolution actually delayed the growth of a very fruitful artistic movement that had already started decades before the 1979 revolution. One could even say that Iranian art cinema grew *despite* and not because of post-revolutionary censorship, nepotism and dogmatism. The only positive side of the revolution for Iranian cinema (and any form of art and literature in Iran today) is its ability to advertise films in the West and the rest of the world, although Kiarostami sees this as a 'negative phenomenon'.

Kiarostami believes that the revolution had no influence whatsoever on his art. Although he sees himself very much as an Iranian citizen, he cannot relate to post-revolutionary cinema and does not see his films as part of a post-revolutionary cinematic movement. The revolution did not create a favourable artistic or intellectual environment in which he could make his films; the revolution was just an event – a historical event – that passed him by, and he does not regard himself as part of a genre that is sold as 'post-revolutionary Iranian cinema'. In other words, he is neither a 'revolutionary' nor a 'post-revolutionary' film-maker. He knows that he is often accused of 'escapism', of not reflecting the reality and the *zeitgeist* of post-revolutionary Iran in his films. This he attributes to the fact that he strives not so much to understand the phenomenon of the revolution as to get closer to the reality that surrounds him. In pursuing this goal, he 'depicts' life in Iran sometimes in a very realistic and sometimes in an otherworldly, poetic manner.

This milieu is vital to his art and, in a way, his reason for staying in Iran. In his view many important film-makers, such as Golestan, Shahid Saless and Naderi, have been unable to make the films that they deserved to make precisely because they left their native country and were unable to establish roots in exile. This is why Kiarostami, despite much hardship, has stayed in Iran.[2]

His beginnings as a film-maker, he reminds me, go back to the 1960s and 1970s – the years in which he worked with the Kanoon (Institute for the Intellectual Development of Children and Young Adults) under the management of Lili Arjomand and the auspices of Queen Farah Dibah. I tell him that I am aware that his pre-revolutionary films from these decades, such as *Nan va Koucheh* (*The Bread and Alley*) and *Gozaresh* (*The Report*), made respectively in 1970 and 1977, introduced him to the world as an important film-maker of the Iranian New Wave. However, it was only after the revolution that he became known as a world-class cineaste: he was awarded the *Palme d'Or* for his film *Taste of Cherry* 20 years after the making of *The Report* and 18 years after the 1979 revolution. Kiarostami reacts to this observation with his unique sense of humour. Who knows, he muses, he might have won the *Palme d'Or* just the same without a revolution! There is no way of proving whether the revolution facilitated, however arbitrarily, his success at the Cannes Film Festival, since the revolution had already taken place by then. From his point of view, the purported connection between the revolution and his films has been fabricated by people who secure their living through close ties to the government and its so-called cultural institutions. These fabrications, Kiarostami says, are enhanced further as universal 'truth' by the naive post-rationalizations of scholars, critics and academics in the West. They have, however, no connection whatsoever to reality.

I seize on the clues I discern in this remark and invite him to help me find out the truth or myth behind statements about his role in New Iranian Cinema. He replies that reality is itself a fabrication and I am reminded of his frequently quoted aphorism: 'Lie. The shortest way to truth is to lie.' After a short pause he politely agrees to be interviewed by me and contemplates my questions with artistic and intellectual curiosity, in the hope of getting closer to the truth.

Note

The interview with Kiarostami took place during three long sessions in his house in north Tehran – a house filled with old Persian rugs, glass and ceramic ware, modern European furniture, Kiarostami's own photographs and books, and, most importantly, as Kiarostami proudly points out, two prints on the living room wall by Kurosawa, dedicated to Kiarostami by the master himself.

Initially Kiarostami was not very keen on giving an interview and said that in the last ten years or so he had not given any interview for publication in Iran, on account of the shameful treatment he had received at the hands of the Iranian press after winning the *Palme d'Or* for *Taste of Cherry* in 1997.[3] In the beginning he suggested giving me a photograph as an answer to each of my questions (Kiarostami is a celebrated photographer whose work was shown at a major exhibition at the Museum of Modern Art in New York in 2007). He said that he distrusted words as a means of expressing the truth and felt he was 'clumsy' with them. I reminded him that, his own assessment notwithstanding, he has quite a reputation among the connoisseurs of Persian poetry as someone who knows how to work with words.[4] We finally agreed that I would not record his interview. For this reason Kiarostami's answers to my questions are not presented as direct quotations.

Shiva Rahbaran: I start by explaining to Abbas Kiarostami that the aim of this project is to understand the influence of the Islamic Revolution on New Iranian Cinema and the influence of this cinema on the post-revolutionary society in which it is produced. I want to approach this question from the viewpoint of those film-makers who live and work in Iran. Iranian film, I suggest, has turned into an alternative identity card for a country that is mainly represented in the Western media by angry, *chador*-clad women and bearded men burning flags in front of Western embassies in Tehran. My first question is, how do film-makers in Iran see their role in changing the rules of the game in Iran itself (and thereby creating pockets of freedom), on the one hand, and changing the perception of Iran in the West (and the rest of the world), on the other?

Abbas Kiarostami does not deny his Iranianness at all. He says that he can only work so long as he lives in Iran, in the framework that he has created for himself in this corner of the world. During the interview he refers to this framework as his own self-made paradise. However, he cannot see any relation between his films and post-revolutionary cinema. He believes that the revolution has passed him by.

SR: How could he claim such a thing, I object, when his films are mostly highly realistic and, like a delicate seismograph, record the psychological and emotional condition of individual Iranians within their social and natural surroundings?

AK says that the films he made before the revolution had exactly the same quality. Neither the revolution nor the war changed his way of film-making. This does not mean that he as a citizen did not come into contact with these disturbing events. He too had to stand in long queues in the early years after the revolution to get milk-rationing coupons for his young children. Like hundreds of thousands of Iranians, he too had to leave Tehran in haste with his family for the Caspian shores in search of the shelter that the Alborz mountains offered during Saddam Hussein's missile offensives against the capital. However, none of these experiences forced him to make a film about the revolution or the war.

SR: I ask him whether he therefore denies the importance of the 1979 revolution for the development of Iranian cinema and its popularity internationally.

AK clearly believes that the theory that the revolution promoted the international success, progress and appeal of Iranian cinema is an instance of post-rationalization – an academic myth that has been created by so-called 'intellectuals' and 'scholars' both inside and outside Iran who are dependent on the regime for their livelihoods and for funding their research and symposia on Iranian cinema. It is very difficult to undo the myth of the usefulness of the revolution for the progress of Iranian cinema. Too many people make a living by promoting the myth. They want us all to forget that the Iranian New Wave had actually started two decades before the revolution and was highly regarded internationally. No one can say for sure that the revolution was the catalyst for the attention that Iranian cinema enjoys today. Kiarostami is convinced that the revolution has, in fact, distanced him as a film-maker from his Iranian audience, or severed the ties between his Iranian audience and his films. The official and unofficial means of censorship have hindered his artistic activity and damaged his relationship with the people of Iran. He jokes that perhaps the only positive thing that could be said about the usefulness of the revolution to his films was that it honed his ability to turn a negative situation into a positive one. Good can come out of evil, God willing. The revolution forced him to use his imagination and turn a bad situation into a positive one by taking refuge in his paradise – his house and studio in the breezy outskirts of northern Tehran, his peaceful retreat amidst the hot, unstable and easily excitable Iran, where he could live, paint, take photos, make films and write poetry. In this paradise he can turn what he witnesses in society into art. The revolution has not influenced his film-making but it has *accidentally* (as it has no *will*, despite the claims of the revolutionaries) produced a climate in which he's been able to use his imagination and make his films. But for that, he concludes, he must thank himself and not the revolution!

SR: But, I persist, he cannot deny that this event – be it an accident or 'the will of history' or that of Allah – was a very good PR agent for Iranian cinema worldwide and especially in the West. The most important festivals in the West are very eager to show Iranian films, perhaps because Western audiences have always been very curious about the fact that such wonderful productions can come out of such a 'monstrous' country.

AK does not deny that the West, with its insatiable appetite for sensation and 'news' from post-revolutionary Iran, has always been influenced by publicity and propaganda. However, he insists that one should not confuse the attention that Iranian films receive at

Western festivals with the progress and quality of this cinema since the revolution. That applies especially to his films, where the revolution had hardly any influence on their development and style.

SR: I challenge this assertion: how can he ignore the influence of this global attention – which he attributes to the attractiveness of the revolution to the sensation-addicted West – on his artistic development?

AK clarifies that he does not ignore at all the influence of global attention on the development of his films, because this attention has spared him to a great extent from the sanctions and restrictions that many Iranian film-makers in Iran are forced to grapple with. Unlike the majority of his colleagues, he does not have to get 'permission' from the Ministry of Culture and Islamic Guidance in order to make a film. He jokes that, now that he has turned into a 'world-class' film-maker, partly thanks to the negative perception of the revolution, he can make his films in Iran but have them produced and distributed abroad.[5] However, he explains, this does not mean that the revolution as a historical event has affected his *style* of film-making. He is not a revolutionary film-maker whose style was revolutionized after 1979. It wasn't the revolution that enabled him to make good films. His first feature film *Zang-e Tafrih* (*Breaktime*) was screened in 1972 – seven years before the revolution. The film's realist and minimalist style, together with its poetic flights, was admired by international critics. This small example, he argues, shows clearly that it was not thanks to the revolution that he has become what he is today.

SR: So, in a way, I ask, the revolution 'freed' him from the revolution and its constraints by attracting the attention of the West – albeit unintentionally – to Iranian cinema in general and his films in particular?

AK reminds me that the Iranian New Wave started in the 1950s and 1960s. Mehrjui's *The Cow*, released in 1971, for example, won the International Critics' Award at the Venice Biennale[6] some seven or eight years before the revolution. He also reminds me that his own taboo-breaking film *The Report* (1977), which contained explicit bedroom scenes, was made three years before the revolution. In the early years of the revolution the films of important Iranian cineastes were not only subjected to censorship but some were burnt in their entirety and there are no surviving copies. So one could say that the revolution did not help our cinema to progress but in fact put it back by about seven or eight years. It took more than seven or eight years, he explains, before he could make a film such as *Where is the Friend's Home?*. Many such films spent years in the vaults of the Ministry of Culture and Islamic Guidance before being screened.

SR: I go on to say that many of his successful films were made during the years that Mohammad Beheshti was in charge of the Farabi Cinema Foundation. Several critics and scholars believe that this institute played a considerable role in the promotion of New Iranian Cinema both in Iran and internationally. In the interview he gave me for this book, Beheshti claims that the Farabi was like a gardener that prepared the ground for art films by weeding out Hollywood films, shallow foreign films and cheap Film Farsi productions.

AK replies that many scholars and critics are responsible for the 'Farabi Myth'. An institute such as the Farabi is interesting to an academic researcher who has to examine Iranian cinema in a political or historical or sociological framework. People who can get their academic teeth into this subject will find it enlightening. On the other hand, we have the 'exile' critics, who may well denounce those Iranian film-makers who depended on the Farabi as accomplices of the regime. And last but not least, he adds, the Farabi offers regime-friendly critics and scholars the evidence that New Iranian Cinema is one of the many fruits of the 'Glorious Islamic Revolution'.

SR: I counter that the Farabi acted as a sort of mediator between the fanatics at the Ministry of Culture and Islamic Guidance and the film-makers. I ask whether he doesn't think that the Farabi was quite successful in modifying the ministry's policies and making it possible for people like himself to make good films in a hostile environment.

AK replies that the Farabi did not owe its existence to the revolution. The Farabi's role model, he explains, was the Kanoon (Institute for the Intellectual Development of Children and Young Adults), an organization under the excellent management of Lili Arjomand, who was a true mediator between the royal court and art film-makers under the shah. Of course, the Farabi did try to take on a similar function under Mohammad Beheshti, who had a genuine interest in cinema. He did try to be a good 'gardener', as he claims, weeding out immoral, decadent foreign and home-grown films and preparing the ground for art films to flourish. However, he was not as successful as the Kanoon. The reason for this, he suggests, was mainly the ideology of the post-revolutionary regime. The majority of the mullahs and Islamic functionaries had a fundamental problem with cinema per se and believed it to be a decadent Western artform at odds with Islamic values.

SR: I put it to him that, despite Islamic censorship, many good films that broke a lot of Islamic taboos were made in those years.

AK explains that censorship in Iran is very different from that in other Islamic countries. In Iran it is a personal thing; the rules are made according to the tastes of the person in charge, not according to a clear set of rules and regulations. One censor might allow something that another censor had strictly banned a couple of years ago – or vice versa. In Kiarostami's eyes, the Farabi did not really succeed in moderating most aspects of censorship. It hardly had any influence on the wheelings and dealings of the Ministry of Culture and Islamic Guidance. All the Farabi ever did was to give funding to some film-makers, while other films had to stay for years and years in the vaults of the ministry before either being destroyed or given screening permission, but only after numerous scenes had been cut out. This alone is evidence enough that the

Farabi had little influence on the mechanisms of the Ministry of Culture and Islamic Guidance.

SR: Even though he may not agree that the Farabi contributed to the development of New Iranian Cinema after the revolution, I ask whether he will admit that it had considerable influence in introducing it to the world. I tell him that Mohammad Beheshti recalls the difficulties he faced when Iranian films were sent to foreign festivals. According to him, the restrictions of the regime were not too bad compared to the 'censorship' he had to grapple with in Western countries, namely, the quiet 'sabotage' of Iranian films owing to the political sentiments of the festival coordinators. They would either delay the screening of the films for a variety of reasons – he remembers that 'Iran' was spelt 'Iraq' on quite a few occasions – or they would say the film was of poor quality. All in all, he remembers that he had to fight for years after the revolution before a few independent minds realized the high quality of these films and could force them through the barriers of censorship and nepotism.

AK does not really think much of this. He remembers the difficulties Iranian films faced at festivals but that, he says, was not because the coordinators were negatively inclined towards Iran but because of the poor quality and technical shortcomings of the films themselves. Many of the audience left the cinema soon after screening began, either because they could not make out what was being said or because the old and substandard celluloid kept melting in the projectors. He believes that the most important reason for the miraculous survival of Iranian film is the exact opposite of what Beheshti claims: it only survived because of the few curious Western viewers who watched the films in their entirety, perhaps because of their curiosity about the negative aspects of the revolution. They asked themselves: how could such films come out of a country in the grip of an anti-Western revolution? The revolution had turned Iran into a land of mystery for them.

SR: I ask him whether, apart from this negative perception of the

revolution, which made Iranian films interesting to Western viewers, Iranian cinema also benefited from post-revolutionary censorship, in the sense that regulations and restrictions encouraged
creativity – in other words, that necessity was the mother of inven-
tion.

AK repeats that the Iranian New Wave started more than two
decades before the revolution and was not created by it. He also
notes that cinema had to grapple with censorship under the shah
too – although back then censorship was not directed against
cinema per se. He agrees that censorship benefited creativity but
only to a very limited extent. For example, architects might say
that they built their best houses on a very difficult piece of land
or with very limited financial means. However, the censorship
that post-revolutionary Iranian cinema had to grapple with went
beyond 'restrictions'. It had and still has a very strong ideological
streak that is fundamentally against art in general and cinema in
particular. As far as he's concerned, he never benefited from the
policies of the post-revolutionary art and film institutions. They
neither encouraged him nor gave him financial help nor promoted
his films. Not only were his films not subsidized but they were
restricted, in the sense that they were granted only very short-term
screening permission and therefore were unprofitable for large
cinemas that could only cover their costs by showing the films
for longer periods. He would go so far as to say that the policies
of the Ministry of Culture and Islamic Guidance and the media-
tions of the Farabi even managed to distance his Iranian audience
from him. Maintaining his sense of humour, he declares that the
great favour that these institutions did him was to promote him –
inadvertently – outside the country as an 'underground' Iranian
film-maker! Such a promotion brought him a lot of attention from
real cinephiles, such as Gilles Jacob,[7] who never wavered in their
enthusiasm for his films.

SR: Changing the subject, I tell him that one of the most obvious facets of censorship in Iran concerns the image of women.
Some critics believe that post-revolutionary censorship had a posi-

tive effect on the image of Iranian women in cinema; that the new parameters freed Iranian actresses – and thus women – from their role as sex-objects. In other words, I suggest, these scholars believe that 'cutting out' the decadent, sexual dimension in films enabled female actors to portray themselves as complete human beings.

AK does not agree. He believes that 'cutting out' the sexual aspect of female characters has had an adverse influence on viewers. This policy – whether it is applied on the big screen or on the streets of Iran – has led society to pay even more attention to the sexuality of women. He believes that women today are looked at and look at themselves much more voyeuristically than under the shah, where they themselves could decide how to convey their sexuality. In his view, post-revolutionary censorship has made it much harder for film-makers to approach the imagery of womanhood in a realistic, authentic manner.

SR: I tell him that he's often accused by his critics of being unin-terested in women's issues at all. Some, I add, even say that his lack of interest is calculated because by concentrating on showing chil-dren and men in the lovely Iranian countryside he's been able to manoeuvre himself away from the attentions of the Islamic censors.

AK finds this view very unfair. He protests that he does not like to display the wounds that Islamic censorship has inflicted on his films and on his soul just so as to be celebrated by the Iranian dias-pora as a martyr! He completely disagrees with the idea that he is a calculating and self-promoting film-maker. His interest in children as protagonists goes back to his work with the Kanoon in the 1960s and 1970s, where he was one of the founding members of its film-making department. As far as his interest in women goes, films such as *The Report* (1977), *Ten* (2002) or *10 on Ten* (2004) testify to his intensive preoccupation with what it's like being a woman in today's society. However, he's not too bothered by such accusa-tions; he knows that sensitivity to women's issues in Iran can be partly traced to Islamic censorship after the revolution but has its roots in the private and unofficial censorship that overshadows all relationships between men and women in this country. To a large extent, the problem of portraying women stems from a deep lack of knowledge of the female sex among most male film-makers in Iran. Most film-makers grew up in very traditional, religious families, where, as the saying goes, 'even the bare heel of a woman' is taboo. Although he doesn't believe that this justifies the severity of official censorship, to some extent it can account for the difficulties that even 'liberal' film-makers like himself face when it comes to showing – despite official censorship – erotic scenes. He and his colleagues in Iran could never do a convincing nude scene à la Bertolucci!

He goes on to explain that, aside from that, what preoccupies him with relation to the image of the female sex in films is the fundamental question: what does it mean to be an Iranian woman? What is the common factor or the difference between an affluent, Westernized Tehrani woman and a Baluchi woman with a *niqab* covering her face? As far as he can judge, the uptown Tehrani woman identifies more with what she sees in a Hollywood film than with the cinematic image of a nomadic woman.

SR: This brings me to the issue that is central to this project, namely, the role of the Iranian film-maker as an 'identity maker' for Iranians outside Iran. After the revolution, I explain, the Western media started to create and satisfy the permanent thirst of audiences for sensationalist news from hostile Iran by simplifying the complex political, social, cultural and historical issues facing the country. They did this by showing images of angry black-clad Iranian men and women punching the air and Western flags being burnt in front of embassies in Tehran. At the same time, Western festivals provided a platform for Iranian films that showed the image of 'the other' Iran to the world, thus projecting a different Iranian identity. Does he consider himself part of this group?

AK replies that he can agree with this observation only to a degree and goes on to answer my question with another: what is Iranian identity? He points out the enormous gaps between urban and rural Iran, between affluent, modern northern Tehran and the brutally poor slums on the peripheries of the cities and the deserts. Furthermore he cannot measure his own influence on shaping the identity of Iran, since the very idea of shaping an identity presupposes social engagement, being an *engagé* artist, and he confesses that he does not see himself as *engagé* in the traditional sense of the word.

SR: I put it to him that when one thinks of films such as *Where is the Friend's Home?* or *Taste of Cherry* one is not really convinced by this answer. In those films, I argue, pain and hope are shown in a very poetic but realistic manner. Watching these films one is convinced that the film-maker definitely does not subscribe to the principle of art for art's sake.

AK explains that, from his point of view, a socially engaged artist makes films according to a political or social ideology. For such a film-maker the film is only the medium for sending a message. He admits that, having chosen not to leave his country, despite numerous opportunities, he cannot be ignorant of what happens around him. However, when he depicts the reality in which he lives, he only does so because the aesthetics, dynamics and logic of his work force him to do so. No meta-structure or ideology is involved. In *engagé* cinema, in the classical sense, the exact opposite is true: ideology dictates the film-maker's path. On second thoughts, he says, perhaps he does have an indirect or incidental obligation towards the society in which he lives because he feels emotionally obliged to defend people's aspirations – he feels the pain, the happiness, the sadness of those among whom he lives. However, he does not seek to educate his audience as an *engagé* film-maker would do. The greatest risk that politically committed film-makers run is that of making propaganda films. He, on the other hand, feels committed only to the truth and nothing but the truth. Some accuse him of 'selecting' his audience, of approaching only 'elitist' viewers, but the reaction of audiences in Iran has proved the exact opposite. He has been approached by so many 'ordinary' people because of his films that he cannot accept the allegation of being elitist. The public love his films because of their portrayal of human suffering and human happiness, and it is these things that determine his artistic path.

SR: I go on to say that some of his critics and fellow film-makers claim that his modern and experimental films are made according to European tastes (see, for example, Hatamikia's interview below). In the West, I add, he is regarded as a world-class cineaste, but in Iran few cinemas show his films at all and even if they do then only for a short period because they do not enjoy the same popularity in his own country and are therefore unprofitable.

AK is well acquainted with these critics and often asks himself how it is they don't see the contradictions in what they say. On the one hand, they accuse him of artistic dishonesty and of applying self-censorship in order to sidestep the policies of the Ministry of Culture and Islamic Guidance, and on the other they see him as a film-maker who has sold out to the West!

SR: Yes, he is accused of having his cake and eating it, I say.

AK retorts that this must be the biggest compliment he has ever received. In that case, he adds, he is tempted to think of himself as a world-class magician.

SR: I add that from the beginning, film-makers were accused of being magicians.

AK is aware that such accusations are directed not only at him. He tells me that most film-makers, artists and writers who work in Iran and enjoy a certain degree of success must endure such negativity. This is what artists and intellectuals of every country in political turmoil or under revolution have to endure, whether in their own country or abroad. This situation has now reached a peak in Iran and especially within the large Iranian diaspora. Those in exile seem to accuse any Iranian film-maker working and living in Iran of betraying democratic values, while for many Iranian critics, artists and scholars, a film-maker who enjoys success abroad has sold out to the decadent West. His own message to critics on the right and on the left, in or outside Iran, is that art does not have any borders. Artists must first and foremost be committed to themselves, to what they consider the truth. Only in this way can artists be original.

SR: I move on to a different point. His films are extremely 'meta-fictional', I suggest. The viewer is constantly aware that he or she is an observer. His actors constantly show that they are only acting a part. This is especially obvious in films where he uses real people – such as the *Koker Trilogy*. In other words, his films project an awareness that these are only films. I ask whether such self-consciousness hinders the viewer from 'getting into' the film, from being immersed in the story. Is he not obstructing the emotional reaction of the viewers?

AK answers this question with another: why should he turn his viewers into hostages to their emotions? Immersing viewers in their emotions is something that he and his comrades-in-arms have been trying to fight against from the beginning of their careers. They have always fought against – not all that successfully it seems – the Hollywood and Film Farsi productions that lulled the consciousness of cinema goers by appealing to their emotions. He wants to free the viewers by liberating them from their addiction to emotionalism. He wants to force them into observation and self-observation and to ask questions instead of drowning them in sentimentalism.

SR: I also query the seeming liberation of his films from the narrative framework, of the story with a plot.

AK replies that he does not want to tell stories. He wants to write poetry. Poetry, in contrast to a novel, needs neither a hero nor time nor space nor a storyline. He remembers how Lili Arjomand, the head of the Kanoon, talked about his first feature film, *Breaktime*, before the revolution in the early 1970s. She called it a *poème*, he says, using the French word that apparently she used at that time.

He personally finds that his *Where is the Friend's Home?* is a poetic response to the great poet Sohrab Sepehri, just as his *Life, and Nothing More* was a contemplation on Forough Farrokhzad's poetry.

SR: I say that I find it interesting that Kiarostami, the most modern, or as some (such as his colleague Hatamikia) believe, Francophile film-maker, locates the roots of his films in Persian poetry.

AK says that having roots in a traditional Iranian art is at once at odds with modernity and necessary for achieving modernity. He repeats that he does not feel that he belongs to post-revolutionary Iranian cinema. However, this does not mean that he has no connection with Iranian heritage and tradition. The Iranian heritage is his fate. His main preoccupation in his own poetry is this tradition – the works of poets such as Saadi and Hafez. He experiments with form while keeping an eye on these masters of the genre. At the same time, he says, the art and cinema of Europe, America and Asia are also part of his personal heritage. Without them he would never have been able to make his own films.

SR: I point out that the interesting aspects of his heritage are his Iranian roots, his focus on contemporary Iranian society and his radical modernity. The difficulties that this society has had to grapple with ever since the revolution and Kiarostami's very 'French' take on modernity lend these aspects an even greater significance. Exile is a keyword for modern Iranian artists and film-makers, I suggest. The great Iranian avant-garde film-maker Ebrahim Golestan, for example, found both the Iranian authorities and Iranian viewers not mature or modern enough for his works and left Iran over a decade before the Islamic Revolution.[8] Artists such as him often believed that contempt and exile are an inevitable precondition for being modern artists – especially in countries such as ours.

AK replies that every artist has his or her own unique sensitivities, but he cannot deny that Sadegh Hedayat, the most important scholar, researcher and writer in modern Iranian history, chose to leave his motherland and live in Paris, where he took his own life in 1951. Especially in Iran, avant-garde art has never been welcomed with open arms, but, still, exile is often unwelcome to Iranian artists. Golestan, Shahid Saless and Naderi stopped receiving due attention when their inner exile was transformed into actual exile, compelling them to leave Iran for good. What he can say for sure is that contempt for and separation from the environment in which an artist lives – whether because of political shenanigans, censorship or the artists' own emotional inclinations – reduces creativity and that is exactly what the authorities have been trying to achieve since the revolution: force the artist into inner – and preferably actual – exile.

SR: I point out that judging by his persistence and prolific output since the revolution, he cannot say – as he did at the beginning of this interview – that the revolution just passed him by.

AK explains that when he says that the revolution passed him by he means that the political and social climate – the sensationalism and ideological excitement of it – had no effect on him. He is neither pro- nor counter-revolutionary. He is not committed to a revolutionary idea. Unlike many artists, poets and intellectuals, he did not 'lose' himself and his grip on art in the hurricane that struck Iran after 1979. His job, he says, is to observe and show what he sees, without a social or political agenda. People should remember that art – whether realist, or poetic or surrealist – is always about constructs and artefacts. In other words, art is always a 'lie' through which the artist and the recipient of art attempt to get closer to the truth. The most important aspect of artistic work is honesty, not the subject matter or the style. Revolutions emotionalize things. from whence artistic honesty can perish and that is most dangerous for the quality of art.

SR: I remind him that he is seen both as highly 'realist' and highly 'escapist'. His film *Through the Olive Trees*, about the earthquake in Roodbar (northern Iran), depicted the natural beauty, dreams and hopes of the victims instead of their sufferings and the problems caused by the catastrophe. Furthermore a number of critics and some of his colleagues (such as Hatamikia) accuse him of not having been interested in the eight-year war between Iran and Iraq and of having turned instead to the idyllic scenery of rural Iran.

AK is once again astounded by the contradictory nature of these accusations. He appears amused by the labels 'realist' and 'escapist' because, in his view, these are mutually exclusive. His answer to these critics is decidedly Platonic: art must show beauty. Beauty is the only 'idea' that the human eye can see. The only thing that compels him to take photographs or make films or write poetry, he says, is beauty; for example, the beauty of an old man who prepares for Noruz (New Year) by planting violets in the ruins of his devastated street after an Iraqi missile attack.[9] The reality is the bombarded town but the truth is the old man planting violets in the middle of this reality. What's more, he adds, making films about the 'reality' of the Iran–Iraq War is futile in Iran. First, in comparison with, say, Hollywood, there are hardly any film production companies with sufficient financial and technological means to make an interesting war film. War scenes in Iranian films are embarrassingly 'amateur' when compared to those of international productions. Therefore, he reasons, the only thing that an Iranian film-maker can do is to try to turn this shortcoming into an advantage, which is hugely difficult.

Second, he explains, Iranian viewers are not interested in war films. They are too painful to watch – the war is still part of their reality. Even in Europe people needed a decade or two before coming to terms with their war 'as it was'. That is to say, Europeans were ready to see the misery of war depicted on the screen only after they had achieved a certain degree of national peace and welfare. In his eyes, the distance in time and space from the event of war is necessary to the artist – otherwise the end result is either propagandistic or just plain boring! That is why he treats the subject of war only indirectly in his films, like Michael Curtiz did in his masterpiece *Casablanca*.[10] That film, he explains, was made while the war was raging in Europe, but it completely refrained from showing war scenes. *Casablanca* was successful because it was honest art. That is to say, it showed that the truth of life is living it. And all true art exists because of the human hope for survival. It is the duty of art, he concludes, to show this 'beauty', especially in times of war and destruction.

4

DARIUSH MEHRJUI b. 1939

Islamic Ideology and Post-revolutionary
Intellectual Films

DARIUSH MEHRJUI DOES NOT IDENTIFY the beginnings of New Iranian Cinema or the Iranian New Wave with the years that followed the revolution. Pointing to the international success of his experimental film *The Cow*, which won the International Jury Prize at the 1971 Venice Biennale, he believes that the wave of modern non-commercial Iranian art films had already begun a decade before the 1979 revolution, when, both within Iran and internationally, there was a definite awareness that a new Iranian cinema was emerging. He vehemently disagrees with the idea that the revolution and the specifically Islamic parameters of censorship cleansed Iranian film of the decadent, facile productions that abounded during the shah's reign and thus opened the way for experimental and intellectual film-making. He reminds us that if Ayatollah Khomeini had not happened to appreciate *The Cow* and declare publicly that cinema per se does not go against Islamic values, the fate of Iranian film-making would have been different. According to Mehrjui, that verdict saved Iranian cinema from a horrible fate at the hands of fundamentalist Islamists, who believed cinema to be an instrument of corruption and Western decadence.

Mehrjui sees himself and his art as part of Iran, its people and its culture. Like many of his colleagues, he too is forced to

79

accept the role that most artists in totalitarian regimes have to play, namely, that of a socially committed and critical artist whose works inevitably are conceived from a socio-political point of view. In other words, he must carry the burden of the *engagé* intellectual. From his point of view, the regime tries to restrict Iranian cinema both through censorship policies – he mentions in this interview the 'dismembering' of his recent masterpiece *Santouri* (2007) – and by reducing the number of film theatres. The latter policy places film-makers under financial pressure and creates a division between them and their works on the one hand and the audience on the other. This division is the biggest tragedy that has afflicted the film industry in Iran since the Islamic Revolution.

Shiva Rahbaran: The main purpose of this project is to understand the influence of the 1979 revolution on Iranian cinema and the influence of this cinema on post-revolutionary society. Unlike poetry and literature, for the understanding of which you need a certain level of literacy and cultural awareness, cinema is an artform that can reach people of all social classes regardless of their background and education. In that sense the aim of this project is to look at the art of film-making in Iran after the revolution from a historical and sociological point of view rather than an aesthetic one.

Dariush Mehrjui: Cinema is an artistic medium and, like any other form of art, its influence on social movements, that is, on the political, social and historical consciousness of society, is always indirect – if it's meant to be considered art and not propaganda, that is. This is what characterizes art: it can only determine the cultural atmosphere – unlike propaganda, which dictates an ideology or a certain way of life and thinking. Now, among all forms of art, cinema has the widest influence and the strongest tool with which to exert such influence – namely, the moving image. Cinema can reach everyone: it is both 'popular' and 'elitist', it is commercial and entertaining as well as artistic and experimental, and it can reach people as a blockbuster or as an auteur film. In our country it was actually the auteur film – the elitist cinema – that managed to take root and develop after the revolution. Whereas in other countries commercial and mainstream cinema developed first, in our country it was 'artistic' cinema that saved our film industry after the revolution. And today this is recognized internationally.

Following the revolution, when most types of public entertainment were forbidden, cinema became increasingly popular. That's where a very important quality of cinema comes in – entertainment. Cinema going became the sole means of amusement. After the revolution all foreign films, with all their advanced technology, were considered vulgar and were banned.

What did this mean for us? It meant a great stroke of luck for our cinema! On the one hand, we no longer had any serious competition in our home market and, on the other hand, we stood before an audience thirsty for film! Thus Iranian cinema was able to stand on its own two feet and go forward in complete freedom. Unfortunately, however, today, more than three decades after the revolution, Iranian cinema is bankrupt and struggling to keep alive. Without help from government institutions it won't survive.

SR: You mention government institutions, so let's talk about the Farabi Cinema Foundation. In the course of this project I spoke to Mohammad Beheshti, who, as you know, was head of that foundation for many years and under whose aegis quite a few important films were made. He told me that Iranian cinema developed because of a paradox, namely, the Islamic government's ideology, which was basically against cinema, and the fact that we had many really good film-makers who could not thrive under the shah because of censorship and also, as you mentioned, competition from Hollywood and beyond. Beheshti sees this division between government ideology and the art of cinema as the space in which Iranian cinema grew after the revolution. In his opinion, the government and intellectual film-makers had one thing in common and that was their rejection of commercial film. However, one was against cinema while the other was for it. The Farabi, according to Beheshti, was able to take the intellectual film-maker's side and play a constructive role in making the government understand that cinema per se is not vulgar or anti-Islamic. Thanks to the Farabi's mediating role film-makers were able to produce works that won international acclaim.

DM: It depends on which period of Iranian cinema you're looking at. At the beginning of the revolution, Iranian cinema was nothing. All the studios, film institutes and film theatres were dead. No one knew what to do until, by chance, Ayatollah Khomeini watched my film *The Cow* on television. The next day he made a speech in which he said that we are not against the art of cinema at all. We are in favour of educational and cultural films such *The Cow*!

Remember that one of the very first revolutionary acts was the burning down of a cinema (see Introduction, p. vii). Why? Because the fanatics thought that film theatres were centres of immorality, vulgarity, corruption and Western decadence. So we entered a dangerous impasse: fanatics burning down cinemas and intellectual film-makers saying that they wanted to make films! It was a most precarious situation; we were on a knife-edge. This brought the film business to a period of stagnation for about two or three years. Television, however, still continued to show films, as long as they contained no erotic scenes or beautiful women, of course. Then one day they showed *The Cow*. And after Khomeini's speech, Islamists realized that you could make films within a certain framework. Thus cinema was no longer seen as fundamentally at odds with Islamic values. That was the beginning of the new neo-realist movement that drew on the lives of the lower classes, those people who had been exploited by the rich elite.

Gradually things improved for cinema. However, we need to bear in mind that the main beneficiary of this new movement was the social elite. The films we make – the films that have given New Iranian Cinema its name and reputation – are intellectual, not mainstream or commercial. It was the elite of pre-revolutionary and intellectual film-making that was allowed to continue working, not the directors of facile commercial films. This was when Mohammad Beheshti was head of the Farabi. Yes, he helped us a lot, though we should remember that at the time neither film theatres nor labs nor anything else functioned normally. Nor was it clear that once you'd made your film you'd be able to distribute and show it. Times were extremely hard.

The Farabi came up with the idea of loans to film-makers and of providing them with film stock and equipment. At the beginning the Farabi's support was vital to cinema and that's how auteur films gradually began to be made. Art-house films also provided main-stream and commercial cinema with a gateway, and in the first two and a half decades after the revolution in a way we witnessed the bloom of Iranian cinema.

SR: So we could say that the revolution was good for the develop-ment of cinema.

DM: Well, the revolution affected everything. I do not want to use the words 'good' and 'bad' – these are relative, you know. During the first few years, the government neither understood nor wanted our cinema, but the battle between the government and the film-makers resulted in the creation of our artistic cinema, which was the only good thing that people around the world knew about Iran. You know, the government was not made up only of funda-mentalists and fanatics. There were and still are people who have common sense, who are rational. Even among our religious leaders there are some who are educated, who like literature, cinema and modernity, and who think that it's possible to have both religion and modernity at the same time. There were and always will be such people.

On the other hand, there were also those who burned down film theatres. In the middle of these struggles Khomeini said, 'There is no conflict between cinema and Islam!' These words opened a route for us and thus educational films – children's films in partic-ular – were the first kind of film to be made after the revolution. Over time we watched Kiarostami, Beyzaie and the rest make their post-revolutionary films after six or seven years of silence, and thus a 'universal' Iranian cinema was born. Remember, it could have died instead had the fanatics, whose verdict on cinema was death, won the battle. So at a very sensitive stage after the revolution, we were able to save Iranian cinema through the artistic movement and turn it into something universal.

SR: Yet, as you mentioned, we saw that this artistic movement opened the gates to commercial and mainstream films as well. Some directors, such as Farmanara, believe that what we have today is the Islamic version of the trivial and vulgar pre-revolutionary Film Farsi!

DM: Well, this is the peculiarity of cinema – it attracts different classes of society with different levels of awareness and intelligence. *The Cow* was not mainstream. At first it was screened in just one theatre. Of course it was popular among people of a certain class, but during the revolution a wider group were attracted to the film. The revolution, at least in the early days, did something for people's awareness. Many people – who normally only watched commercial films – now enjoyed this auteur film because they could somehow see themselves in it. Furthermore, because the film was about exploited peasants and showed poverty and desperation, the new government supported it. It was seen as a good example of educational cinema.

SR: So, in your opinion, does cinema have a commitment towards society? Should it be educational?

DM: In my opinion, yes, it should be educational. If you look at my *Dayereh ye Mina* [*The Cycle*; made in 1975, released in 1978] you'll realize that it was made in order to raise awareness. It's about a criminal organization that buys blood very cheaply from drug addicts and then sells it at a very high price to hospitals. The film has an entertaining plot but is also educational. It had a great impact back then and accelerated the foundation of the blood transfusion centre before the revolution. Dr Ala, who was the founder of that centre, was a great fan of *The Cycle*.

I must also add that the script was censored and the film itself banned for three years before getting permission for release. What I mean is that my films are not made on the basis of 'art for art's sake'. I don't make action films or worthless sentimental films for the sake of entertainment. I admire the works of Robert Bresson and Andrei Tarkovsky. Yes, a good film should be entertaining to some extent but at the same time it should try to increase the level of awareness in society.

SR: What is particularly interesting to me is that when you talk about inspirational directors you mention Bresson and Tarkovsky. You do not mention Iranian film-makers. Furthermore what is interesting to me is that in a country where poetry is the 'national art', cinema – a Western, imported form of art – has managed to develop to such an extent in comparison to poetry. It seems as if our poets, writers and scholars are working in isolation. In your opinion, what's the reason behind the success of cinema in Iran as compared to literature?

DM: If we look at cinema in the West from a historical point of view, we realize that it is a novelty there too. It's only a hundred years old! And don't forget that almost as soon as it was invented there, cinema was introduced here. A few years ago, we celebrated the 100th birthday of Iranian film. Cameramen filmed the king, the court and various Iranian landscapes during the reigns of Nasser al-Din Shah Qajar and Mozaffar ad-Din Shah Qajar in the late 1870s and 1880s. We were involved in the art of cinema almost from the beginning. That's what characterizes cinema, as I told you before: it belongs to everyone regardless of their culture, background, literacy and wealth. The first films in the Persian language date back to the early 1920s – the first Iranian sound film, *The Lor Girl*, was made in the early 1930s. So our cinema is almost as old as that of the West.

Now, to get back to your question, today all around the world – regardless of whether you're in the East or the West – the image is replacing the word. In my opinion, there is a 'universal culture' – both in democratic and undemocratic countries – that is dominated by the image; the image is swallowing up everything. The computer is on all day, there's terrestrial and satellite TV and videos running on the internet constantly. We are experiencing an unprecedented historical phenomenon – the image is colonizing people's souls. As a result, the word is gradually retreating. This is the problem with our literature. In the West poets are also isolated. Modern poetry is really poor and then, when you look closer, it's mostly reliant on the visual medium. Now poets write their poems hoping that they can be turned into images. Writers write their novels as scripts or hope that they will become scripts. Writers themselves are becoming film-makers. Image rules!

SR: There has always been a lively exchange between literature and cinema in the West. Writers have often written their novels with a view to them becoming scripts, while film-makers have always tried to turn great works of literature into films. Works such as *War and Peace, Pride and Prejudice* and *Jane Eyre* and many others have been filmed many times, but this process hardly ever happens in Iran, except for a few films such as Farmanara's *Prince Ehtejab* [1974], which was based on Golshiri's masterpiece of the same title, or Kimiai's *Dash Akol* [1971], which was based on a story by Hedayat, published in 1932. How come the stories of great Persian novelists such as Simin Daneshvar [1921–2012] or Bozorg Alavi [1904–97] are not filmed?

DM: Basically, except for the few names that you mentioned, we don't have many good novelists and, remember, Hedayat, Daneshvar and Alavi had their heyday over 50 years ago! We're done with them! It's true that their works still represent the best of our literature. I mean, no one has ever been able to create anything that surpasses Hedayat's *The Blind Owl* [1937], Alavi's *Her Eyes* [1952] or Daneshvar's *Savushun* [1969], but for Iranian cinema, which is a completely modern movement, these novels are now outdated. Of the few writers we now have, Esmail Fasih[1] is, in my eyes, our best contemporary novelist – but that's it, really.

SR: A lot of our great poets and artists have always felt alienated from their society. I'm thinking of people such as Forough Farrokhzad and Sadegh Hedayat or a film-maker like Golestan, who have always been in a kind of inner exile that has often led to them living like expatriates. In your opinion is this alienation necessary for creating good art or avant-garde art?

DM: In my opinion, alienation is quite worthless when it comes to creating good art. The artist is always in conflict with his environment. You, as an intellectual, must know that the 'job' of artists is to be in conflict with their society. I mean, they should always question things, they should always search for something better, they should always try to initiate some change or movement. In fact, this is the nature of intellectuals and artists. As to whether a real avant-garde artist can only create art when he or she is in exile within society I say 'no'. Creating art is a natural thing – it is a talent; some have it, some don't. Talent is not something that is created in special circumstances or something that you can force onto people. You cannot decide to go into a kind of inner exile and then hope to create good art!

Creativity is a treasure that you possess and its workings can probably be found mostly in the subconscious. So the process of creativity has nothing to do with your country turning its back on you or with you turning your back on it. I would even argue the opposite: if you take a good look at our history, you'll see that creativity does not increase in exile – it may even decrease. Those who have spent most of their time in exile have hardly produced any cultural gems – Golestan, Naderi and Shahid Saless actually stopped making good films when they left Iran. The same can be said of our writers and poets. You see, I've a good deal of experience of America, France and other European countries. The people of our generation – those who were born and raised in this country – who live abroad dry up! They cannot adapt to the environment and culture of the country of their exile. They are away from their own culture. By the time they have learned the language of that country and got the hang of its culture, it's too late for them to do anything! And even if they can speak the language, they're still unsuccessful because they cannot connect with any subject of interest in the West.

I've had this experience myself. In Paris I received a very interesting proposal. They had sent me a few scripts through my agent and were waiting for my reply so that they could go ahead with the funding. Yet, no matter how hard I tried I saw that I could not do it, even though the subject interested me greatly. The scriptwriter was very professional and had worked with Claude Chabrol, the famous French film-maker. The script was similar to Albert Camus' novel *The Stranger.* It was about a young Algerian boy who lived in Paris and tried to make it in the hard and violent environment of the Parisian suburbs. It was a good script but, despite much effort on my part, I saw that I could not go near such a project. You see, some of you people in exile have managed to grow roots in those societies and cultures. You have gone abroad at a stage in your life when you were able to understand that new society and adapt yourself to it and create a meaningful existence in it. First and foremost, a film or a piece of writing should have a meaning for you as an artist. For me, a film is like a novel. It has got to come from the depth of my heart, and I can only do this in Iran. I must point out again the fact that our film-makers and writers who are in exile have not created anything worthwhile so far.

SR: Many Iranians abroad and in exile believe that those intellectual film-makers who did not leave Iran after the revolution – such as you and Abbas Kiarostami – have paid a heavy price, namely, their intellectual integrity and honesty. They have adapted to the Islamic environment that developed after the revolution, meaning that they have made compromises with the ideology of the Islamic Republic, so to speak. For instance, Hamid Naficy writes: 'The price of adaptation and evolution, however, was accommodation and the charge that the film-maker[s] had sold out. For example, the endings of Mehrjoee's [Mehrjui's] films *The Tenants* (1986) and *Hamoun* (1990) which seemed to contradict the body of the films have been criticized because of the perception that the director had caved into the authorities and changed his original endings.'[2]

DM: This gentleman is being unfair. I actually wrote the script for *Hamoun* before the revolution – the framework is exactly the same as in the film. The atmosphere in the last few days before the revolution had got to all of us – we were all attracted to Islam and spirituality and so on. In the film I depicted the atmosphere of that period. I did not change any part of the film. Mr Naficy's opinion is typical of the exiled Iranian community in the West. They look at you from the outside. It is a politically and ideologically charged point of view. So it's not me who is being ideological but the critics who want to label me.

SR: All the same, people who accuse other famous film-makers of Islamization also accuse you of having sold out to the West. They say that you make your films according to the tastes of Westerners and their idea of art films and auteur cinema. In other words, they are saying that people like you want to have their cake and eat it. You always choose subjects that are both OK with the censorship authorities in Iran and at the same time are to the taste of Western festivals and their perception of Iran.

DM: So what do you suggest that I should do now? I serve both God and Mammon, they say. So what? They call everyone who is successful an opportunist, but if you fail to succeed both in Iran and in the West, why, then you have preserved your integrity! You see, it is important for us to be able to make films here, in Iran, in this setting. That is very important to me because it is my fate. It is my fate to make films *here*. Personally I was not a revolutionary, but the revolution happened. This is the historical fate of anyone who is from Iran. I cannot run away from it.

SR: So is the revolution an inseparable part of your work?

DM: As a historical event, yes, it is. Look, I did not want to come into this world in the first place. I fell into this world – was thrown into it. This revolution is the same. This revolution threw us into today's society. Of course we had an alternative, which was to live in the West. And I too have done this once, but there's no escape there either from the roots I have in this land. So I came back. Many of us came back. It was our fate – you could call it whatever you like. We started to make films here. None of the writers and film-makers of our generation who is in exile – I repeat this – has actually created anything of note. It is the same with music. Even our pop music, created in the very land of pop music – the USA – is mostly a reproduction of the pre-revolutionary variety. So the idea that exile is necessary for artistic creation is wrongheaded. Those artists who left and did not succeed need to justify themselves in some way.

SR: Yet you cannot deny that the harsh and irrational censorship policies in Iran try to silence the artist and force him into some sort of inner exile.

DM: Yes, you are right. However, regardless of censorship, I do think that artists live in a kind of exile within their own society. The artist is always in conflict with the ideas of those who want to rule everything and want to change everything according to some 'ism'.

SR: So, after all you *are* living in a sort of exile?

DM: Well, yes. But I did not choose this exile. It's where I have to work. You have no other choice as an artist.

SR: In your opinion, has this exile – the result of censorship from the top – been beneficial for Iranian film? Some people believe that censorship fertilizes the creativity of the artist, because he or she must look for creative ways of getting around it.

DM: Not in the least. What benefit? What are these people talking about! In my own country I have not seen anything other than an oppressive censorship apparatus looking over my shoulder the whole time. We have always lived under the blade of censorship – both before and after the revolution.

As soon as I opened my eyes in this land – in this land where my roots are – I've been suppressed and censored in all sorts of ways. All my films, made both before and after the revolution, have been banned for between a year and over a decade. I even had to change some of my titles. For example, *The School We Went To* [1986] was originally called *The Backyard of Adl-e Afagh School*. At first they played around with it, then cut it and finally banned it for 11 years! I was later told to change its title if I wanted it to be released. My next film *Baanoo* [*The Lady*; made in 1991, released in 1998] was banned without explanation for some seven years. When it finally did come out it had been chopped into pieces! Censorship is the symbol of cultural mayhem and bankruptcy. And today this mayhem rules in our country more than ever.

I should also remind you that ever since the revolution, censorship in our country has been based on personal taste. Today under Ahmadinejad [2005–09, 2009–13], censorship has become harsher than it was under Khatami [1997–2001, 2001–05], for example. There was censorship back then, yet we had more room for manoeuvre.

SR: Mr Beheshti tells me that in his day censorship worked in the opposite direction than it does today – a sort of a reverse censorship. Then scantily dressed women and dancers dominated the perception of womanhood in cinema and hardly left any space for a different portrayal. After the revolution, however, those in charge struck out the sensual, 'vulgar' dimension of womanhood and made room for a different perception. Do you agree with that?

DM: No! Look, at the end of the day, we are living in a society that keeps telling us, 'Don't talk! Don't look! Don't wear this! Don't eat that! Don't listen to music! Don't play music!' In other words, the regime has banned all five senses! At the same time, all banned things find expression somehow or other – at private parties, in underground movements. The fact is that all these 'don'ts' have not changed or educated the young nor have they made model Islamic citizens out of them. The government's guidelines only work on a theoretical level; in practice – in reality, as we live it in our homes and in our own spaces – they are nothing. Our civil society is not the same as that of Saudi Arabia. Our women are fully active in all areas of life. Why should we not show a woman as she is in reality?

SR: That's right; you are not able to show women in their own personal spaces – as they live their lives.

DM: If we make a film about villagers or about religious and traditional families, we can show things as they really are. For instance,
a peasant woman wears her scarf even at home and a religious
woman covers her head at all times. I remember, my grandmother
always had her scarf on and my mother would always wear a scarf
or *chador* when the pond cleaner or a stranger came in. I remember that we kids never saw our grandmother's hair. Now, maybe
she was bald, I don't know! Anyway, having a scarf on was normal
for a woman in that setting. To take another example, when I was
a child, I never saw my parents cuddling, kissing or flirting. There
was a kind of decency, a form of behavioural *hijab* in many families
and that's still the case. This is a part of our culture and, as I said,
still exists in many families. I personally cannot show bedroom
scenes, I cannot show a man and a woman making love. Even if I
were free, I don't think I could do it because, since my childhood, I
have never seen anything of that sort in my own family.

You know, the films that were made before the revolution did
not show such things either. For example, there would be cabaret
dancers in our films, but there would be no sex scenes. Yet in those
days we *could* show a woman in her bedroom! I wish that today we
were able to show a woman going to bed in her nightgown. If you
watch our stupid TV series in Iran, which feature modern middle-
class or upper-class women, you'll see that, because of censorship
guidelines, we cannot show how these women behave in their natural surroundings. We cannot show them taking off their scarves
before going to bed! We have to cover the entire neck and all the
hair, and so on. All this is ridiculous. In my opinion, the film-
maker should not do that. He or she should avoid interior scenes
as much as possible. That's what makes someone like Kiarostami
prefer villages. In our villages, women have always worn scarves;
they wear them in a more natural way than the up-town, urban
Tehrani women, who, since the revolution, have been forced to
wear them. So you wouldn't be lying as a film-maker if you showed
a woman going to sleep in her scarf! I mean, there were and still
are some taboos that you always had to be careful about, regardless
of censorship from above. For instance, you could not be disre-
spectful to clergy in your films – even in the shah's time. We live in

a very closed society. Now, however, censorship, especially when it comes to the portrayal of women, has reached nonsensical proportions.

SR: Would you say that your work helps create pockets of freedom in this closed society?

DM: I try to be effective. My aim is to create such pockets of freedom; just to open society up a little. That's why my films are always censored and get banned. I get punished! For example, I made a film, *Sara* [1993], about a religious woman who lives in a modern city. Her husband is also religious and works in a bank. But he's not a good husband and Sara revolts against him. She tells him that he is an idiot and that she does not want to live with him any more. I thought they'd ban it, but, as I told you before, our censorship guidelines are to a large degree dictated by the tastes of the persons in charge and I was lucky with those in charge back then. They did not cut the film into pieces and did not ban it either! This was the beginning of a series of films in which I showed rebellious women. My next films, *Pari* [1995] and *Leila* [1996], were on the same subject. My aim is, yes, to create pockets of freedom.

SR: This shows that it is possible to create socially committed art.

DM: Yes. In fact, that's how it should be. The best kinds of cinema have developed in a similar atmosphere. Eisenstein made *Battleship Potemkin* in 1925, at a time when the Soviet regime hardly let artists such as Eisenstein breathe! Yet he made a cinematic masterpiece. Or, for instance, look at the Eastern European cinema of the 1960s and 1970s, when the system of Russian dictatorship still ruled. Many of the masterpieces of Krzysztof Kieslowski belong to that era.

SR: Some people – yourself included – are labelled 'festival filmmakers'. How much influence do foreign film festivals have on your work?

DM: First and foremost, I make my films for myself and for my society. Now, if a film attracted foreign attention that would be great! Indeed, 'festival film-makers' do exist. On the one hand, there are films that are only released here; on the other hand, there are films that are never seen here and are made especially for consumption abroad – much like the pistachios and dates that are for export only! They are beautifully wrapped and the subjects are what you might call 'festival subjects'. Unfortunately this trend is ongoing, as we can see. The foremost requirement of these films is to show poverty – extreme poverty sells even better. The film has to be about poor, miserable people and poor villagers, and so on. Now, a sort of naturalism has also become trendy. You see very strange subjects – for example, a ship that's stuck in the middle of a desert that used to be a lake, or something like that. Festival directors don't even care about the film being screened in Iran. There are many such films, and the festivals send representatives over here to pick some of them for screening. Now, my problem is that I don't like this naturalism; I like to build the reality myself, to create it myself. I'd like it to be a new reality – a reality that suits *my* world view.

SR: So do you choose a different audience? Do you solely make films for the Iranian audience?

DM: No. I don't think about the audience at all. I try to make a film that *I* like, above all. My first question is: what kind of film would *I* like to watch? For instance, a subject comes into my mind and stirs my interest; then I start working on it and manoeuvring around it. I want to make something that won't bore me. I don't want to sit for half an hour watching a scene in which nothing happens. I don't like such films. Of course, the feedback you get from audiences, critics and film magazines is wonderful. You know that you've started a dialogue and suddenly hundreds are replying to you. So begins a rewarding cultural give-and-take that's instructive for me and at the same time motivates the audience and the critic. But this cultural give-and-take is not the reason for my choice of subject; it's a side effect. First I choose my subject and then, if I'm lucky, this wonderful dialogue – the give-and-take – happens.

SR: Haven't the government's censorship policies made it difficult for you to enjoy this give-and-take? Have they not created a
distance between you and your audience?

DM: Whatever attention I get in Iran creates a connection that
energizes me. Abroad they show your film once – only once – and a
bunch of strangers sit there, ask four questions and get up and go.
They write one or two reviews and that's it. There is no feedback,
no exchange. It's just a meeting. They usually show your film somewhere in a run-down cinema in the backstreets of a city like Paris.
Every time you go there, you see that there are no more than 20 or
30 people in the auditorium. And that doesn't give you anything.
It's not energizing. But here in Iran you see long queues of people
gathered outside the cinema long before it opens. People here are
thirsty for our cinema. Here the passion and excitement are of a
different kind. Take the Fajr Film Festival, for example. Come and
see for yourself! Despite the fact that this festival takes place in
winter, in the cold and the snow, there are so many young people
who come to watch the interviews with the press – this is lovely. At
the same time, you should bear in mind that the government is
not keen on this synergy between us and young viewers. No, they
don't want our films to be received as enthusiastically as that. Take
my film *Santouri* [2007], for example. They really hassled me when
I was making it. The title was supposed to be *Ali Santuori*. They
forced me to cut out the name 'Ali'. Now I'm still not sure what will
become of it.[3]

SR: Apart from hassling you, what else do the state authorities do
for you?

DM: Sometimes they give small loans to film-makers. It's a sort of
start-up loan that's supposed to support you when you set up something. That's all the help they give. The rest is just hassle. But then,
at the end of the day, Beyzaie is making films, I am making films,
Farmanara and Kiarostami are making films. Everyone is somehow

making films. In a way, they compromise with the situation. It's not as though we were better off before the revolution. Now the young generation is writing and making films and producing plays.

SR: Has the quality of Iranian film improved since the revolution?

DM: Yes, it has. In my opinion the quality has improved.

SR: Some people, such as the director Bahman Farmanara, believe that many of today's films are made according to the Film Farsi recipe from the period before the revolution – the only difference being that the actresses now wear scarves instead of miniskirts. These films are concerned only with entertainment. At the same time, we see films being made by directors who are considered world-class intellectuals. Considering your success in Iran, have you managed to build a bridge between Iranian popular cinema and Iranian art-house cinema?

DM: Yes, I have managed to do so. Rakhshan Bani-Etemad has managed it as well. Or even Farmanara. But Kiarostami has not managed that balancing act; many film theatres don't even show his films.

SR: Why? Is it because of censorship by the state authorities?

DM: No. That's not the only reason. Kiarostami has trouble finding a theatre to show his films because his films are unprofitable. In a way, cinema owners censor him financially! After the revolution the number of cinemas in Iran decreased. Cinema owners want their theatres to be sold out. There's no longer a cinema where you can screen an experimental film. That is one of the big tragedies of our culture: the bankruptcy of the cinema industry. They destroyed many film theatres or turned them into malls; they have not been rebuilt. Thus the number of cinemas in our country is very low. So you can see that the government has not done anything for the film industry – except for granting some small loans.

Of course, the regime's relation to cinema is schizophrenic: for instance, they did not want our films to be sent to festivals, but the Farabi would somehow send them without the government's approval. The success of our films abroad somehow made the government's brain click into gear – that this could actually be to their own benefit too. In other words, they realized that the popularity of Iranian film could reflect positively on the regime. This is exactly what happened with Kiarostami's *Taste of Cherry* [1997]. That was sent to the Cannes Film Festival at the last minute and it won the *Palme d'Or*. That's when the gentlemen realized that, yes, you can score points this way.

SR: That brings us back to the issue that we talked about earlier: in the eyes of many Iranians in exile, you are an ally of the regime.

DM: Yes, I know. You in exile believe that anyone who lives in Iran is a traitor. But that is not true. You see, the government is not a coherent unit; there isn't a fixed line on art. Take Mr Khatami for instance. Iranian cinema took off when he was minister of culture. Film-makers started to make films and go to festivals. It was in that period that the government gradually realized that awards reflect well on its own reputation abroad, so it welcomed contemporary Iranian cinema. It even insisted that Iranian films, like Iranian ambassadors, should show the world what was really happening in Iran. At the time when Iranian cinema took off – in the late 1980s and early 1990s – the government would even organize Iranian film weeks through its embassies in different countries. I was present at some of these, in Athens, Tokyo, Belgrade. You see, we would make the films and the government would support us, in the sense that they wouldn't prevent the films from being submitted to festivals. For example, Panahi's *Offside* [2006], which was a very critical film and was forbidden to be shown in Iran, was screened abroad with no problems. The director lives and works in Iran too. It's a schizophrenic situation that we have here. You see, the mentality of Iranians abroad is programmed so that they don't register reality in Iran. They make up their own reality. They also live in a schizophrenic situation. On the one hand, they reject the reality in

Iran and, on the other, enjoy watching films that come from Iran; they write reviews about them, screen them and make money out of them!

It has always been like this for us artists living and working in Iran. Even during the shah's time it was the same. For example, when *The Cow* was smuggled out of Iran and shown at the Venice Festival in 1971, leftists demonstrated in front of the cinema arguing that the film, which had been made under the bloody regime of the shah, should not be shown. I was attacked as a traitor by the left. I would say, 'Look! This film is critical of the shah's regime; it has caused problems for the government; it has been banned; it has been censored!' But to no avail. They'd say, 'No! The fact that you are working in Iran, under the shah's regime, means that you are betraying the cause.' You see, this is the ideology of the so-called left which still rules outside Iran. Iranians abroad are still using the same jargon they used 40 years ago. They want you to use film as a propaganda machine. They want you to insult certain persons and institutions. In fact they don't want you to make films at all. In their eyes, the fact that we picked up a camera and worked here means betrayal; it means that we have made deals with the government. So the 'real' writer or artist, in the eyes of these people, is the one who does *not* write or produce any work of art. The 'real' writer or artist should either be in exile or should have been killed or should have committed suicide.

SR: As you mentioned before, our writers and poets who live in exile, away from their society, language and culture, have not created anything worthwhile. You have mentioned a few times in this interview that the artist should have a direct connection with his or her society in order to make good works of art, especially if he or she is a committed film-maker like yourself. Now, the question is, why has one of the biggest historical events of the last 30 years – the Iran–Iraq War – not been reflected in your films?

DM: Many films have been made and are still being made about the war, but people don't like watching them, firstly, because they are badly made and, secondly, because people have bad memories of the conflict – in fact, they don't want to remember that the war happened at all. Thirdly, the Iran–Iraq War was one which, by international rules, we lost. No matter what the regime's propaganda machine says, we did not win it – we finished as the losers.

SR: So, do you mean that we are not prepared for critical films about the war?

DM: The government is very sensitive about the war and consequently about war films in general. They only want you as a filmmaker to praise it. You should always say that the war was fought in 'sacred defence'! If you so much as hint that it was a bad thing, the government will quickly stop your film. You see, here the level of tolerance is very low. They pose as a popular government, but that's not the case at all. They have no tolerance in any area.

'Tolerance' is a very important word, but unfortunately they do not understand it. If you want to be popular or have democracy, you must be able to tolerate the opposite view. We must get out of this black-and-white dogmatic thinking.

SR: In your films you want to encourage tolerance and show a way out of this black-and-white dogmatic thinking.

DM: Yes, because of my rebellious spirit I have always worked in that way. I am always pulled towards those who don't accept oppression and extortion. For instance, before the revolution I concentrated on the oppressed and disgruntled working class, and my ideology and philosophy were based on Marxism and the socialist ideologies of the time. Jean-Paul Sartre and his supporters were my role models. After the revolution, as you are aware, the class for which I fought became dominant, so addressing that group was ridiculous – useless in fact. That's why we no longer understand films made by the likes of Makhmalbaf.[4] We don't even know what he's saying. You see, the former 'oppressed' have now invaded all walks of life. The people that Makhmalbaf's films address have now become dominant. So now I concentrate on the middle class, the bourgeoisie – especially bourgeois women. Universally, women do not have the

same rights as men, but in the post-revolutionary Iranian society
and under the pressure of religious fanaticism, Iranian women face
worse deprivations than women elsewhere. The compulsory wearing of the *hijab* in Iran has become a symbol of oppression globally.
It's interesting for me to see what a woman can do in such a situation, what means of manoeuvre she has. By now I have made five
or six so-called 'women's issues' films – such as *Sara* [1993], *Pari*
[1995], *Leila* [1996], *Baanoo* [1998], and so on. I did not make these
only because I'm interested in women's issues, but also because I
am very sensitive about social injustice. For instance, in *Santouri* I
highlight a horrible disease that has spread and penetrated our
society to a large extent, namely, drug addiction. Heroin is so
cheap in this city that it's destroying the youth. This film is about a
bright and talented person who suddenly hits rock bottom because
of the easy accessibility of drugs. Of course, since the film is highly
critical of post-revolutionary society, the authorities have banned it
and are now busy cutting it into small pieces!

(2 0 0 7)

BAHMAN FARMANARA
Exporting New Iranian Cinema

IN THIS INTERVIEW, BAHMAN FARMANARA POINTS OUT the contradictory policies of the Islamic regime on Iranian cinema. All the same, he does see a positive side to these policies. First, he believes that the ban on the films of Hollywood and European directors – who have always been the most important role models for Iranian film-makers – after the revolution was enormously beneficial to their Iranian counterparts. It offered them a golden opportunity to make films without having to put most of their energy into competing with the giants of Hollywood and Europe. Furthermore, Farmanara feels that the ban forced Iranian film-makers to leave the ivory towers they had been inhabiting before the revolution, from which the reality of life in Iran was barely visible, and make socially committed and critical films about the society in which they lived.

Farmanara does not believe that censorship is exclusively the 'speciality' of the Islamic regime. All totalitarian regimes censor art. Under the shah, intellectual film-makers also faced many obstructions. In Iran, intellectual film-making has always been a political activity; after the revolution its politicization only increased along with the Islamic regime's restrictions on and invasions into public and private life. Now 'Islamic' film-makers are favoured, while erotic subjects have been added to the taboos that existed also under the monarchy. The difference, however, between the film-maker's situation under the shah and under the Islamic government is the overall climate of excitement and rebelliousness. This climate caused chaos, contradictions and heated arguments on censorship, but it also opened up the space for some important films to be made. Like many of his colleagues interviewed here, Farmanara also insists that the Iranian New Wave had already started before the revolution through the artistic activities of people such as Golestan, Beyzaie, Kiarostami, Shahid Saless, Mehrjui, Kimiavi and himself; however, the great success story of this wave was born out of the experiments that took place in the chaotic aftermath of the revolution. Farmanara goes on to explain that another positive effect of the revolution was the 'negative propaganda' it created for Iranian films. He agrees with Kiarostami that audiences in the rest of the world were quite perplexed by some of the wonderful films that came out of the 'black hole' of Islamic Iran. In this sense, the revolution helped boost the popularity of Iranian cinema world-wide, but it has not given film-makers the necessary space to work.

During our meeting he mentioned that under Ahmadinejad the atmosphere was so poisonous that he decided to give up film-making altogether. His films *A Little Kiss* (2005) and *A Familiar Soil* (2008) suffered badly under the censorship policies of the regime and now all he cared to do was research cinema's history in Iran and participate in lectures and symposia. A few years after our meeting, however, news of his renewed optimism following Hassan Rouhani's election reached my ears. He had even decided to participate in the International Fajr Festival of 2015 with a new film called *I Want to Dance* (2014). The circumstances of the film's screening, however, show that 'artistic freedom' in Iran under Rouhani's presidency is still a far cry from how Western democracies conceive it. Farmanara had to omit the verb 'to Dance' from the title, as dancing is frowned upon in the Islamic Republic.

––––––––––

Shiva Rahbaran: Mr Farmanara, I'd like to talk to you about the beginnings of New Iranian Cinema and the reasons for its international success, the influence of the revolution on its development and its influence on Iranian identity, both inside and outside Iran.

Bahman Farmanara: Oh, that's quite a big, multifaceted topic! First things first: we need to look at a few historical facts before we tackle this question. Above all, we need to look at the situation our cinema was in before the 1979 revolution. Then it was mainly the big foreign companies from Hollywood, Bollywood and Europe that had offices in Tehran. These companies either owned big film theatres or secured contracts with them and could thus show their productions widely. There was an unwritten law, however, which obliged them to invest a lot of money in dubbing their films into Persian – otherwise the big theatres wouldn't screen them.

Alongside these films, we also had Film Farsi, which did quite well. As you can imagine, most Iranian people, like most people around the world, prefer to watch their own dramas and tear-jerkers on the big screen and on television. So our cinema was firmly in the hands of dubbed foreign films and Film Farsi. In such restricting conditions, which became even harder to bear for intellectual film-makers, because of the royal government's refusal to fund their films, we still managed to have film-makers such as Kiarostami, Sinai, Beyzaie, Kimiavi, Mehrjui and Fereydun Goleh. These people succeeded in achieving recognition from Iranian and foreign cinephiles and there gradually grew a current – an underground, independent current – called the Iranian New Wave. While they were in the process of establishing themselves, the 1979 revolution took place. The new government banned most foreign and Film Farsi productions – not immediately, of course, but quite soon after the revolution. Now, compared to the situation under the shah, where the government not only did not fund our films but actually gave our much stronger rivals – Film Farsi and dubbed foreign productions – more room to grow, intellectual Iranian film-makers were faced with a dramatic challenge and a unique chance. The Islamic government said, 'We will subsidize Iranian films but only if, first, there is no sex in them, second, if there are no beautiful women, third, no murders, fourth, no Hollywood-style heroes, and, fifth, no insults to God's religions and prophets' – this included the Jewish and Christian religions.

At the same time the number of film theatres didn't change much; it even decreased – especially if you take into account the growing Iranian population. In any case, these cinemas needed material. After the revolution and all the suffering, people needed entertainment. There were no cabarets and 'dens of sin' left! TV programmes were not as well made as they should have been, so people started going to the cinema. Those who had always looked down on home productions as cheap copies of Hollywood and European films now had no choice but to go to the cinema to watch Iranian films.

This was a very important 'paradigm shift' in Iran. You'll only appreciate the weight of it if you recall how hostile the pre-revolutionary climate was towards art-house Iranian films. For example, screening my film *Prince Ehtejab* [1974], which had won the Grand Prix for best film at the 1976 Tehran Film Festival, was really difficult. Finally, Mr Ataollah Rohani, may he rest in peace, who owned a few film theatres in Iran, agreed to screen it in one of his cinemas. He told me that he was only doing this because the film had won the Tehran Grand Prix but that he couldn't show it for more than a week or so because otherwise he'd be risking the reputation of his cinema and would lose money! Imagine: showing Iranian art-house films was a risk for business in the days before the revolution!

SR: Do you mean that in those days the owners of film theatres censored you?

BF: That is exactly how it was. I didn't accept Mr Rohani's offer and looked elsewhere. I went to Cinema Bahman, which had a seating capacity of 2,000. They took the risk and *Prince Ehtejab* was very successfully screened – for nine weeks! Yes, that was the situation then. But it changed after the revolution. Foreign films were mostly banned. The films shown in cinemas had to be Iranian – of course, they had to comply with the regulations that I mentioned earlier. All those cinemas that refused to screen our films before the revolution now had no other option except to screen our films. Thus

– and perhaps unwittingly – the post-revolutionary Islamic government gave us the security that the pre-revolutionary government
wouldn't and that's how, out of an underground current, a major
artistic movement was born.

All the same, we should bear in mind that the first group whose
films enjoyed great popularity was the same group that had made
internationally recognized films *before* the revolution. In other
words, Iranian post-revolutionary cinema was a continuation of
pre-revolutionary independent, underground cinema – the same
current that had started with people such as Kiarostami, Mehrjui,
Kimiavi and me. The second group to come along were those who
started making feature films only after the revolution – people
such as Bani-Etemad, Majidi, Panahi, Makhmalbaf and Hatamikia.
These young film-makers were riding on the wave of the artistic
success of the first group.

What I said about the change in our situation does not mean
that our situation became ideal. Far from it! We still had difficulties
convincing private Iranian investors that they could make money
from Iranian cinema! So, in the early days we were mainly dependent on state subsidies. As I said before, in those early days cinemas
did not have the right to choose which films to screen. Everything
was completely controlled by the government and advertising was
limited to television. There was a fixed rule that any film, good
or bad, popular or unpopular, had to be on screen for only four
weeks! The question for us was, why should a film that's selling well
be pulled from theatres? Unfortunately such rules still exist today;
their implementation is weaker, though.

Another obstacle, especially in the early 1980s, was the government's plan to spend the largest part of its cinema budget on films
dealing with Islam and spirituality, or 'the cinema of the holy war',
as they called it – you know, the films about the Iran–Iraq War
in the 1980s. The government would in effect tell film-makers to
make propaganda films about the war if they wanted to get decent
funding. There were those who'd say: would you like a war film? No
problem, I'll make one for you! Would you like an Islamic film? Do
you want a spiritual film? Yes? I'm going to make such an ambigu-
ous and spiritual film that no one will understand any of it!

SR: From what you've just said, I get the impression that Iranian film grew rapidly after the revolution. So, can we say that the revolution and government bans and sanctions have been good for our cinema?

BF: We always suffered from censorship – the situation was no better before the revolution. For example, five minutes of my film *Prince Ehtejab* had to be cut after it won the Grand Prix at the Tehran Festival – otherwise it wouldn't get permission for release. Those oh-so-Westernized, modern pre-revolutionary authorities explicitly said, 'No! We are not pleased that you won the Grand Prix because this means that we have to release it!' However, the difference between censorship before the revolution and censorship after was that formerly you were not allowed to touch four themes: the royal family, the constitution, Holy Islam and the military. According to the authorities, the sequence that was cut from *Prince Ehtejab* insulted Holy Islam. It showed the female protagonist masturbating while a religious ceremony was taking place. What happened after the revolution was that the government not only told us what not to show but also what we *should* show!

SR: So, you had to propagandize for the system?

BF: Of course they didn't succeed in this but they made things very difficult for us. They told us to make films about war and religious heroes. They wanted to dictate to us the subject of every film. This kind of prescriptiveness meant the end of all creativity, so it hit a concrete wall and did not succeed. Some of us refused to continue working in those harsh years. I left Iran and stayed away for years because I believed I couldn't work under such conditions. Eventually they had to compromise. However, their red lines regarding religion – especially the depiction of women, Sharia law and Islamic practice – remained in place and led to the most peculiar, illogical compromises in our films!

SR: Is the film-making climate better for you now, after the revolution?

BF: I'd say so.

SR: Besides ideological prescriptions and sanctions, what sticks out in Iranian film – as you mentioned yourself – is the issue of women's sexuality and erotic love. Women have to wear a *hijab*, lovers can't hold each other, husband and wife cannot touch each other even in the privacy of their bedrooms! Are these some of the peculiar and illogical compromises that you have in mind?

BF: Yes, but these are issues that we have now almost got used to and learned how to deal with. I'll tell you how the censorship of sexuality began. First, a religious group founded a film-making company called Ayat Film. They were funded by the Hosseiniyeh Ershad.[1] On the board of trustees were some very religious people from wealthy Bazaari backgrounds – people such as Seyyed Mir-Hossein Mousavi, who later became the prime minister of Iran,[2] and Mostafa Hashemi, who later became the minister of industry. In the early days of the revolution, this centre released a film by Mohammad Ali Najafi called *Jang-e At'har* [*The Battle of the Pure*, 1979], which was supposed to tell the life story of Dr Ali Shariati.[3] My company was to distribute it. When I saw the film, I jokingly asked the director, 'Why doesn't the female protagonist take off her scarf? After all, she's supposed to be married to the male protagonist in the film!' Mr Najafi said, 'Are you kidding me? The woman who portrays Shariati's wife is my wife in real life!' So, you see how illogical compromises were already taking hold because of the religious influence that had already started to contaminate the minds of our intellectuals before the revolution. *Jang-e At'har* could only be released after the revolution, but it was made during the shah's time.

With the exception of the very vulgar, commercial films, even before the revolution we couldn't dwell much on female sexuality. Sex scenes were not even shown in Film Farsi, and heavy sex scenes in imported films were censored. And as far as the *hijab* is concerned, it was a fixture in our society even before the revolution. You saw more black *chadors* when you walked down the Tehran Bazaar area than you see today. In smaller towns and villages it was even worse. Ninety per cent of women wore a *hijab*. Only a small percentage who lived uptown and in posh areas of the city didn't. What I'm trying to say is that after the revolution we suffered greater cultural disasters than the compulsory wearing of the *hijab*. Was it not equally objectionable when they enforced the ban on the *hijab* under Reza Shah in the 1930s? That was a disaster too. My grandmother, for example, didn't leave the house for three years because she didn't want to go out 'uncovered'.

SR: So it's not the *hijab* itself that's a sign of backwardness, but the diktat from above?

BF: In reality most Iranian women are religious and that's why they wear a *hijab* – regardless of decrees from above. The insult – the cultural disaster – was the behaviour of the Islamic regime towards the nation, telling women that, starting tomorrow, you *have* to wear scarves and, no, you have no choice! This bullying mentality could have crippled the cinema. A bunch of amateurs with vague Islamic ideas wanted to force us to make *their* films. If an amateur film-maker was a zealously practising Muslim, they'd fund his films and leave the professionals to fend for themselves! Yes, they honestly believed that praying devoutly would teach you how to make films! In our time, before the revolution, a lot of young people experimented with cheap 16mm and 18mm film and made some short productions. After the revolution, everyone who was a good Muslim and said his prayers and fasted punctually was given money to experiment with the more expensive 35mm film. Out of this group five or six good film-makers, such as Majidi, Hatamikia, Mirkarimi and Makhmalbaf, emerged.

SR: So, fasting and praying was useful after all!

BF: Of course, all this widespread experimentation and all this practice taught us how to make things that we simply used to import from abroad. But it was experimentation and practice that did it, not praying and fasting!

SR: And not only Iranians but also the 'arch-enemy' of the newly born Islamic Republic – the West – appreciated the high quality of Iranian cinema.

BF: If you look at our image in the rest of the world, you'll see that it's so dark that our country has turned into a black hole. But out of such a place comes a film like Kiarostami's *Where is the Friend's Home?*. There is so much elegance and delicacy in this film that people in the West wonder how it's possible for such beauty to come out of such a jungle. And we have managed to keep it going and pass our knowledge on to the next generation. Today it is not only Mehrjui, Kiarostami and I who are successful because of the breadth of our experience. We have active film-makers from three generations after our own who are making great films. Yet at the same time it must be said that the negative perception of the revolution made Iranian films more interesting. It was a sort of negative advertisement for Iranian cinema as such.

SR: Yes. Handing this legacy down to the younger generation is so important for New Iranian Cinema to progress. For example, cinema in Italy today – a country that produced one of the greatest waves of cinema ever, with people such as Visconti, Fellini, Antonioni and Pasolini – is so anaemic.

BF: That's right. No doubt we'll produce enough good Iranian film-makers for the next 30 years. There is this love affair between us and cinema that hardly exists in any other country.

SR: Considering the young age of cinema in Iran, its worldwide success is quite a phenomenon. My last book, *Iranian Writers Uncensored*, was about contemporary Iranian literature and, although I spoke with many famous writers and poets, in the end it became clear that Persian literature is isolated, both in Iran and abroad. Many believe that the dominance of languages such as English, German and French has inevitably limited the field for Persian literature abroad, and if a novel or a collection of poetry is successful, it takes so much money and effort for it to be translated.

At the same time, there are some works that are successful despite the language barrier and the translation costs – Orhan Pamuk, the Turkish novelist, is a good example of this. His works have been translated from Turkish into all the main languages of the world and a few years ago he actually won the Nobel Prize for literature. Why can't we produce a Persian Pamuk? Why is contemporary Persian literature, with its 1,000-year-old background, treated with neglect here and abroad whereas Iranian cinema, despite its short history, is much more attractive to both Iranians and foreigners?

BF: There are lots of young writers and poets. However, there is a big difference: the writer writes for one person – usually himself or herself – whereas the film-maker 'writes' for hundreds of thousands of people. So it's the extent and the scale of the work that we should look at. Why is the first thing that most dictators do is to take over television and cinema? We should bear in mind that all Iranians, regardless of what they do, have a shared literary and historical memory. Even illiterate people know verses by Saadi and Hafez by heart. They might not understand the poems in all their multilayered complexity, but they know them. This shared memory – or as the Europeans call it 'collective memory' – that has been carried from generation to generation through literature and is the basis of our identity should not be ignored when we talk of films. Regarding our literature, the number of people who speak our language worldwide is not high. Even in Asia the domain of Persian is not what it was some 200 years ago. However, in at most one or two decades, translations of works by Golshiri, Jalal Al Ahmad or Dolatabadi will be widely available worldwide and receive their due respect.

SR: Translations are available but they are not duly recognized.

BF: I think our poet Ahmad Shamlu should have won the Nobel Prize. But the problem is that if you compare Shamlu with Neruda, for example, who actually won the Nobel Prize, you'll see that the latter wrote his poems in Spanish, which is spoken by half the world.

SR: Orhan Pamuk writes in Turkish.

BF: All right, he writes in Turkish, but you should compare the money spent on translating Pamuk's works with the situation we had and still have in our country. Our governments have never been interested in doing this and don't encourage it. All the writers I know whose books have been translated had to rely on their own resources. For example, they may know someone in England or America – they get in touch, and this someone decides to translate their work. The government never supported this. It's not as if Mahmoud Dolatabadi and Simin Daneshvar are not great writers.[4] Our literature, though, has always been the victim of the government's political games. This leads to such absurdities as Madonna singing the verses of our Persian poet Rumi to us, or the Turks claiming that Rumi is actually Turkish because his grave is in Turkey! They make a fuss over him without understanding a single verse of his. What do we do for this poet in the eyes of the world? You can see for yourself that, because of our isolated position in the world and because of our government's politics, we have never been able to deal with such issues properly with serious support from the government. That is the sort of tragedy our literature faces.

SR: Yet Iranian films win top awards at international film festivals, despite what you've just described and despite the censorship they struggle against. Why has Iranian film been smarter in managing to find its way than contemporary literature?

BF: It's because of the medium of cinema. Anywhere in the world, the image, because of the speed with which it's conveyed and the simplicity of its use, is more pervasive than literature. It is much easier to consume than books. Cinema has known waves of growth in many countries at different times. We've had the Italian, Japanese, Swedish, German and French waves – you name it. All these have come and gone. This Iranian New Wave will pass too. Compared to other waves, though, our situation is different. We should bear in mind that in the rest of the world not one positive word is said about this country, except for its cinema. Our cinema has managed to find a way to the festivals and to an international audience. Yet the films that have attracted great attention mainly suit the tastes of Westerners and their view of us, except for Kiarostami's experimental works, whose strength lies in creating a completely different way of looking at cinema and revolutionizing an artform in which we thought that everything that could be said had been said. For example, Majid Majidi – whose film *Children of Heaven* [1997] was nominated for an Oscar – shows images of Iran that are much more congenial to foreigners than to ourselves, of Iran as a country where one pair of shoes is shared among four children.

SR: That's exactly what I want to get at: Iranian identity outside Iran. The cinema of Iran plays a considerable role in forming the identity of Iranians abroad. As you mentioned, some like to watch Kiarostami's delicate films. Others, however, like to see poverty and hardship in the films made by Makhmalbaf and the like, through which their feeling of superiority towards Iranians is confirmed. All these films show a multifaceted Iran to the world.

BF: A few factors should be considered here. The most important of all is the power of the festivals. Next is the fact that in the West they are trying to fit us into a framework they have built up of who we are. In the eyes of the world Iran is like a child who's making trouble in the class and the teacher chooses to either send him to the back of the classroom or throw him out so that the rest of the children don't follow his example. You see, before the revolution, we were seen as a child that behaved well in the classroom. If America coughed, the shah would catch a cold. Today our government, at least in public, tells America to go cough itself to death. They don't care about America and they're quite hostile towards them as the 'world police'. This is frustrating for the West. And then you have these wonderful films coming out of this 'dump'. It's confusing! Nothing fits! To confirm what you were saying earlier, an American critic wrote a review of my *A House Built on Water* [2001] in which he said something like, 'This director stubbornly insists on showing us another image of Iran than the one we are used to! Hence be prepared to be astonished!' That's how this gentleman described my film.

Now, the characters in my films are artists and intellectuals. I show poverty and I show wealth. If my main character is a surgeon, for example, he's also a politicized surgeon. You cannot accuse any of my characters of agreeing with the regime's policies. However, I do not make political statements. The films, while observing aesthetic standards, also look critically at daily issues. In *A House Built on Water* I talk about AIDS, about the surgical restoration of virginity and about the chain of assassinations of opposition leaders in Iran during Khatami's presidency in the late 1990s. That's why that critic calls me 'stubborn'. I make films for Iranians whether you like it or not, whether it fits your worldview or not, whether you give me awards or not. My main audience are Iranians.

SR: What you've just said brings to mind the 'classless' audience of cinema. Unlike poetry and literature, which are elitist arts, in the sense that you need at least to be able to read and write in order to enjoy them, cinema is an art that everybody, regardless of their background and education, can enjoy; so it can reach a much greater and more diverse audience than literature. With that in mind, what influence do you think film has on Iranian society as a whole? Do you consider yourself a committed artist? Do you try to educate your audience through your films and help them grow culturally, or do you think that art should only be made for its own sake?

BF: In a country where 65 per cent of the population is under 25 years old, regardless of my intentions, there is 'education' through cinema whether you like it or not, inevitably. Young people are thirsty for knowledge and learning. Whether deliberately or not, I 'educate' through the subject I choose and the way I present it. At the end of the day, I hope that my films have influenced the audience – no matter how little. What I want a young audience watching my film to understand is that for an artist it is easier to be executed than to be banned from working. Being alive and not having a connection with the audience is much more agonizing than dying.

SR: The censorship policies of Iranian governments – be it during the shah's time or right now – have always aimed at shutting up artists and separating them from their audience. A person like you may say that this is fatal for a film-maker and for an artist. However, someone like Ebrahim Golestan shows disregard for his Iranian audience and considers them idiots. I think it was during the 1969 Shiraz Festival that he went as far as to hurl abuse at his audience! He saw himself as a misunderstood artist who was not appreciated in his native country and eventually felt that he'd been forced to leave. And this had nothing to do with the government's policies. How do you compare yourself with someone like that?

BF: The snobbishness you see in Ebrahim Golestan belongs to a generation before our own. But I suppose we ought to try to see things from Golestan's point of view as well. At that time over two-thirds of the country's population were illiterate. If you had been to school or were educated or, as in Golestan's case, spoke a foreign language, then you would have looked down on Iranians and felt misunderstood. Golestan is the embodiment of that attitude. However, we should never forget that many new trends in film-making in Iran started with Golestan. He was a successful pioneer. Yet he looked on life with hatred.

SR: How much anger and hatred do you need to be able to make films on the same level as Golestan in such a 'backward' country?

BF: In my opinion, if Golestan is interesting, that's because of these contradictions. His daughter tells us that he refuses to set foot in Iran, yet at the same time he wants to know how much the syca-more trees that he planted in his garden years ago have grown. If you are not interested in Iran, why are you interested in the size of your sycamore trees? He's always been a contrarian. He defends himself by offending you, by saying that you don't have the brains to understand what he says! For him, the best defence is attack, be it against the government or against the audience. But let me tell you this: if the government really wanted to hurt me, they would send me away into exile. I draw energy from my audience here. For instance, when I go to Tabriz University to talk, 1,800 people come to the main lecture hall, which has a capacity of only 500. Where else in the world would I get that? This brings me back to that love affair between our people and their cinema. Our people have a special relationship with film-makers and for me this relationship is life-giving.

SR: In your films you concentrate heavily on social issues. Do you consider yourself a politically and socially committed artist?

BF: Of course my films are mainly political – they always had a political aspect. That's me, really. For example, in my most recent film, *The Familiar Soil* [2008], I address the youth of this country directly. I tell them, 'You are the first generation who wants to harvest without planting anything in the first place!' That is not possible. Throughout history, no one has been able to do that. What I mean is that our country has turned into a place where you pay money and import goods. This new generation doesn't want to produce anything. It doesn't even want to plant wheat or rice. Everything has to be imported from abroad.

While in my films I hold a mirror to society, at the same time I try to tell a tale so that I can entertain the audience. For example, in *A House Built on Water*, when I show a young woman who wants to have her virginity artificially restored, I'm not talking only about her case; I'm talking about a political issue, and when such issues are brought up, you have to put up with people's reactions. They are usually harsh because there are so many 'red lines' for artists in this country. The people of Iran – the audience of our films – are completely aware of that. The fact is that our audiences are much cleverer than we give them credit for.

Another thing I want to say is that not taking religion into account was and is foolish. Religion has strong roots in our country. Many intellectuals and friends with modern ideas have always criticized me for this, but I believe that religion is a reality that we must take into account, like it or not. My problem with the Islamic

Republic is not their religiosity but the fact that their ideology interferes with the most personal part of my life, my inner life – no, I don't mean my sexual life, but my relationship to God. No one has the right to interfere in this matter. If I see a flower and admire its beauty, I start to believe in something beyond – I start to search for meaning within myself. I do not want them to tell me what to believe. I do not want them to tell me that I have to do what they say in order for me to go to heaven. I do not believe in heaven and hell anyway! My faith tells me to leave the world in the same way it was given to me – with a bit of luck, perhaps in a slightly better condition. The rest is rubbish. Everybody asks, well then, why do you make so many films about death? I reply, because I think a lot about life.

SR: Your films are indeed very spiritual.

BF: Spirituality does not have much to do with exploring religion. It is more about confronting mysteries – unanswerable questions. In the twenty-first century humans are used to finding a solution to every problem – the unknown seems not to exist for us. The fact is that eventually something will be left unanswered. Take this canary, for instance. With a larynx as big as a fingernail, how does it make such sounds? They say it is the work of nature. I can grasp this kind of thing. I understand the logic of it as well. I just do not understand why. Why are all religions of the world alike? Why do they keep repeating their stories? Is it that God wasn't creative enough to make a new story? Was God's imagination limited? All religions are connected. You show me a religion that says it is good to rape your neighbour's wife or it is good to kill. My way of looking at religion is moral. Religion was made for the sake of social morality and yet people are still tearing each other up. Imagine the disaster if such morals and rules did not exist. This is the framework within which I view religion – as a set of rules.

SR: To what extent does Persian literature, classical or contemporary, provide an artistic background for you?

BF: I cannot separate myself from Persian literature. I read a lot. We have lots of very good stories that lend themselves to film-making. We have people such as Esmail Fasih, who is not only an excellent novelist but also a very good screenplay writer. His works have a visual quality; his novels are 'cinematic'. However, because of the flawed infrastructure of our film industry we cannot use people such as him as much as we would like. Iranian produc-ers are mainly at fault in this respect. When you tell a producer that you want to make a film based on one of Fasih's novels, he asks, 'Why should I pay five million to Fasih?' He'll tell you to read the book yourself and modify it and work on the first and the last chapter and then turn it into a script! So eventually the film-maker has to write the script himself, as I have done in my last three or four films.

Apart from the financial aspect, there is also censorship to consider. Personally I would really like to adapt a novel such as Fasih's *Winter of '62* into a film. I really like this story but if you passed on the script to those in charge, they wouldn't allow it to be made into a film because the book itself was banned after it had been given permission to be published! This is the depress-ing situation of art and literature in this country. That's why, in complete desperation, I sat down and wrote *Smell of Camphor, Scent of Jasmine* [2000]. Fortunately there isn't much rationality or logic when it comes to censorship policies in Iran, so they accepted the script and allowed me to make the film. To cut a long story short, the reasons for the lack of exchange between literature and cinema in Iran are government censorship and producers' unwillingness to invest in good novels and have them adapted into scripts. The situation is so sad that it makes you want to throw yourself from the twentieth floor.

SR: Under these circumstances didn't the Farabi Cinema Foundation play a positive role as producer and distributor of Iranian films?

BF: The Farabi bought the rights to some novels. However, it did not discuss this matter with any film-makers beforehand, so no one agreed to make any of these novels into films. It was as though the Farabi wanted to give support to certain writers rather than to film-makers. If I, as a director, decided to make a film I would choose a story and say that *this* is the story I want to make into a film. For example, I wrote a script based on a story from Golshiri's collection of short stories *Dark Hands, Light Hands* [1995], but they rejected it! I wrote a script based on Fasih's *Winter of '62*, but again they rejected it. They did not want such stories. The truth is that they wanted to force on film-makers the stories they had already bought!

SR: Many experts and some film-makers believe that New Iranian Cinema owes a lot to the Farabi, especially while it was under the aegis of Mohammad Beheshti. What do you think about that?

BF: To some extent that is true. At the beginning the Farabi did invest in our films and encouraged us. Many films were made through their funding but, because they wanted to dictate to film-makers what subjects to make films about – as I mentioned earlier, they had bought the rights to the novels they wanted us to turn into films – they stood in the film-makers' way. That's why many of our good film-makers didn't make many films.

In the last two or three decades the Islamic Republic has become stronger in many areas and has spread its control over all parts of our lives. If we move an inch further than they permit, they will hit us hard. They tell us what to do, what to wear, what to eat and drink! They do everything they can to control our newspapers, books and films. However, what they have failed to realize is that culture cannot be controlled. It will always find a way out.

SR: What was the Farabi's role in relation to cinema?

BF: It was like starting the engine of a car – a car that has been idle for a long time. Because of funding problems, no one would invest in Iranian film. The private sector thought that investing in the post-revolutionary film industry was a big risk (the same thing happened in other industries). So they backed off – it was safer to open a café or a restaurant! The Farabi wanted to restart the engine. To begin with, the best thing it did for Iranian cinema was to invest in and encourage us to make films. After those films had been made and some proved profitable, the private sector saw that it was possible to gain from this. So gradually they started to invest and the Iranian film market started to develop. It's now about ten or 12 years since the Farabi has done anything except send films to festivals or rent out film-making equipment and buy film stock for the whole country.

SR: Was this after Beheshti?

BF: Mostly, yes, but they had already started making cuts in subsidies in the last few years of his management. During the first seven or eight years, though, when no one was willing to invest, the Farabi played a wholly constructive role. Even more important than the investments was the support they gave Iranian films abroad. The Farabi was able to convince the authorities that the only thing the West and the rest of the world were positive about when it came to Iran was its cinema! Those in charge got the message quickly and this made our lives a little easier – just a little. I must say that the Farabi was very active in this sense.

SR: Was the Farabi the puppet of the Ministry of Culture and Islamic Guidance – the Ershad?

BF: The Farabi's funding has always come from the Ershad; it has never been an independent institute. The Ershad established the Farabi because the best film-makers would not work for the ministry. So they decided to create an institute – something like an intermediary – and appoint the most intelligent of their people and Islamic intellectuals, of which Mr Beheshti was the best example, to it. The Farabi was thus separate from the Ershad, though funded by it.

The budget of the Farabi has always been part of the annual budget of the Ershad, so the Farabi is not at all independent, though to outward appearances it has always seemed so. And that was its positive point. Instead of talking to an official at the Ershad, film-makers now talked to Mr Beheshti. This gave the Farabi the key role. Even today, if anyone is looking at something in connection with a film, he'll contact the Farabi straight away. The Farabi had two weapons: one was to invite important people from abroad to the Fajr Film Festival in Tehran, and the other was to send Iranian films to big foreign film festivals. These two weapons were used very successfully under Beheshti's management and thus Iran was put on the cinema map.

SR: So did film-makers have to submit their films to international festivals exclusively through the Farabi?

BF: That's how it was then, but now you can do so via other channels as well, although film-makers still give copies of their films to the Farabi, which can send them anywhere it wants. But now that you can send your films abroad through other channels, the Farabi has lost its meaning. It is still there, it still creates jobs and its staff travel to festivals, but it no longer has a meaningful role to play – as is the case with a lot of government institutions that have outlived their usefulness.

SR: The interesting thing is, why was an organization such as the Farabi ever founded for the promotion of cinema in Iran after the Islamic Revolution? The Western view is that Islam is against images, so cinema is against Islamic principles.

BF: Those in charge wanted to control the images.

SR: They could have said no to cinema – as they did in Saudi Arabia.[5] They could have forbidden it.

BF: They could have done no such a thing.

SR: How can you be so sure?

BF: You cannot stop culture in this country. So instead they decided to set up a body they could trust to ensure that no films against the regime would be made.

SR: But you said earlier that during the early years of the revolution Iranian cinema benefited from the Farabi.

BF: They realized that they could use film as a strong medium for the promotion of Islamic values. However, things are always much more complex than one thinks. There were and are hardly any independent producers for such propaganda films because they don't sell well. So this responsibility was assigned to television, which has both the budget and the means. Independent religious films could not be made in Iran, so the task was assigned to state-controlled organizations: responsibility for so-called moral or religious productions was handed over to the state itself and to television. The ordinary viewer, though, is not interested in such films. At the moment only 10 per cent of films made are of a religious or spiritual nature. The rest is commercial. It's interesting that a lot of the banned Film Farsi productions that were very popular before the revolution are now being remade with new actors but without the erotic scenes! We no longer see popular actresses such as Mahvash dancing or Foroozan in a miniskirt,[6] but the storyline is the same. If you watch Ms Milani's *Cease Fire* [2006], you'll see that it's an ordinary story but with two very good-looking actors. It's about a husband and wife who are having problems and the girl looks very much like the most popular singer and actor from the days of the shah – Googoosh.[7] So, after the revolution we took to remakes. We found look-alikes of all the popular singers and actors from the shah's time –

SR: – Who are now dead or are mostly active in Los Angeles and London –

BF: Yes, we have found people who can imitate Ebi's voice, people who can sing like Dariush or Golpayegani[8] but we do not allow the originals to perform in Iran. In cinema, too, we are back to the same point we were before the revolution. Popular TV series and

films were made before the revolution and so were auteur films –
masterpieces such as Kiarostami's *The Report* [1977]. So it took us
28 years to end up with the same formula we had at the start.

SR: Throughout the interview you've been saying that the revolution did influence our cinema – especially its global status. Even
Kiarostami, who is very sceptical about revolutions of any kind,
believes that the Iranian revolution, as a kind of advertisement, has
been positive for Iranian cinema. You did mention this yourself in
the beginning of our interview. On the other hand, people such
as Mohammad Beheshti say that our revolution led Westerners to
censor us because they resented the revolution and still do. For
that reason it took a long time for our post-revolutionary films to
get into festivals in the West and, *despite* Western political attitudes,
win awards there.

BF: Mr Beheshti and those in charge of institutions such as the
Farabi still wrongly believe that if *they* – meaning the usurping,
imperialist West – would let us, we could beat America. In June
2006 there was a meeting between a group of cinematographers
and Ayatollah Khamenei. Some of the religious film directors
begged him to ask the government to fund their projects so that
they could overthrow Hollywood and thus America as a whole!
That's a naive vision, because they don't know who they're dealing
with.

When I say that no country has a film industry except for
America, everyone objects. My answer is that every film industry
has to have a distributor. We cannot produce and not distribute.
We do make good films here but as soon as we finish a film we
have to take it to European and American distributors such as MK2
or Miramax, go home and wait for the cheque! And why is that?
Because we don't have the means to distribute films worldwide. But
the Americans have offices even in Burkina Faso; *they* release their
films and *they* take the money. They also have offices in France,
Italy and China. Everywhere they are in control of their own products and thus in control of homegrown products as well. American
cinema is an industry that cannot be overthrown! Even France

cannot truly claim to have a film industry. If a film of theirs is successful in France, the Americans will buy the story, do a remake in Hollywood and sell it to the rest of the world as a blockbuster. The original will be forgotten and, if it ever does get released, it will, because of the problem of subtitles, be screened in no more than a dozen American cities – the most important market for films. These are the facts, at least now. Not even the Chinese can compete with that. Anyone who doesn't understand this dynamic could say things like, 'The West stopped us because of their fear of the glorious Islamic Revolution; otherwise we could have stormed the market with our own cinema!' That's just not possible. The best thing we can do is support our own cinema abroad, just like the Japanese have always done. When I was a student in America, the Japanese embassy rented a cinema in Los Angeles and showed Japanese films there. As film students we were thus able to see films by Kobayashi, Ozu and Kurosawa.[9] This is something that the Iranian government could do for our films abroad.

SR: How important are festivals for introducing Iranian film to the world?

BF: There are five important festivals: Cannes, Venice, Berlin, New York and Toronto. There are also film festivals in London and Locarno, which are national rather than international, yet they are good starting points. French critics have always been opinion-makers in the domain of European cinema and we were lucky that they liked Kiarostami! At the height of New Iranian Cinema Godard, the famous French director, said that cinema ended with Kiarostami.

However, claiming that festivals turn us into good film-makers is wrong. The jury and the audience watch films for ten days in a row and then hand out awards. This plays an important role in introducing cinema – especially the cinema of the Third World – to the rest of the world, but it doesn't make us into what we are. You see, only the Cannes winners can score a box-office success. And in the most important market for film – the USA – only a fraction of cinema goers would buy tickets to watch subtitled films.

So festivals don't matter much for our film industry as a whole. Yet for us 'Third Worlders', who don't have much leverage in the global market, festivals – especially European ones – have been quite helpful because of the influence they have on film-lovers and also because Europeans are used to subtitles, which is good for us.

SR: I'd like to get back briefly to the issue of the artist being exiled from his or her own society. Many film-makers who stayed in Iran after the revolution continue to work despite a thousand obstacles and have become internationally renowned. But those who left, despite all the opportunities and freedoms abroad, have not been able to produce popular films.

BF: There's one main reason for that. The Eastern artist has roots within the soil of his culture just as European and American artists have common roots in the West. I'm not talking about the new Eastern – Iranian – generation who went abroad en masse because of the revolution and the war when they were six, seven, nine or ten years old and now live there – and, yes, are establishing roots outside their motherland. I'm talking about the people who came of age in Iran and then went abroad for further education – like myself. When Amir Naderi left, for whatever reason, he made a big mistake. He does not even have formal training in film-making. I don't think he even finished high school. His strength was that he was from this land. He made amazing films about his own life – *Harmonica* [1974], *The Waiting* [1974] and *The Runner* [1984] are masterpieces of New Iranian Cinema. How is he supposed to make a successful film in America, where he's unfamiliar with the language, the culture and the history? I mean, you cannot make a film there that would interest Americans if you can't relate to them. If Amir Naderi came back now, they'd roll out the red carpet to welcome him, yet he's being stubborn.

You see, his case isn't about politics, as it is for many Iranian writers and artists who cannot return home. The latter haven't produced any good literature and art in exile either and all of them live sad lives or have practically died of depression. This is mainly because the societies in which our artists are exiled don't accept us culturally. After living in Germany for 50 years, you are still an Iranian; you are always an alien. It's true that there are institutions that fund artistic activities regardless of your nationality, but you still cannot be successful there if you come from my generation and your roots are in Iran. Here, for instance, when you get into a minicab, the driver will tell you all the latest rumours, all he's seen and heard during the day. Where do you think I get my dialogue from? As an artist you have to be where your roots are. You might say, wait a minute, the novel *The Remains of the Day* [1989] was written by a Japanese writer. I'll reply, Kazuo Ishiguro went to England when he was only two years old and he's completely immersed in the culture of that country. Another example is Salman Rushdie, who first became acquainted with the English language in very early childhood. As for me, I first went to England and then America when I was 16. I studied and lived in both countries, so my English has always been fluent – but it was too late! I didn't recognize their songs. I was an alien. When after the revolution we left Iran for a few years and my children went to school in America, I would look at their first-grade school books with amusement and astonishment. But I know everything that comes from this place, from this water and soil. I know everything, from a mother's lullaby to the rhymes and complaints of canal and sewer cleaners walking up and down our streets and offering their services! I know what conditions are required for good yogurt-making. It is from here that I take my cultural sustenance.

I daresay that more than a hundred films have been offered to a person like Kiarostami to make abroad, but he always declines.[10] Shahid Saless, who was a very good film-maker in Iran, also made films in Germany and Austria which were no different from typical German films. Yet he never really got on track. His only successful films in the West were those that conveyed the atmosphere of *this* land, such as *A Simple Event* [1974]. In fact, Kiarostami and other Iranian New Wave film-makers were greatly inspired by Shahid Saless's cinema. But Shahid Saless was a special case. He left Iran before the revolution – that was his end! You think you must become like them in order to be successful. But that's a trick! You become like the Germans or the Americans, but the chances of you being successful are very low because you are only an imitation, not an original – because you have been formed in *this* land. I had a friend whose surname was Asgar; when he became an American citizen he changed it to Oscar. Now, what was wrong with Asgar?

RAKHSHAN BANI-ETEMAD
Cinema as a Mirror of the Urban Image

RAKHSHAN BANI-ETEMAD SEES THE 1979 REVOLUTION as a key event in the growth of Iranian art-house cinema. She has no doubt that New Iranian Cinema emerged more than a decade before the revolution took place, but adds that it was the revolution that opened the way for a truly original cinema that is still admired greatly through-out the world. She is convinced that neither the progress nor the worldwide success of Iranian cinema was planned by the Islamic regime; in fact, the contradictions and ideological conflicts that followed the revolution gave rise to a sort of creative chaos within which some film-makers found the opportunity to work. She sees the period immediately following the revolution as the key moment in the life and death of cinema. It was a stroke of luck that the arguments of moderate religious intellectuals (such as Mohammad Beheshti, who ran the Farabi Cinema Foundation from 1983 to 1994) won the day against the fundamentalists.

Another factor that enabled the growth of Iranian film despite censorship, she adds, is that, in contrast to European countries under fascist or communist regimes, in Iran there has never been a single set of rules that had to be enforced meticulously in order for a film to get permission to be released; it was more the censor's personal tastes and beliefs that determined their fate. Of course, the downside of this policy was that films could also be banned for trivial reasons. This is why during the presidency of Ahmadinejad, Bani-Etemad largely stuck to documentaries, unwilling to make the compromises necessary to get a feature made. Now that Iran's government under Rouhani seems to be more 'culture-friendly', she has released her latest film *Tales* (2014), for which she received the Golden Lion for best script at the Venice Film Festival in 2014.

Although Bani-Etemad discerns traces of Persian poetry and literature in Iranian art films, she believes that the films that stand out for international viewers and critics are those that deal with the reality of day-to-day life in Iran rather than those that take a poetic or surrealist approach. In Iran, she believes, the definition of the artist is different from that in prosperous, democratic Western societies. In Iran an artist has social and political responsibilities, whereas in the West artists must be committed only to their own art or their own personalities. This is why she worries greatly about the film-makers' lack of interest in the Iran–Iraq War. In her view, this is a cultural and historical catastrophe that was due mainly to the regime's exploitation of the war for ideological and propaganda purposes, which in turn led good film-makers to avoid it altogether as a subject.

Shiva Rahbaran: The main purpose of my book is to examine the influence of the 1979 revolution on Iranian cinema and, in turn, the influence of that cinema on post-revolutionary Iranian society, from the point of view of those film-makers who are now living and working in Iran. In this sense, Iranian cinema is examined from a sociological rather than an aesthetic angle. Bearing in mind that cinema is considered a 'popular' art that can communicate with people from all backgrounds regardless of their education – as opposed to literature, for example, which requires that people possess a certain level of literacy – how do you see the influence of cinema on society?

Rakhshan Bani-Etemad: I don't think that there is a clear boundary between our art and our literature. They have always fed from each other. Regarding the influence of Iranian cinema on post-revolutionary society, we should start by looking at our pre-revolutionary cinema. Although the dominant genres then were Film Farsi and Hollywood blockbusters, during that same period film-makers such as Golestan, Ghaffari, Kiarostami, Mehrjui, Shahid Saless, Taghvai, Kimiavi and Beyzaie were active. They represented a cinema that in many people's eyes was very poetic, in that it fed off Persian literature and poetry. If you look at the works of these film-makers, you'll see that they are actually timeless – like all good works of art. But at the same time you'll see that they have been slightly elitist – like poetry. Their brand of cinema did not necessarily communicate with the masses but appealed instead to a certain intellectual segment of society. Although intellectual cinema – also called the Iranian New Wave – was still a niche market and had not yet grown into a movement, it was still very important for the birth of contemporary Iranian cinema as we know it.

What these pioneers had in common was their very delicate and poetic way of depicting life. So, the roots of a major strand of New Iranian Cinema can be found in the ideas of the intellectual film-makers who were active before the revolution. However, before the revolution there weren't many opportunities for them to thrive – in particular, finding private producers for their films was difficult and government funds were meagre. And yet, some of the films made during that period are among the best in the history of our cinema. Personally I believe that Kiarostami's *The Report* is one of the best films ever made.

SR: You say that cinema is an expensive industry and that the scant government funding before the revolution limited the production of art films. Why, then, did Iranian cinema thrive exactly at the time when, because of the revolution, the sanctions and the eight-year war with Iraq, the economy was at a very low point?

RB: The economic constraints that you point out, together with cultural and social problems, made it hard for us to make our films. However, it's not as if the revolution or the Islamic regime suddenly offered intellectual film-makers great opportunities to overcome these obstacles. What happened in Iran after the revolution was the birth of a contradiction that proved to be fruitful for film-makers. Censorship and bans on foreign and pre-revolutionary home productions – Film Farsi – gave cinema the opportunity to develop. It was a kind of abnormality – a paradox, as it were. Yet it opened the gates for the Iranian New Wave.

Pre-revolutionary Iranian cinema also struggled with restrictions, but these were different. Film-makers were not allowed to look at the reality of their country from a critical point of view. The worst obstacle was the mainstream and blockbuster films produced in and outside Iran which had invaded our cinema. They left hardly any room for auteur films. But after the revolution we were given the opportunity to look at social issues, not only because there was a need for such scrutiny but also because erotic films and love films were not allowed. You see, it is very difficult to talk about such things; it's difficult even to discuss this subject in an interview. What I am saying could easily be put in a political context and then I would get grilled for it by the left and the right inside and outside Iran! You must see things in Iran for yourself. You must be in Iran. You must look at the situation firsthand.

During the early years of the revolution there was not only an ideological but also an existential discussion on cinema. There were those who said that cinema was *haram*, meaning that, from the viewpoint of Sharia law, it should not be consumed and had to be destroyed. That was a crucial time for the continued existence of this artform. The good news was that those who took the side of cinema as a form of social art won the argument against those who saw it as no more than vulgar entertainment. This triumph was crucial for the survival of a cinema that went on to become a world-class phenomenon.

One of the most important events of that period was the launch of the Farabi Cinema Foundation under Mohammad Beheshti. The Farabi went into battle for the right of cinema to exist. The battle had to be fought against those who held key positions in the Ministry of Culture and Islamic Guidance and who thought that cinema was a nest of immorality. Fortunately the intellectual film-makers managed to hold their own in the battle. The paradox of it all was that the struggle made us side, to a certain degree, with the 'fanatics' – the enemies of cinema – against the old, vulgar cinema and rediscover the artform as a new, realistic, as well as poetic medium that reflected our social and individual realities. Those were strange times; one had to be there to understand it.

Of course, as I said earlier, the roots of this cinema began almost two decades before the revolution. Then film-makers looked at the world around them from a social as well as a poetic point of view. After the revolution this small current turned into a large stream, into a major movement. It's true that there were lots of disagreements between the film-makers and the authorities. I mean, a film-maker could get into big trouble by trying to present the simplest of subjects – such as a love story. However, if we look at our cinema over the past two decades, we can see that it has successfully overcome a historical challenge – one that could have cost it its life if a wrong turning had been taken.

Through this challenge, Iranian cinema learned how to deal with the issues of our reality and society in both poetic and realistic language. What I mean is that Iranian cinema developed the language of a kind of poetic realism, through which the film-maker could show social reality with sharp precision. The various restrictions and censorships could have led Iranian cinema towards a sort of symbolism, which was often the case in pre-revolutionary art cinema. The films of Golestan and Shahid Saless are some of the more prominent examples of that symbolism. Luckily, however, as we can see, this didn't happen and our cinema never lost contact with reality.

SR: Are you saying that the fruitful contradiction you speak of was the child of harsh censorship?

RB: I never said such a thing. That would mean attaching value to something negative. Just because our cinema found a way of surviving harsh censorship does not make censorship a good thing. It's much more complicated than that. In my opinion, the most important thing at that time was society itself. Our society needed a cinema with a different point of view, and it was only thanks to the vigilance of our film-makers that good films were made, despite the constraints that could so easily have forced them to veer towards dishonest and propagandistic cinema. I think that if it weren't for the intelligence and independence of directors, the inclination towards inertia – of 'moving with the flow' and making propaganda films – would have been much stronger. As I said, the new movement's beginnings lie in a time well before the revolution, but it evolved mainly because of a need that was felt deeply in post-revolutionary society. Cinema grew towards a kind of realism and poetry that represented social issues. It may seem to you as though I'm saying that censorship made Iranian cinema grow, but actually it was the non-existence of uniform censorship that enabled film-makers to find their way through religious and political constraints.

SR: Can you elaborate on that, please?

RB: We never had a law that defined censorship, as was the case in, say, Nazi Germany or fascist Italy. We have always had various restrictions based on different circumstances and different tastes. Under one minister of culture, representing social issues might be more difficult than showing a close-up of a woman's beautiful face, but under another minister the opposite might be the case. In that sense, we've had more leeway than film-makers in other totalitarian regimes.

SR: When we look at some of our neighbouring Islamic countries, such as Saudi Arabia, which, in contrast to Iran, is regarded as an ally of the West, we see that all film theatres were closed down there in the 1970s.[1] But when we look at Iran's image in the world today, we see pictures of men and women in black, filled with hatred, burning Western flags. Surprisingly, the most delicate yet bold films come out of this country – a considerable number were made by women like you. In view of these contradictions, what kind of a country do you live and work in?

RB: To answer this question, it is necessary to take into account the historical and cultural state of our society.

SR: You mean the gap between civil society and government?

RB: Exactly! We need to compare the historical and cultural backgrounds of societies to each other. When a woman in Saudi Arabia is not even allowed to drive, how can she act in a film? In any case, there is a very different sort of censorship in Iran compared to that in Saudi Arabia. There has been throughout history some degree of freedom in our country and women's issues have always – up to this day – been on the agenda. In the past 100 years or so, women here have been allowed to work and thus have a status different from Saudi women. Although some women's activities were banned after the revolution, our society will not allow these boundaries to relegate us to the position of women in Saudi Arabia. We have a different social, historical and cultural background.

SR: It is felt that you personally grow and thrive in the gap between civil society and government.

RB: I think that even the government itself has come to accept some realities and this has forced it to adopt a different attitude towards certain boundaries. You cannot forget the historical conditions; in any case, it is within these contradictions and gaps that the roots of alternative thinking are formed. Even in the government there isn't a single, fixed point of view; so existing censorship does not necessarily comply with the government's own laws! Boundaries have always been set through guidelines – sometimes stricter than others – but when something is not based on the law, then, as an artist, you may interpret it in different ways.

SR: So the Ministry of Culture and Islamic Guidance [the Ershad] sometimes allows you freedom and sometimes ties you down.

RB: The Ershad never allows any freedom to anyone. We had to fight for our freedom. *I* push the boundaries; they wouldn't give me freedom as a gift – neither to me nor to any other artist. I don't think this is the case only in our society. I was talking to an activist film-maker in Italy. He was saying that in Iran if our pitch is not approved we know which institution has rejected it, whereas his pitch would get sent to a large organization, such as a TV station, and if it got rejected he'd never know why!

My aim is to fight for human rights in the twenty-first century. I gave the example of the Italian film-maker in order to highlight the problems that film-makers who cherish freedom have not only in Iran but also in the West, namely, to show what they see as the truth. Of course, our problems and obstacles are way larger than those of film-makers in the West. But I want to point out that there are discrepancies – gaps – between the official line of the Ershad and the reality of film-making in Iran. It is within these gaps that we search for our freedom and try to gain it bit by bit.

SR: A lot of people in the West say that if there is censorship in Iran, how can Bani-Etemad make a realistic film such as *Mainline* [2006], about drug abuse and prostitution among middle-class youth in Iran, or *Nargess* [1992], a film that not only deals with a woman's sexuality and lust but goes a step further and represents the male protagonist as the sex object of that woman? In other words, you reverse the traditional relationship between man and woman in that film. Again, in *The May Lady* [1999] the relationship between the boy and his mother has erotic undercurrents that are depicted in the most lyrical language. In your films you manage to hint that nothing is what it seems. Your subjects are taboo not only in Iran but also in the enlightened West. You can transport your audience into a state of shock and awe not only because of the taboos you break but because they are acutely aware of the fact that the film is from the Islamic Republic of Iran – a fanatical Islamic regime, the arch-enemy of artistic freedom.

RB: Absolutely! I agree with you. These films do bring up these questions and, frankly, answering them is always difficult. The reality is that they are never made with the complete approval of the censors. I never know what may happen at a future screening of one of my films. We make our films in full awareness that the person in charge of censorship might change his mind, or be replaced by another soon after the film comes out, and that a film that has been granted screening permission may be pulled from cinemas without warning.

SR: Yes, in Iran films are often banned after they've been on for only a few weeks. That explains the long queues in the first weeks of screening!

RB: That's right. *Nargess* was released initially and then after two years was allowed to be screened again. Altogether it was banned for seven years! And when it was finally released, the film copies had decayed. A few years ago at the Fajr Film Festival there was a retrospective of my films. When we tried to show *Nargess*, the copies were so damaged that we had to interrupt the screening probably 30 times because the film kept tearing. After the screening I told the audience that what they had just witnessed was evidence of cinema's lack of freedom in Iran! Let me tell you, though, that the most heart-warming and encouraging thing in the middle of this fiasco was that the audience stayed and watched the film in its entirety. The house lights had to be switched on at least 30 times while the film was fixed again and again, but the audience persisted and applauded at the end!

You see, this shows the arbitrariness of things in Iran. A much less controversial film might have huge problems and yet a film like *Nargess* be allowed – at least for a few weeks – to be shown! As I said before, one reason for this is the lack of a fixed set of censorship rules. The second reason is the censors' personal interpretation of the subject matter. That is, the review committee that approves the release does so on the basis of each member's own personal ideology and sensitivities. For example, the review committee for *Mainline* was concerned about addiction among young people and thought that the film had educative value, so it was passed. But it was not worried about the other taboo subjects in the film. However, a different set of people on the committee would have banned it.[2] It's as simple as that! It is within the gaps between these different points of view, ideologies and 'tastes' that we find the space to realize our films. However, the gaps can close just as fast as they have opened. I wrote my first script when I was pregnant with my daughter Baran. It was called 'Touba'. I wrote and re-wrote it many times until the Ershad finally approved it for production. By the time I got to make the film, Baran was 16! Of course, during that time I kept on working and made other films, some of which were released. I just want to give you an example of what it's like to work in Iran today. A lot of energy is put into making a film and by the time you finish it you may have broken down physically and mentally. So, I repeat, the idea of censorship fertilizing Iranian cinema is a lot of nonsense. Censorship in Iran can break a film-maker. Some of them, though, learn to develop strategies and through their intelligence, resistance and dynamism succeed in making a film – which, again, may have a short screen life. But that's not the way it should be.

SR: Don't you get fed up with such difficult conditions and don't you feel yourself pulled into a sort of inner exile that could easily lead to physical exile? I'm thinking of film-makers such as Golestan, Naderi and Shahid Saless.

RB: No, I do not think so. I suffer a lot from injustice in Iran. I suffer to the depths of my soul because we are denied even the simplest and most common rights of citizens. All my films reflect this pain – the pain of my society and the people who live in it. Yet, I would not call this being 'fed up'. The role of an artist in this society is different from that of an artist in another society, like the free and affluent countries of the West. As an artist I am responsible for the conditions that prevail in my society. Rakhshan Bani-Etemad is no different from any other woman in Iran. I can see the inequality and it hurts me. There are many women with a lot of intelligence who are more creative than I am but who have not had the opportunity to flourish. For some reason – put it down to my hard-headedness and my thick skin – I got the opportunity to work. So that makes me responsible for others in my society who have not been able to do the same. The hearts and minds of these people have nurtured me and I believe that if I can represent an issue pertinent to my society in a way that brings about the tiniest bit of awareness or the tiniest change in the authorities' point of view then I have done my job. I think a film-maker living in a country like Iran is responsible for her country.

SR: So, in your opinion, art has to be responsible and shouldn't follow the philosophy of 'art for art's sake'?

RB: For me, art is only a medium; cinema is not an end – not in the slightest. It is of no importance to me whether or not my name is recorded in the history of Iranian film-making. I want to see the effect of my films on my society while I'm still alive. I want to see the effect of my films on people both at the Enghelab Square cinema [Iran's largest cinema situated in Tehran] and in the smallest town. If I see that *Mainline* has succeeded in keeping just one young person away from drug addiction then that's my reward. It's a bit of an affectation to say that I am a 'committed' film-maker. This is a label mainly used by political artists; you could call it instead 'artistic commitment'. I see society from a social point of view. I feel that I'm indebted to this society and its people because I am moulded, like them, from the same unjust state of affairs.

SR: Would you be able to make films outside Iran as well?

RB: I prefer to make films in Iran because the most important thing for me is to touch the heart of my Iranian audience. For me, first and foremost, the Iranian audience – whether inside or outside Iran – needs to gain a much more realistic view of circumstances here. I'm not saying that winning awards at foreign festivals doesn't make me happy! However, it is not as important to me as success within Iran.

SR: Many Iranians who live abroad say that all the well-known Iranian directors are 'festival directors' who have been nurtured by the West. They believe that many Iranian films are made according to the tastes of Western film critics. But that does not apply to your films, which are popular both here and abroad.

RB: In my opinion it is unfair to talk in this manner about Iranian film-makers who are admired abroad. It is not fair to say that if a film-maker is successful in the West it is only because he or she knows how to appeal to Western film festivals.

SR: Cinema is a Western, imported artform compared to poetry, for example, which for many Iranians is the quintessence of our culture. Persian literature has a background that spans more than 1,000 years and our contemporary novelists and poets can call on a mountain of story-telling and epic poetry. Yet, despite such deep roots, our writers and poets seem rather isolated, as if they have fallen behind. Iranian cinema, on the other hand, seems to be doing well despite its relatively short history.

RB: I think that the most important thing might be that the roots of our cinema – the source of the progressive force of our cinema – are found at the very heart of our society. What I mean is that our cinema has been and is still being influenced by the reality we live in. This is very important. As you mentioned yourself, the image of Iran in the Western media is dramatized and sensationalized – it is not realistic. Compared with that, Iranian cinema is like a small window onto real life, to the real people of Iran and to the issues that they have in common with the rest of the world. The desire of the world for images of Iran is satisfied through the window of cinema. We also live in an age of high-speed communications; it is much easier to satisfy our curiosity by watching films than by reading contemporary novels. A Persian novel needs to be translated, too, so the novel or poem is inevitably a 'slower' medium than cinema.

SR: Let us go back to the 'schizophrenic' image of this country in the Western media – the angry fundamentalists versus the strong women of your films.

RB: You cannot describe the situation in Iran in a few words. For example, when you make a film in a country like Sweden, because the middle class is large and homogenous you will see considerably fewer social contradictions and conflicts. If my camera looked at life in Zargandeh Street (where I live) and then at daily life in Zafar Street, which is only ten minutes away, you'd see two completely different worlds – the former is more like a street in a small town – almost a village – with a smaller middle-class population, whereas the latter is a highly urbanized street in a highly affluent area. And there are many dramatic disparities between the two, particularly the differences in people's behaviour. As you know, there is a horrific class gap in our society and you can easily see that in the way people act and carry themselves. The disparity is so deep that it creates a lot of potential for drama – perhaps a blessing for the film-maker. Even the image of those flag-burning women in black is a part of our society. Yes, even the image of our society that Westerners have – regardless of how little they actually *know* about us – is part of our reality.

Yet this reality exists next to other realities which many Westerners cannot believe exist in an Islamic country like ours. I'll give you an example. A few days ago I received an email comparing Tehran to London. It was a comparison between the *hijab* of Muslims in London and that of Iranian girls here, where the *hijab* is compulsory. The Tehrani girls look pretty chic and almost '*hijab*-less' compared to their Muslim 'sisters' in London, who are covered from head to toe in black clothes. At the root of this situation lies the difficulty of implementing laws and regulations in our society. In most countries, when you park your car on a zebra crossing, you will be fined and that's that. No matter how much you beg, you will still be fined. In Iran, on the other hand, you might get away with a terrible crime through bribery but could be sentenced to prison for the smallest of misdemeanours. This resistance to complying with the law and this tendency to interpret or bend it exists in all walks of life in our country. So it's natural for a Western audience to ask how these films are made in a country where Sharia is supposed to be the bedrock of the state's legal system. You cannot explain these contradictions to a Western audience; you can only baffle them!

SR: The resistance towards accepting laws also offers a degree of freedom to the artist.

RB: At least it offers us the possibility to find a way of escape. In most other areas of social life this attitude could cause chaos and abuse, but in the realm of culture – especially in a totalitarian system – it can provide you with an escape route so that you are able to say what you want to say.

SR: You mentioned that you want your films to have an impact on society. But in a totalitarian society, where a film may enhance the awareness of the viewer, it also becomes a threat to authority. So, is the film-maker in such a society an activist as well as an artist?

RB: Definitely. By dealing with an issue from within our society and by breaking cultural taboos the film-maker creates room for discussion – discussion about issues that have been hardly touched on before. A strong film can even make the censorship officer think about his own place in society. The medium is the film-maker's means of fighting for freedom and bringing awareness to society. That is my job. Not that I think that a work of art can launch a revolution. Works of art are like water dripping on a large rock. Eventually it will wear down the rock but cannot be expected to make it explode instantly like a bomb. At the same time, the effect of slow dripping is much deeper and more enduring than that of a bomb and will clear the way for democracy in a much more lasting manner. That's the difference between cultural activism and political activism. Cultural activism is able to clear the way for democracy over time.

SR: Many Iranians living in the diaspora consider being culturally active in Iran as a form of support for the regime and its censorship. They say that when you choose to stay and work under a totalitarian regime you actually sustain it and work according to its guidelines and limitations.

RB: I don't believe in the necessity of exile for artistic freedom.

This is an old, dead theory. Many people in Iran take a different view: they say that those who left Iran did it for their own benefit and to save their own skins. In my opinion this theory is also problematic. You cannot separate the Iranians in Iran from those in exile. It is destructive to try to do so. We all share the same fate, more or less. I am not claiming that those of us who stayed and worked in Iran are more important than those who are active in exile. We all work in some way and hope for better days for our country. However, some of us who work in Iran have more impact on its society than those who work outside. Of course, many of us have no choice but to work abroad. We should put this 'inside/outside' issue aside. I will not waste my energy on addressing such issues. History will judge us.

SR: Your films mainly have urban settings. Is this riskier than making films that concentrate instead on the beauty of Iran and the innocence of childhood?

RB: I may take more risks but that doesn't mean that someone whose film is set in a village is less committed than I am.

SR: So, in your opinion, the film-maker who represents the beauty of Iran does not evade the ugliness and social reality of the country?

RB: This is a politicized point of view. Perhaps I take more risks. I might get to the heart of a situation and thereby cause friction, but that is not the reason why I choose such a subject. My reasons are of a social nature. If I see an increase in drug abuse in my society, then that issue also becomes *my* issue because I live in that same society. For example, I made *Gilane* [2005] because I realized that we were forgetting our victims of war – and it was only in 1988 that the war ended. Shrapnel will stay forever inside the bodies and souls of war victims, especially the women, and no one wants to know about it! No one wants to know about the woman who pushes the wheelchair on the pavement. No one cares about what she's going through. Unfortunately, because of censorship, there is a sense of indifference towards war films. Often one even senses a sort of a loathing for those who went to war.

SR: Yet you cannot ignore this eight-year war as a fertile source for film.

RB: During the war the regime tended strongly towards a kind of wrongheaded heroism with Islamic pretensions. In other words, the 'you're either with us or against us' issue was very prominent. It's true that many of the kids – yes, they were teenagers – who went to war, even voluntarily, came from a religious background. Yet there were many who didn't. The children of people like you and me also went to war. They did not go in order to defend Islam; they went in order to defend their country – it's as simple as that! Yet the image presented on TV was that of young people clutching the Qur'an and carrying the key to heaven around their necks.[3]

But despite this climate of political religiosity, our young people kept their feet on the ground. They were from this earth – not from some sort of spiritual heaven. They had girlfriends, they had lovers, they had fiancées, they listened to music and they went to the movies and dreamt of the sweet life. The regime's war propaganda, however, represented them as having no attachment to anything on this earth, as creatures who had only one aim in their lives – to die in the name of Islamic ideology. No doubt, one who goes to war has a certain ideology – for example, he thinks he's defending his country. Defending your land is no joke and we did it for eight years. I believe that there were quite a few opportunities where the war could have been brought to an end but wasn't – we have to ask the authorities why! However, despite all this, those who fought for Iran, those who came from non-ideological backgrounds, like you and me, fought on right till the end. Yet the TV showed images of soldiers who cared for nothing on earth – martyrdom was their only goal. An imaginary world was built on the regime's propaganda, a world in which a soldier's only wish was to get killed. Now look what this did to our young people! When I was in London I saw people wearing poppies. I asked why. I was told that it was in remembrance of the victims of World War I. You see! World War I!

I was in tears, not for the victims of World War I in Europe but for the forgotten victims of our own war. The absence of sympathy for victims in our country made me cry – a war that came to an end just 20 years ago. I'm glad that *Gilane* brought the war survivors to the public eye. Through watching this film Iranians remembered what they had been through.

SR: So we could say that the Iran–Iraq War was hijacked and became the government's war.

RB: The regime's lies and hijacking of the war opened up a huge gap in our society and caused us to feel no sympathy for the soldiers, nor for the tens of thousands of women who were raped and ruined for life by Iraqi soldiers. Luckily, history inevitably moves us towards enlightenment and awareness. The government may have managed to slow down this progress at times, some values may have been lost and bloody wars may still be fought around the world, but you cannot deny that the world generally moves towards awareness. That's also true of Iran. Why did I make *Gilane* some 15 years after the end of the war? First, I needed that gap to distance myself from my emotions. That is very important for creating art. You should also bear in mind that I made the film when the US was at war with Iraq – the same Iraq that had attacked us. In this film I question war as a whole.

This brings me back to your question about why I don't make films abroad. It is true that I make films in Iran and concentrate specifically on Iranian issues, but the emotion that watching my films elicits is universal and not exclusively Iranian. When *Gilane* was shown in Toronto to people of various nationalities, I remarked to the audience that the cinema was a bit like the United Nations. I saw that all those people from all those different backgrounds – each with personal experience of war and destruction – were touched and all spoke of a common pain. We were talking about the war in Iran, but in that film theatre in Toronto we saw that war is a universal issue.

SR: So, your films appear to be Iranian, but the deeper you go the more universal they become.

RB: My films are the same on the outside and the inside. When you look at lots of well-known and important films from all over the world, although you may not have much in common with the cultural background of the film-makers and not know anything about the places where the films are located, by empathizing with the characters you feel closer to the films. I think that this empathy is rooted in the common pain of human beings.

SR: Your films are mainly about the lives and fates of women. We did talk briefly about this before, but I'd like to discuss it a little further. How much does being a woman influence your films?

RB: My beliefs are the main source of my creativity. These are the result of my view of life and my experiences. My gender also influences those beliefs. I never deny my gender but I do not like to put everything down to sexuality. Film-makers are not separated into categories according to whether they have green eyes or black eyes. That would be like what the regime claims: that women are separated from men on buses so that women can sit more comfortably! That is not right. We must learn how to stand next to each other while respecting each other's personal space. Separation and compartmentalization upset me. So I don't understand why people reduce my ideas and thoughts to my gender. Some people may like being categorized in that way but I don't. I have picked up traces and waves throughout life which have turned into thoughts and experiences. I try to look at the world through these thoughts and experiences and make art out of them. But sexuality is only one part of them. Sometimes, when we give a female artist more credit than a male artist it is because we don't expect her to be that good! Both positive and negative discrimination is essentially discrimination. I am very sensitive to women's issues because I think I am more familiar with their world and am better at making films about it, but you can't claim that a male film-maker cannot make films about women's issues. He could look at women from a different point of view than me.

SR: Suffering is the main subject of your films. Is it easier for you to make films about suffering than about happiness? Do you know suffering better than you know happiness?

RB: My choice of subject depends on how I see the world at the time. I haven't been as lucky as it may seem. It's not as though, because of my success, I don't know what suffering and agony are. Being successful doesn't mean that I got where I am easily. That's not the case at all. I may be happy with my films in general, but I haven't had an easy life at all. I have enjoyed life very little and the pain that I've been through to become who I am is probably much greater than you can imagine. I know pain; I know it with every part of my being. Nothing has been handed to me on a silver platter and I've always wanted to achieve things through my own strength. However, I must emphasize that this doesn't mean that I necessarily base the lives of my heroines on my own life. What we have in common is that none of us is a warrior, holding flags and swords. None of us does what heroes do. Nevertheless, we come from different backgrounds and layers of society. My heroines are usually women I respect. They are women who try to be true to themselves and shape their lives despite all sorts of difficulties. There are many such women in our society. They live under diffi- cult circumstances but they fight back. Sometimes they may not succeed but they are strong. They hate being passive, they hate to give in, and if you look at them closely you'll see that they are not the kind of women who will surrender apathetically to the status quo. They fight and they may be sacrificed but they don't give in. For example, if they have a problem with the divorce laws in this country, they will look for a solution. They don't shout, they don't use big, ideologically laden words, but they quietly try to find a way to save themselves and their families. If a film has a message, this would be the most hopeful message to bear.

(2007)

MAJID MAJIDI

The Revolution and the Cleansing of Film Farsi

MAJID MAJIDI'S INTERNATIONAL RENOWN is an exception to the rule.[1] Whereas many important figures of New Iranian Cinema – such as Kiarostami, Beyzaie and Mehrjui – have generally started their careers before the revolution and are strongly critical of the Islamic regime, Majidi is a leading pro-establishment film-maker. His latest film, *Muhammad, Messenger of God* (2015),[2] is the most expensive film in the history of Iranian cinema and received its funding from regime-friendly sources such as Bonyad-e Mosstazafan,[3] a charitable organization under the auspices of Ayatollah Khamenei, the Leader of the Islamic Republic and the highest authority in the land. The film has been severely criticized and even condemned as sacrilegious by Sunni authorities such as the Egyptian Al-Azhar University and Saudi Council of Senior Scholars.[4]

Majidi believes that the 1979 revolution was the single key event in the progress of New Iranian Cinema. In his view, the revolution breathed rebelliousness into the weak body of pre-revolutionary art cinema. Under the shah, censorship was much worse and more destructive than under the Islamic regime. Indeed the worst type of censorship of Iranian art films before the revolution was the dominance of Hollywood and the so-called Film Farsi of the 1960s and 1970s – cheaply produced copies of Indian, Turkish and Egyptian films that showed scantily dressed women dancing on tables in cabaret clubs and men drinking alcohol and having knife fights. For him the 'present restrictions' – the term he uses for censorship policies – are much more in line with the ethics and culture of the Iranian people, the majority of whom are faithful Muslims.

From his point of view, every people must find its place in the modern world in its own way. This does not mean that Iranian society should isolate itself politically in order to find its way. On the contrary, Iran must learn from the West and from the world at large, and at the same time feel its way along its own path. Majidi believes that Iranians are now learning to experience freedom and democracy – not the sort of democracy that the West 'prescribes' for them but a democracy that is characteristically theirs.

Censorship under the Islamic regime should be seen as a protective measure against the hegemony of the foreign mass market and against decadent homegrown films. It is thanks to this kind of censorship that the way for Iranian art films has been opened up. The number of committed film-makers, he observes, has increased in the last three decades after the revolution – by 'committed' he means those socially but not politically engaged. Iranian cinema today depicts a much more authentic image of Iranian life; it is now freer to convey the true Iranian identity to the world than it was before the revolution.

————————

Shiva Rahbaran: Mr Majidi, this book examines the influence of Iranian cinema on society since the 1979 revolution and, conversely, the influence of society on Iranian cinema during the same period. What are your initial thoughts on this?

Majid Majidi: First, let's look at cinema's place in and influence on society. During the last 30 years – that is, since the revolution – we haven't witnessed such a surge in any other artform. One reason is that, essentially, cinema is remarkably influential and popular. Nowadays millions and millions of people watch films. Before the revolution, however, Iranian cinema was not as influential as it might have been because it was so idiosyncratic. At the time there were two kinds of cinema. One was Film Farsi and the other was what is often called 'intellectual cinema'. Culturally, the former had a very destructive effect. This was because religion, especially since the Safavid dynasty (1501–1736) and its central role in spreading Shi'a Islam in Iran, has always played a key role in this country. Film Farsi, with its anti-Islamic depictions of women and everyday life, never really suited the Iranian people and their needs. It was entertaining all right but could never reflect the reality of life here. As a result, despite its large presence in our cinema, its influence was slight; it was seen as cheap entertainment, not meaningful art.

Parallel to this, another kind of cinema grew, which became known as 'intellectual cinema'. This type could not really grow in the shadow of Film Farsi.

In my opinion, the revolution created much potential in all areas of art, including intellectual cinema. You see, the revolution, being by nature an audacious act, brought out the bold artist in us! This boldness had a great influence on post-revolutionary film-makers – especially those, like me, who were young then. One felt one could do what one wanted to do. I was 18 or 19 years old at the time of the revolution and had just enrolled at university to study dramatic arts. As a matter of fact, the revolution as a process was for us like a film in which we took the leading parts. We were present in every scene. This dynamic environment helped people, especially the young generation, to fast become part of the cultural and intellectual movement. After the revolution there was a big cultural gap in our country. Prior to that, heavy censorship had greatly limited the cultural field but the revolution opened it up to us. A lot of potential was generated, especially among intellectual and educated people, and I was one of those students who felt the need to enter the cultural field more strongly than ever. That's why we witnessed such a big surge in Iranian cinema in the 1980s. Of course those in charge at the time, such as Mir-Hossein Mousavi, whose team included Mohammad Khatami, the then minister of culture, and Mohammad Beheshti, the director of the Farabi Cinema Foundation, had a great influence on the progress of Iranian film.[5] You could say that that's when it all started – the 1980s.

SR: Could you talk a little about the history of cinema in Iran compared to other artforms? Film-making is really a Western art but Iranian film-makers have flourished better than contemporary novelists and poets, even though the latter have 1,000 years of history behind them and cinema is only about a hundred years old. Iranian films are famous worldwide but contemporary Persian poetry and novels hardly get noticed. In your opinion, why have Iranian film-makers been able to do so well worldwide?

MM: As I mentioned earlier, all this has to do with the people's thirst for film and the whole atmosphere that emerged after the revolution.

SR: Yes, I understand. But why wasn't this the case with our contemporary poetry and fiction?

MM: That's because of the influence of cinema. My own field of study was theatre and I really like it, but theatre could not stimulate my thoughts as much as cinema and I could not communicate with the audience through theatre as much as I could through cinema. As soon as I got into cinema I realized that it was like an ocean compared to other media and could express subjects much better and more effectively. Before the revolution there were restrictions on many film subjects, so cinema could not properly develop. Our cinema then was either Film Farsi or of the rather elitist and inaccessible intellectual variety. Take a look at Sohrab Shahid Saless's films, for example. They were screened at film festivals and celebrated as important works – his *Still Life* [1974] won the Silver Bear at the Berlin Film Festival. However, they were hardly accessible to a wider Iranian audience. The time was not ripe for such films to flourish before the revolution, but afterwards things changed. Except in the first few years, when most films were about oppression and injustice or meant to expose the shah and his decadent regime, the situation changed in favour of intellectual cinema. Gradually cinema split into political cinema, social cinema, comedy (to a lesser extent, though) and, when the conflict with Iraq started, war cinema. A wide variety of strong subjects were introduced. You could say that this was the beginning of a new era for Iranian cinema and that the kind of films that became successful internationally belonged to 'humane' or poetic cinema – the kind of cinema that is somehow close to poetry.

Now I come to your question about the artistic history of cinema. Literature is always close at hand in this country. A film-maker doesn't need to be a specialist in literature – it is present in our everyday lives. There is no house without a *Divan* of Hafez, Saadi's *The Rose Garden* and Ferdowsi's *Book of Kings* next to the Qur'an. Hence, our culture, literature, poetry and cinema are all inter-twined. Many critics at foreign film festivals point to the humane, moral and contemplative aspects of Iranian cinema. This humane theme comes from Persian poetry and literature. As a result of modernism, the West today faces a decline in social communi-cation, and thus Iranian films, which deal with human relations, love and affection, have a special attraction for the West. Indeed we've seen that Iranian films which touch on these subjects have managed to captivate the whole world.

SR: Meaning, the West is hungry for love?

MM: Yes, exactly. This hunger exists and the West has been able to find it in Iranian films. At many film festivals people talk about how the treatment of love in Iranian films has touched them. In any case I've always believed that art, especially in its contem-plative form, resides in every human. It's eternal and inherent. God has not separated human beings in this part of the world from those in another part. All of us have some human features in common: love, affection, forgiveness and devotion are all contemplative characteristics that God has put inside us all. It is art, through which we can get close to these characteristics. Why does Hafez have a universal language – not only for us but also for all human beings and in any language? Or, for example, Rumi, Saadi, Ferdowsi – their language is timeless and universal. That is because they have come close to the core of human nature. This is a language with no expiry date and, as long as humans exist, they can communicate fully through it.

SR: And it's interesting that contemporary Iranian film-makers have managed to get closer to this language than poets and writers. When I spoke to some Iranian poets and writers, they said that one of the reasons why Iranian literature has not spread worldwide is the Farsi language. In their opinion, Farsi is a limiting factor and that 'universal' languages such as English, French and Spanish are hard to compete with. Yet people such as Mohammad Beheshti say that this is just an excuse: Hafez wrote in Farsi too but his appeal is universal. From Beheshti's point of view we can't say that the Farsi language impedes the growth of contemporary literature. Yet it's interesting that our film-makers have managed to introduce the heritage of Hafez and Saadi to the world through cinema, an imported artform, rather than through the poets' works themselves.

MM: Yes, but time is also a factor here. If Hafez were alive today, he might have chosen to express himself through film. We should look at the era we're living in. Consider Western literature between the sixteenth and eighteenth centuries, or even nineteenth-century Russian literature: today there is probably very little comparable with the literature of those times. Our perception of things and our forms of expression are very different nowadays. I think that cinema is the most modern form of art. One of its characteristics is that it is much more communicative than other artforms, such as poetry and novels. This is the age of the image as language. We should study people in the context of their own times. We live in a complicated world that leaves us little time for reading poetry or novels. We need peace and quiet to undertake such activities. You can communicate faster through film, connect with the audience faster. Because of this power of cinema, it can bring together other types of art such as literature, music and painting and bridge the gaps between them.

SR: Many European and American films are based on novels, but this is hardly ever the case in Iran. The exchange between literature and cinema that we see in the West doesn't exist here.

MM: This is because contemporary literature does not have a strong base. It hasn't gained a foothold in our cinema because it is not strong enough to do so. For example, in Russia – or in France or Germany – novels play a key role in film. But here the language of poetry pervades our films because Iranians can relate more to poetry than to novels. That's why the West thinks of our films as being very close to poetry and describes them as a form of poetic realism.

SR: This trait is obvious in your own films. When we watch them we witness the spiritual dimension of love, but you don't seem to show its physical manifestations. Is this only because of official censorship or is it that you do not do romantic films?

MM: I mentioned earlier that censorship should be defined in the context of the social and cultural circumstances of a country. My belief is that even if our government were more open and less religious and if the country had never become an Islamic republic, because of my spiritual perception of human beings I would still have followed the same path. So, I assure you that government policies have not influenced me as such. Censorship should be defined in relation to the culture of a country. 'Freedom for Women' is perceived differently in our country than in the West. And both traditional and modern Iranians do not have the same view about women's freedom as Westerners. Promiscuity, for example, might be a kind of freedom in the West but in Iran it is definitely not talked about as something positive. What I want to say is that there should be boundaries – moral boundaries. You might be able to set certain boundaries in the area of politics, but in the area of morality, censorship is defined in relation to the people of Iran. Even before the revolution there were films that Iranian society didn't accept and to which it objected.

SR: Yes; I remember when I was no more than six or seven, the grown-ups of the family were talking a lot about *Dar Emtedad-e Shab*,[6] the sensational and erotic film starring the popular singer Googoosh. Films like that did provoke strong reactions. Religious people and religious intellectuals objected strongly. Society could not accept such things. But these objections caused film-makers to turn to the world of children in order to depict the themes of love and affection. A lot of good films draw on these. There's a feeling that because Iranian film-makers cannot show the erotic side of love, they turn to the innocent world of children. For example, in your film *The Willow Tree* [2005] when the hero, Youssef, comes home, the audience expects him to make love to his wife but he can't even take her in his arms.

MM: Yes, we do face certain boundaries – moral boundaries – which limit the artist dramatically; this, however, is not a sign of weakness. I believe that it's all to do with creativity. You often lay your viewpoint open to view, but this is less effective than when you seed an idea in the minds of the audience and thus the audience becomes creative too. The audience may even put themselves in the hero's shoes. For example, in *The Willow Tree*, the first night that Youssef and his wife come home, Youssef, after taking a look around the house and at his books and desk, stares at his wife. The woman feels there's something lewd in that look and although she is clothed she becomes uncomfortable, as if a stranger were eyeing her. Then Youssef asks her, 'Don't you want to change your clothes?' If I had had the woman simply change her coat and put on her ordinary clothes, I would not have communicated the strangeness of the situation – the trepidation – to the audience. Yet in this scene I manage to create very strong emotions – partly due to the fact that censorship would not have allowed the woman to take off her *hijab* and put on her everyday clothes. Because I am forced to take this approach, the scene has a much deeper effect. Or when the woman, upon hearing a thunderstorm, runs and stops in front of the mirror and looks at herself as if she's looking at someone else. She looks at the man she's lived with for years in a sort of shy, bashful way, as though he's a stranger.

SR: But in the Paris scenes of the film you show women with sleeveless tops and blond hair over their shoulders. The audience is led to believe that the moral boundaries apply only to Iranian women.

MM: I show women within the moral framework of Iran, within the geographical boundaries and the boundaries of tradition. If you show an Iranian woman naked and without the *hijab*, well, then you go against tradition and morality. But the cultural structure of the West is different from ours and the *hijab* plays no key role there. So showing nudity in a Western setting is not against Sharia law.

SR: Like many other Iranian film-makers you make use of idyllic settings. For example Beyzaie's *Bashu, the Little Stranger* is set in a beautiful area in northern Iran and your Youssef in *The Willow Tree* lives in a quaint house in old Tehran. In these films you don't show Tehran as it really is. Wouldn't you call this a sort of self-censorship? Do you find it difficult to show negative images of the city or do you not want to show them at all? Your approach in this regard is quite different from Bani-Etemad or Panahi, who make a feature of the ugliness and the problems of urban life.

MM: No, not at all. These 'ugly' aspects, as you call them, are just not relevant to the making of a film. Basically, location has a dramatic function; I certainly don't see beauty from a touristic point of view. Locations serve particular functions. For example, the beautiful scenes in my *The Colour of Paradise* [1999] serve a strongly dramatic function in that they express the film's very concept. The father is able to see beauty but is unable to grasp it. He turns beauty into blackness – he makes charcoal. His job has a symbolic function in the film. It's all symbolic: the father turns nature, in the form of wood, into blackness, in the form of charcoal, whereas the boy, although blind, can grasp the beauty of the world. So, it is as if the father is the one who's really blind rather than the boy. What I mean is that in this film nature and those beautiful locations take on a dramatic form. The father feels nothing about the beauty of nature – the only thing he doesn't see in nature is beauty itself. So, you see, my choice of location has a dramatic purpose. The blind boy conceives of nature as if he were reading nature – it reminds us of the way the blind read Braille. That way the boy communicates with nature – he communicates with the voices of nature through Braille. Likewise the woodpecker pecks three times. This

forms a combination and the boy, using this combination, is able
to communicate with the woodpecker. So the various elements of
nature have a dramatic function. If we had filmed in the desert, it
would have been a completely different story.

SR: So we see that one of the secrets of the 'universality' of Iranian
film is that it depicts love, affection and wisdom and pays attention
to the human dimension. The popularity of Iranian film, especially in the West, is a very interesting phenomenon, particularly
if we bear in mind the hostility of the West towards Iran since the
Islamic Revolution. So what is the secret of Iranian film-makers
and their international success? Do you make your films to appeal
to Western tastes?

MM: Everyone has his own ideology and ideas and I can only speak
for myself. My concern has always been how to present a subject
in a simple way, even if this subject is philosophical or spiritual –
how to translate this subject into a simple form, how to communicate with any social class and any person. For me the Iranian
audience is more important than any other because my roots are
here and this is where I live. Art can only be appreciated globally if it is native and has roots in the artist's home; it should have
its roots in its homeland. I ask myself why Hafez and Saadi and,
above all, Ferdowsi are universal? Why are they famous worldwide?
It's because, above all, they are Iranian. You cannot find a more
Iranian poet than Ferdowsi. He's thoroughly Iranian – he has his
roots here and that is what makes him universal. Now, attending
international festivals and communicating only with a certain,
'intellectual' class of people could be seen as 'good' art by some.
But I believe art is only eternal when it has roots in the home of the
artist – when it is native. Only then has it got a 'real' identity. For
example, you can't separate Kurosawa from his being Japanese. He
is first and foremost Japanese and because he is Japanese he is also
universal. In the West also, family roots are very important to great
film-makers such as John Ford – I must mention here that, in my
view, family is fundamental to society. John Ford is so quintessen-
tially American that he's universal.

SR: But as a film-maker don't you make – invent – this 'native' identity? By portraying what it's like being Iranian, don't you play a big part in actually creating this Iranian identity?

MM: I don't create identities. I work in the climate and conditions in which I live. Languages, accents, morals, appearances and relationships – I live among all these things, which make up my life. No, I don't make them. They make me.

SR: But Iranian film-makers have been able to transcend the boundaries and show the West a different side of Iran – one in stark contrast to that of men and women dressed in black, burning flags in front of Western embassies. Your delicate imagery has managed to permeate the intelligence of Westerners and made them question those negative images.

MM: Actually, this 'delicate imagery', as you call it, is our reality. The images shown in the Western media do not reflect our reality. What I am telling you is, I don't make the images of Iran. I show them. The images of angry men and women are the images of turmoil in a society that has been violated and abused by the West for centuries. The revolution was a historical necessity and the images of people revolting differ from the images of people in times of peace. When I say 'identity', I refer to culture not to politics. Politics is dead. Politics has no soul. In politics, something might be considered good today and bad tomorrow and then good again the following day. That's why politics is not a bridge between people; it's not a foundation on which to build anything. But because culture is part of a society's identity, then when you build something on that it will be meaningful and will last.

I've often heard that we film-makers are the unpaid ambassadors of Iran. In fact film-makers do play a more important role in international affairs than politicians do because their concern is the people's soul whereas the concern of politicians is just politics. I meet many people who haven't been to Iran but have got to know its true identity through my films. They say, all we knew about Iran came through our TV channels and when we watched your films we couldn't understand how it was possible for a nation supposedly full of terrorists, where people get killed daily out on the streets, to produce such films – so full of love for humanity, wisdom and self-sacrifice. They say, how can this identity not be real? You cannot fake such reality – you can only show it. These films are rooted in your social and cultural beliefs and that's how we got to know the true identity of your people through your films.

SR: Now that your films have become part of Iran's unofficial identity, do you think of yourself as an *engagé* artist? Do you want to make way for freedom in your society? You may have changed Western perceptions of post-revolutionary Iran up to a point, but what have you done for the Iranian audience?

MM: First, I am trying to put forward a different picture of our culture from my point of view and through the language of cinema. At the same time, I should mention that we are gradually experiencing more freedom and democracy in our country. We have been under the influence of foreign powers for many years – Russia, Britain, the USA and so on – and their presence created a sense of insecurity amongst us. We are now gradually getting closer to a democracy – not the kind of democracy that Westerners prescribe for us, but a kind that is native to us, specific to Iran and suitable for our own culture. For example, a few days ago we film-makers had a frank meeting with Ayatollah Khamenei [the present Leader of the Revolution]. At this meeting, Mrs Tahmineh Milani said that she was an independent film-maker and that nobody could stop her from speaking her mind! What I'm trying to say is that if we look back we'll see that 30 years ago not even a CEO could criticize the system in the slightest. You weren't even allowed to keep a book that criticized the system in your own house back then – I mean, before the revolution. If you were a student and they believed you to be politicized, they would raid your house and throw your books out. See where we have come from and where we are now.

SR: So, do you think that as a film-maker you have helped bring about this state of affairs?

MM: Absolutely. We shouldn't forget that there are intellectuals in other countries with whom you can have a dialogue. I am not talking about governments. I don't make films so that I can show them to Mr Bush and see what effect they have on him!

SR: Are you hinting at Makhmalbaf's *Kandahar*?[7]

MM: Whatever! I'll give you an example of what I mean about dialogue with people abroad. Between 1999 and 2000 I was invited to a festival in New York for the screening of my film *The Colour of Paradise* [1999]. When I arrived they told me that I would have to be fingerprinted. I said, 'Your people have invited me. I didn't want to come. If that's the case then I'll go back. When you invite someone to your house you don't search his pockets at the door! You may refuse me entry; I'll go back to Iran.' They said, 'Even if you go back now you'll still have to be fingerprinted because you have entered the US.' As it was the opening night, the festival director came to welcome me at the airport. When he heard what had happened he was very apologetic. I said, 'I will not attend the festival's opening ceremony because your country has insulted not only me but my people as well.' I was really angry. They came to me later and said, 'It's the opening night and your film is being screened this evening. Everyone knows you're here so wouldn't it be better if you went on stage and said all this to the audience?' After some consideration I decided to attend the opening ceremony. I wanted to speak before the screening but then I thought it would be better to speak at the end. Before the screening I'd be Majidi the Iranian film-maker, but after the screening I'd be Majidi the creator of *The Colour of Paradise*. So eventually I went on stage and said, 'You are applauding the person who is the creator of this film. His hands have written every scene of this film and tonight these same hands have been insulted.' The audience came close to shouting 'Down with the USA'! The speech had quite an impact.

SR: Recently we've seen Western investors show an interest in Iranian films. Producing them is much cheaper than producing European or American films. How do you feel about this? Do you think that you are worth less than a foreign film-maker? Do you feel that foreign investment would influence your work?

MM: No, no. I've never felt that because my films cost less to produce I am worth less than a Western film-maker! I might feel that way if I thought that they were trying to influence my work through their investment in my films. In fact there is no problem with cultural interaction. Foreign investment will help our film industry, but the minute they try to change our views and attitudes we will not accept that investment. Often they want to invest in our so-called 'festival films'. They know that in these cases they have only to invest a tenth of what they would invest in, say, French films and so do not take much of a risk. In the worst-case scenario they will get their money back by selling the film to a TV channel. But the key to the success of Iranian cinema – any cinema – is to get films released and distributed.

SR: Is that what you're aiming at?

MM: I try, and I am one of the few Iranian film-makers whose films have been bought by Miramax, Sony and Japanese, Canadian and European companies. Some big companies have bought our films and this could help our cinema thrive and last. Unfortunately we are rather cursed by the attention that festivals give us and risk being labelled 'festival film-makers'. This is very dangerous for the next generation of film-makers and a real threat to our cinema. Also some of our film-makers have moved their operations to Kurdistan and Iraq and deal with topics related to those places because such films suit the tastes of foreign festivals. This is also damaging to our cinema. Another threat is digitization. With the advent of digital film-making – which has very low costs – technique and cinema craft are about to be forgotten.

SR: You mentioned the war and how some Iranian film-makers reacted to it. This brings to mind not only how destructive the Iran–Iraq War was but also its potential as a subject for film. Yet when we look at our contemporary cinema we see that, except for a few film-makers who exploit the subject for commercial reasons, others keep away from it, as if neither the people of Iran nor Iranian film-makers have time for it.

MM: Compared to the magnitude of the war itself, the films that have been made about it are a poor reflection. This has to do with the aesthetic perceptions of film-makers. The war-cinema genre is very ideological. In these films one side is always right and one side is always wrong; that is, the approach of Iranian war films is not aesthetic but ideological. The films are quite politicized.

SR: Propaganda films?

MM: You see, many people ask why such films are not shown abroad. I say that if these films do get shown abroad, the effects will be negative for us. For a Japanese person it makes no difference whether the film is from Iran or Iraq. What matters for him or her is the human aspect. Yet in Iranian war films what you see is the destruction and killing on only one side. Hence, these films have negative effects. I ask why I should make films with such 'agendas'? Yes, going back to your question, such 'agendas' turn war films into propaganda films.

Of course some good war films have been made, but unfortunately were only 'one offs' and did not start a wave or movement. For example, Kamal Tabrizi's *Leily is with Me* [1996] or Hatamikia's *The Immigrant* [1990] were good, but were only 'one offs'. They could not create a real genre or the vocabulary necessary for communicating our war experience.

Yes, the war-film genre in this country poses many challenges to us. The authorities are not doing a good job in this matter. Whether they allow a war movie to be released or not is mainly based on the personal taste of the person in charge. The horrible thing we struggle with is not always censorship; very often it is the personal taste of those in charge.

SR: Well, that too is a kind of censorship if film-makers have to tailor their films to the personal tastes of those in charge.

MM: Yes. That too is sort of a self-censorship, whether in the case of Iranian films tailored to the personal tastes of those in charge, or in the case of films that have been and are still being tailored to the tastes of foreign film festivals. In fact it is the restrictions imposed on film-industry management that has stopped Iranian cinema from thriving further.

SR: As Majid Majidi, can you make films only in Iran?

MM: No, I can make films wherever I like.

SR: Do you mean that making films in Iran is your choice and not your fate?

MM: Of course I prefer to make films here, but there is no reason why I shouldn't make them abroad if I wanted to. As a matter of fact I came up with two ideas while I was abroad. One was filming in St Petersburg, Russia, and the other in Kashmir, India. In parts of Kashmir, farmers live their whole lives on floating barges. When they have had enough of one place they move to another. The interesting thing about their moving about is that whenever they do so they take their farm with them! You see, on the shallow parts of the lake, seaweeds and reeds grow. The farmers use the seaweed, reeds and mud to make 'floating farmland' on which they cultivate their crops and vegetables! They tie these 'lands' to their barges and move them from one part of the lake to another! To make one square metre of 'farmland', one person has to work for two months. Now just imagine someone who has a 50-square-metre field and that's all he has; imagine how much of his life he's put into it! Now my idea is to make a film about an old man who lives in this region. The location is beautiful all right, but what interests me is its dramatic quality. For me, that's an important aspect of the art of film-making.

8

JAFAR PANAHI
Cinema and Resistance

IT MAKES ME SHUDDER TODAY to think of the turn that Jafar Panahi's fate took less than two years after this interview. Following the widespread protests against the fraudulent presidential elections of 2009 and the formation of the Green Movement, Panahi was sentenced to six years' imprisonment and a 20-year ban from artistic work. The films he has made in the past two decades not only put him high on the list of the most interesting and respected film-makers worldwide but also incurred the displeasure of the Islamic Republic's courts of justice, where, like many other fearless Iranian artists, draconian punishments awaited him for his insistence on the right to practise his art. The sentence imposed by the regime did not, however, deter him from making some of the best films of his career. He managed to smuggle out of the country the fantastic *This Is Not a Film* (2011) and to shoot *Closed Curtain* (2013). His latest film, *Taxi*, won the 2015 Golden Bear at the Berlin Film Festival. He was not there to accept the award as he is still banned from travelling.[1]

Panahi sees himself as an *engagé* film-maker – an artist with a moral and social sense. He distances himself from all ideological and political involvement, for otherwise he would run the risk of moving into the realms of propaganda. His only commitment is that of a social and historical nature. In his films he tries to depict social and historical reality as 'he feels it'; in other words, he sees his social realism as the exact opposite of politically charged cinema. For Panahi, film in Iran – both before and after the revolution of 1979 – has always been a kind of resistance against ruling dogmas. This resistance is especially effective, as the language of cinema is both broad and immediate; it embodies all other arts such as photography, painting, poetry, storytelling, architecture and music, and can communicate with a large audience directly and imme- diately. Moreover Iranian cinema was and still is to a large extent non-elitist and can generally be understood and enjoyed by people from all layers of society. Indeed Panahi sees cinema as a 'classless' or 'egalitarian' medium, but this should not make the film-maker a slave of the market or the 'masses', who only makes films accord- ing to the tastes of a wide audience. The film-maker must be aware that he is not alone in the making of his art (as, say, a poet might be) and that film-making is a collaborative effort whose output will be seen by thousands or even millions of viewers.

Given the draconian punishment meted out to him by the Court of Revolution for his so-called 'anti-revolutionary' activities and participation in protest movements against the Islamic regime, such as the Green Movement, Panahi has paid a high price for his artistic commitment to his people and country. Being a 'social film-maker', he believes he could only work in a society that he is intellectually and emotionally attached to, despite many offers from foreign production companies. After the revolution, this task became especially important to him. He notes that during the rule of the Islamic regime, more than any other period in modern Iranian history, there have been, through censorship policies, many serious attempts to isolate the artist from his audience. From his point of view, it is especially important now that the *engagé* artist fulfil his foremost task, namely, to resist.

Shiva Rahbaran: Mr Panahi, the aim of my project is to determine the role of cinema in post-revolutionary Iran from the viewpoint of those film-makers who live and work here. So my main question is:

how has cinema influenced post-revolutionary society in Iran, and in what ways has cinema been influenced by society? Our approach is sociological rather than aesthetic. From our point of view, cinema lends itself well to such a study, as it is often considered a 'people's art'. Some even go so far as to say that cinema started off as the art of the masses and remains so today – the artform favoured by the working and lower classes who cannot connect with the more elitist arts, such as poetry and painting, where a degree of education is necessary to enjoy them. Should such a medium aim to bring about changes in society by being, say, educational or morally and socially committed?

Jafar Panahi: The answer to this question can only be found in the work of each individual film-maker. I cannot generalize and speak for others. We have to look at the path a film-maker has taken and the destination he has reached. All I can say about myself is that I make realist-social films. My subjects are social issues – problems and dilemmas that I see every day. These subjects can be of a geographical, cultural, economic or political nature. I take these issues from the society in which I live and then try to work them out in my films. An Iranian realist-social film-maker can only live in Iran. He cannot live outside and make films about the social reality of his country. If he does such a thing, his films will be 'touristy', that is, a view from the outside which by nature is transitory. A 'touristy' film-maker has not lived in the heart of his society, has not felt it through his senses in his everyday life. But a film-maker like me, who lives in this country, faces and feels these social problems on a day-to-day basis. They nudge us constantly. Our reactions to and preoccupations with these 'nudges' are our films. Through our films we see, we show and work out the problems of our society, but where these films lead to – that we cannot know.

SR: This means that you are a politically aware and committed film-maker?

JP: This is where the difference between a politically and a socially

committed film-maker lies: a socially committed film-maker is
not necessarily a political one. I believe that political film-makers
always use their art as an instrument through which to show what
is wrong or right from their party's or ideology's point of view.
So, it is the party or the ideology that classifies the political film-
maker. Socially committed film-makers, we believe, are the opposite of this. The reason why we distance ourselves from political
film-makers is first and foremost the short life of political films. A
political film has only a very short-lived effect on viewers. It has a
use-by date, which expires as soon as the ideology of the political
film-maker has moved on. So, a political film can only be enjoyed
as long as the political ideology that inspired it is in vogue. I do
not believe that any political film can be a lasting one. It dies as
soon as the ideology dies or, at least, diminishes considerably. But
when I say that I am a social film-maker, I mean that in my films
I 'express' society in the way that I have felt and lived it. I do not
express any opinions about what is good or bad. I do not make any
political statements or deliver any moral lectures.

SR: You are saying that a social film-maker is the exact opposite of
a political film-maker?

JP: That is correct. When somebody is dependent on the ideology of a certain party, then any views against that ideology are
condemned. Such a film-maker must turn a blind eye when his
ideology does not work. He must constantly make compromises
with the official ideology of his party. I do not like that. In contrast
to political film-makers, we social film-makers never talk about
what or who is good or bad. We just show the conditions under
which we now live and which have led our society to the state it is
in – with all the problems and issues that come with it.

This does not mean that we are politically apathetic. We are
aware of the reality – the political reality – in which our society
exists. We know that the source of all changes and developments
come from the government. That is about the most political we ever
get. For example, we might make a film about the restrictions that
threaten our artistic activities on an everyday basis and ask, 'Where

do these restrictions come from?' We, too, in the course of our aesthetic endeavour reach politics at the end of the line. I mean, we do not end up accusing one or two officials or Revolutionary Guards! What we want to achieve is to make the viewer find out where the root causes of the symptoms lie – where he can see that religion, politics, economics, culture and even geography are all interrelated and are both the causes and remedies of social problems. All these factors are inseparable. I make films without taking any political position. A political film-maker is, in contrast to a social film-maker like me, always taking a political stand. What I do is call out to the viewer and say, 'Look, this is the society we live in. Now it is your turn to see – according to your own perception, your own point of view – where the roots of our shortcomings are, where the sources of our problems lie.' So, in short, through my films I am doing two things simultaneously: first, giving a nudge to my society, so that it will start thinking about itself, and, second, giving history a report. For example, if you watch *The Circle*, *Crimson Gold* or *Offside*, say, 20 or 30 years from now, you will see that this was the way people in Iran lived at the time and these were the problems and restrictions they faced. So, in that sense, I am giving history a report about Iranians in that particular period of time, when I lived and observed them. I do not need a mediator to tell the story. It is up to the viewer to learn his lesson or whatever else from the report. That is why I do not condemn anybody in *Offside*. The soldier who stops the girls from going into the stadium to watch the game is a member of this society. Military service is by law obligatory in Iran, and a soldier must follow orders. That very soldier could be the brother or the cousin of any of those girls. They are all prisoners of this society and in fact there is no difference between the prisoner and the prisoner's guard.

SR: You and many of your colleagues could free yourself from this prison, from this system and its censorship policies, through your art. By making excellent films you have been able to secure great international attention and in a way become a privileged member of this society with more prospects and freedoms than the ordinary Iranian. There are quite a few artists, critics and scholars who believe that Iranian art and literature in general and Iranian cinema in particular have thrived immensely after the revolution because of the very censorship policies that try to subdue them. They think that censorship has the reverse effect and adds to the importance and popularity of the artist and his work amongst his people. Some even go so far as to say – perhaps rather cynically – that censorship benefits art. What do you say to that?

JP: If we look at things that way, then we are condoning censorship and cooperating with the regime. If censorship is good for art and freedom is bad for it, then are we supposed to introduce censorship to all free countries so that art can thrive? Of course not. By saying this we are working against art. Perhaps one can say that censorship has influenced our art, particularly our films, immensely, but if the artist were not capable and in possession of a good creative imagination then he could not have used the restrictions to his advantage. It is only a good artist who knows how to use his creativity to overcome restrictive policies. That very same artist could also thrive in a free society and learn to use its structures to produce good works – perhaps he would even make better films in such a society than in a closed and highly restrictive one like ours. Perhaps what those who speak favourably of censorship mean is that artists in Iran have to be extremely creative in order to overcome the barriers of censorship and at the same time say what they want to say without irritating the regime too much. However, it is obvious that the authorities get annoyed by our films and artworks no matter how hard we try to bypass their censorship rules. They still refuse to grant us licences to show our films and then try everything they can to sabotage them once permission has been given, even if we have followed their guidelines closely.

SR: In my last book about Iran, *Iranian Writers Uncensored*,[2] I talked to poets and writers who live and work in post-revolutionary Iran about the difficulties they face there. What was especially interesting was the way they compared their own restrictions and freedoms with those of film-makers. From their point of view, censorship was much harder on them than on film-makers. They said that their books would face huge obstacles if they so much as hinted at a love scene or described the face of a beautiful woman or described social dilemmas and unrest. Film-makers, on the other hand, had a much easier time. Many internationally renowned films – despite censorship policies – contain scenes and deal with subjects that would get writers and poets into trouble with the authorities. Is this not a paradoxical situation, especially considering that literature has a much smaller audience than cinema?

JP: Literature is very different from cinema, in that when a writer writes a book that is not to the liking of the Ministry of Culture and Islamic Guidance, they just take it and stop it from being printed! Nobody in the world would notice that or speak out on behalf of the author. Iranian cinema, on the other hand, has now attained an international prominence, so that when a more or less renowned film-maker gets into trouble with the authorities, he can count on worldwide protests, which can force the regime to compromise and show the film in one form or another, either in Iran or at a foreign festival. Perhaps contemporary Persian literature has not yet obtained the same due respect on an international scale as has Iranian film.

Perhaps the fate of my film *The Circle* will make the situation clearer to you. The Ministry of Culture and Islamic Guidance would not give permission for the film to be made. Many national and international newspapers got wind of this and started to criticize the policy: they asked how could the ministry stop a Cannes Festival winner, a Locarno Festival winner, from making his film? This situation continued for about nine months. This was all happening in the late 1990s when Khatami had just been elected president in a landslide victory and the people had great hopes for his reformist policies and promises. Nobody knew how to solve this dilemma. After nine months and many protests, the ministry decided to grant me permission to make the film. I went and made it exactly as I wanted to. I did not abide by any censorship or self-censorship rules; I did not bribe anybody and did what I had to do. When the film came out, I knew what I had to do now! I went to the laboratory and took all the copies before the film was

sent to the ministry. I sent one copy to the Fajr Film Festival just
to check whether they would give it a distribution licence or not.
Some people in the ministry actually quite liked the film and asked
me to meet them and negotiate cuts and changes! But their efforts
were to no avail. So, they refused to show my film at the Fajr Film
Festival. However, owing to the protests beforehand, the film had
already attracted very good publicity and many national and international members of the jury demanded to see it. The Ministry of
Culture and Islamic Guidance, however, refused to show them the
film. Eventually I asked six jurors to come and watch the film in
my house. They liked it immensely and implored the ministry to at
least give them permission to show the film at festivals outside Iran.
The ministry again refused. To cut a long story short, six months
later, the head of the jury of the Venice Film Festival – one of the
six foreign jurors who had seen my film at the private viewing in
my house – announced that Panahi would participate in the festival
with his most recent film *The Circle*! Now the ministry had a serious problem. If they refused to send a copy to Venice, everybody
would know that a film was missing from the competition, right?
Everybody would know that the government had sabotaged this
renowned festival at a time when President Khatami was talking
about dialogue among civilizations and open societies! So, three
days before the festival started, I got permission to go to Venice
with my film.

Now, you tell me, which Iranian writer has access to such worldwide publicity? Such is the reputation of Iranian films today that
international festivals go to a lot of trouble to show them. It seems
as if the world's thirst for knowledge about contemporary Iran
can only be satisfied through film. Films can communicate faster
and more immediately with their audiences, and film-makers have
easier access to multimedia publicity. An author or poet needs
a much longer time span to make himself or herself known; a
reader needs a more creative imagination than a viewer in order
to appreciate a book or a poem. And do not forget, images can be
consumed much faster than words – especially considering the fact
that Farsi is a marginal language today and needs translating. I as
a film-maker can give my audience an immediate, realist depiction

of my society – just as one sees it with one's own eyes. Well, this has a deeper and sharper effect on a viewer.

SR: But you as a film-maker come from the land of flowers, nightingales and sweet poetry! Is this not your artistic heritage? In the case of Abbas Kiarostami, for example, Persian poetry is clearly a source from which he draws artistic sustenance.

JP: Perhaps. Perhaps poetry is part of his artistic background. I, on the other hand, never had a great liking for poetry, perhaps because I could never learn more than ten verses by heart! What I know well is cinema. I studied film-making at college and exercise my profession with an acute social awareness and command of the art of film-making.

SR: Why do you think that film-making, with such a short history, has thrived so well compared to other arts that have a much longer history in this country?

JP: The length of the history of an artform is no guarantee of its success. Cinema is only a hundred years old. Maybe 20 years ago poetry was superior to cinema in this country. Why? Because 20 years ago we did not have the same access to multimedia as we do now. Today an Iranian child, as soon as he opens his eyes, watches moving images; before he can talk or read and write, he accumulates a vast knowledge of films and a deep attachment to those images; he laughs, becomes sad, becomes angry or happy with every image he sees. Films educate him and show him how to understand problems and how to deal with them. He has a much stronger relationship to images that to words. The historical heritage of poetry or cinema is meaningless for him.

SR: So, in a way, cinema reduces or even cuts off the connection of that child with his culture and historical heritage.

JP: No, I am not saying that. What I am trying to say is that image has an Ur-effect on human beings. The more a child develops, the more he realizes that cinema is a profession, where the historical and cultural background of the film-maker is vital to its growth. This is especially the case in Iran. I was a jury member at many foreign festivals and I saw that whenever an Iranian film was shown, there was a higher degree of excitement and enthusiasm amongst the audience. This was due to the freshness of the message and the artistic nature of the film. Iranian films are especially concerned with human suffering and human struggle and so fill a gap that is increasingly missing from Western films. Thus one cannot claim that such films cut off the connection of the viewer with history, culture or humanity.

SR: How do you assess the relationship between cinema and other arts in Iran?

JP: Cinema contains all arts, from poetry to music, theatre, painting, dancing, photography, etc., and can encapsulate and reflect the many centuries of Iranian culture, art and history. Both consciously and unconsciously it is preoccupied with such a rich background. Cinema can see and show things in a myriad of ways. For example, take the very image of you and me sitting in this room; we can place the camera in at least 200 positions and each would give a different picture of our interaction. A non-Iranian might place the camera differently than an Iranian film-maker. The camera's point of view inevitably shows my Iranian historical and cultural background and the influence it has on the image that I convey. The angle from which your camera looks at the world and gives an image of the world immediately reveals your background.

SR: Would you say that through the angle of their cameras Iranian film-makers make a certain Iranian identity?

JP: That is something that critics and social scientists can talk about.

SR: So you do not consciously make an Iranian identity?

JP: I only make films. My films take a certain path. I and the people I work with are certainly under the influence of our subject – our object of observation, namely Iranian society. Whether we influence our subject – that we cannot know. That would be an altogether different subject of discussion.

SR: Many renowned writers and artists feel that they live in a sort of exile in their own country. Writers such as Hedayat or film-makers such as Golestan or Shahid Saless felt this inner exile so acutely that they ended up leaving Iran altogether, although they were not politically persecuted. Is it an ungrateful task to be an avant-garde artist in this country?

JP: Their inner exile was due to their own personalities. As I already mentioned, Iranian films in general and my films in particular can connect with all people from all social levels and backgrounds in different ways. For example, when you see my films you see a group of women who have served their sentences and, once out of prison, have to struggle to find a refuge; or you see a group of girls who, despite being aware that they will not be given permission to watch a football match inside a stadium, dress as boys and struggle to get in. They all end up getting arrested and then unite on the bus that is supposed to take them to prison. This is not fiction; it is a present-day event happening in this country. I have not invented or created a story! Every single Iranian who watches this film has experienced or witnessed such a conflict with the authorities. The masses of Iranian people understand and feel this story. By re-viewing this event on the silver screen, they see deeper layers and discover new meanings. This gives them pleasure. The more aware an audience is the more layers they discover and the more pleasure they feel in the process of discovery. This means that I as a film-maker can connect with a myriad of people according to their level of understanding. I never say, 'Screw the audience! I do not want to have anything to do with you! I have made this film only for myself!' Those who feel in an inner exile have this attitude. And this attitude is a personal thing and has nothing to do with society.

SR: You do not feel in exile in this country?

JP: Not a bit! I am not in exile in my country, amongst my people. From the point of view of the regime, I might be in exile. At the last Fajr Film Festival [2006] they placed me in the part reserved for guests, not for film-makers or jurors or critics. They had thrown me into a 'meaningless' corner. They thought they had thrown me into exile. I answered them in a piece I wrote: 'When some-body invites you to their house, the rules of courtesy tell you to thank those who think of themselves as the owners of the house for their kind invitation. Ladies and Gentlemen, although I feel like a stranger in this festival, I am not a stranger in this place. They throw me into exile, but I belong to this place. They have no right to do this to me.' I want everybody to know that we are the sand at the bottom of the stream. We stay where we are and those who have violently confiscated our dwelling and think that they have thrown us into exile are doomed to flow away – like the stream. The secret of our success is that we have not severed our connection with this land and the people that live in it.

SR: Many believe that the secret of the international success of film-makers like you is that you make films only according to the tastes of Western festivals. You and your colleagues are given the label 'festival film-makers'.

JP: This is one of the tactics of the Ministry of Culture and Islamic Guidance to isolate us both from our people and the international community. As soon as they realized that the interest in Iranian films was growing worldwide, they started to attach such labels to us. They did not know of any better way to confront us, so started to denounce us by playing the nationalism card. The irony of this tactic is that nationalism is at odds with the Islamic ideology of the regime! Let me make this clearer to you. We do not have an Iranian national football team in this country; we have a football team of the Islamic Republic of Iran! In our media we refer to foreign foot-ball teams as the US national team or the English national team or the German national team! We do not call our radio and television national; we call them the radio and television of the Islamic Republic of Iran. We do not call our Parliament national; we call it the Parliament of the Islamic Republic of Iran! All institutions in this country have been given an 'Islamic' label for the past 30 years. It is only when the regime wants to denounce someone or trick someone into doing something against his or her will that the 'nationalist' label is used. Yes, nationalism is completely at odds with their ideology. But as soon as one of our films wins a prestigious prize at a Western festival, they start to denounce it as 'anti-national'! They do not dare call it 'anti-Islamic' because they know that that would not work with the people. You see, a regime in which Islam is on a much higher plane than nationality abuses the national feelings of the people as soon as it decides to throw an artist into exile and sever his connections with his country and label him as an 'anti-Iranian film-maker' or 'festival film-maker'. But we do not give in. We use all our wit and guile to smuggle our films out of the country and show them to the world. If we do not do that, they ban our films and stop them from being seen. All my banned films, such as *Offside*, are available here as pirate copies or on the internet, all because I can smuggle them out of Iran and have them shown at the Berlin Film Festival! My films are being sold by illegal traders everywhere because of the international attention they received abroad. There is a huge underground network that satisfies our people's thirst for film. So, of course the regime tries to sever our connections to our audience by way of these labels.

SR: So the more they call you 'festival film-maker' the more 'people's film-maker' you become?

JP: Yes. They do all they can to force us and our Iranian audience apart. They keep telling them that we have nothing to do with Iran and let ourselves be led by the tastes of Westerners. I myself do not care for anybody's taste. I make films neither for the taste of the regime nor for the West nor for the Iranian audience. I care for nobody's taste but my own. The one good thing that success at foreign festivals has taught me is that the more original, the more 'myself', the fresher the film is, the more successful it is. I do not give in to anybody, not the government, not the people, not the festivals. I do not make films according to Western or Eastern or outer or inner tastes. I only make films according to my own taste. And I only make one film every three or four years, although I could make one every year and earn a lot more money. Unfortunately this is what is now happening for the most part in New Iranian Cinema. I, on the other hand, do not regret having made any of my five feature films; all of them have had a very good reception worldwide.

SR: One of the reasons why you and Iranian film-makers of your calibre are called 'festival film-makers' is the fact that foreign producers are increasingly investing money in your projects. Some believe that Western money confers influence over your work, as it to some extent obliges you to make films according to Western tastes. Furthermore, their investment is seen as yet another example of Western exploitation of our culture, as the money invested in an Iranian film is a fraction of the amount put into a French or American film; consequently the risk/profit ratio is so much more favourable. What do you think of this claim?

JP: I do not agree with it at all. I, for example, always try to find foreign producers but only work with them if they agree to share the production costs. That is to say, the main capital comes from my own production company. The money they put in is not an enormous sum anyway. Actually I do not need their money to make my films. As you mentioned before, the cost of film-making in Iran is considerably lower than in the West. It is so much less that a person like me can produce a film under his own steam. I have now reached such a status that I can *choose* any producer that I wanted in this country and they would probably invest more money in my projects than a Western producer. There is no fundamental need here for foreign investment.

So what do these people mean by calling foreign investment an exploitation of Iranian culture?! If anything, we are exploiting the foreign investors! The foreign investor must accept all the

PR and distribution costs. He must see to it that my film is shown all over the world. He must contact the big distributors – I want my film to be shown as widely as possible in as many countries as possible. I do not understand why some people speak of exploitation when foreign money is invested in Iranian film projects! Don't these people know that the same companies invest money in South American and African films? Why is an Iranian film-maker labelled a 'festival film-maker' as soon as he acquires a certain worldwide status, but an African or Asian film-maker of the same calibre is not? A film festival like that of Cannes or Venice shows hundreds of films from all over the world. Why is it only Iranian cinema that is 'exploited'?

Look, this 'Third World' vocabulary is only used by the Islamic regime because they are implacably against our work. They accuse us of treason whenever they can. They do not like the fact that Iranian cinema is highly regarded in the West. I am sure you have noticed the recent fall in the number of Iranian films at international festivals. This gives the Islamic regime great pleasure. Now they go round saying that the Iranian wave is over! Nobody buys Iranian films any more!

I would like to close our discussion of festivals by saying that a festival is only an opportunity. Yes, I like to finish a film so that I can send it to a festival because an internationally renowned festival is a good showcase for me. It is like a fair! Even big-budget, international and Hollywood projects want to be present at prestigious festivals. Take, for example, *The Da Vinci Code* at the last Cannes festival I went to. It was a big-budget Hollywood production but it still wanted to be at Cannes. Why? Because Cannes can open up many markets for your product! Why should I as an Iranian film-maker not benefit from such an opportunity? Even the regime-controlled Fajr Film Festival is an opportunity to introduce your product to the market.

SR: But is not the Fajr Film Festival a place where Iranian film inevitably gets embroiled in the propaganda machinery of the regime? After all, the West thinks that the films there represent the Iranian state or are there at the behest of the Iranian state.

JP: No, not at all. As I mentioned earlier, the number of Iranian films at important festivals such as Cannes and Venice has dwindled rapidly over the last few years. The authorities in Iran have been celebrating this development in the regime-friendly papers. With worried voices that can barely disguise their glee, they show their 'concern' for the death of the Iranian New Wave in talk shows and round tables! They report that Cannes has not asked our film-makers to send them films! Why? Because there seems to be some absurd law by which internationally successful Iranian films are labelled 'festival films', whereas films from all other nations are not. There is also an absurd law that sees foreign investment in Iranian films as exploitation but sees no problem whatsoever when the same money givers invest in the films of other nations. We have to get rid of this antiquated Third World vocabulary. If we want Iranian cinema to thrive, we have to stop seeing ourselves as members of the Third World Club with no way out.

TAHMINEH MILANI

New Iranian Cinema and the Education of the Masses

TAHMINEH MILANI SEES ART IN GENERAL and cinema in particular as a critical mirror of society. She sees herself as a committed film-maker whose art can only be universal by being characteristically native, that is, Iranian. For Milani, the educational dimension of cinema is its most important trait: cinema has a moral obligation. That is why she thinks that the task of film-makers is much harder than that of other artists. Film-makers, she argues, apart from suffering enormously under the restrictions of censorship, like all other artists and authors, also have great difficulties securing funding for their films and attending important film festivals. Women film-makers in Islamic Iran have to grapple with additional restrictions based on gender. These obstacles, however, pale in comparison to the biggest hurdle of all for film-makers in Iran, namely, the division of film-makers into 'loyalists' and 'the others'. Milani believes that nepotism is rife in the administrative sector in Iran and is especially pronounced in cultural institutions. That is why the majority of good film-makers in Iran have not grappled artistically with many important subjects, such as the Iran–Iraq War, which are 'reserved' for 'loyal' film-makers and artists. Ideological loyalty is more important for the regime than artistic ability.

Milani speaks of the nepotism in Iranian cultural institutions from experience. In 2001 – during the 'liberal' presidency of the reformist Mohammad Khatami – she was imprisoned for propagating 'anti-revolutionary' sentiments in her film *Nimeh-e Pinhan* (*The Hidden Half*). The film depicted the love between a young leftist university student and an elderly man during the last days of the revolution against the Pahlavi dynasty. Thanks to protests from many world-famous directors, including Francis Ford Coppola and Martin Scorsese, she was released, but official charges were never dropped. This seems to have strengthened Milani's determination to pursue her cause as a committed artist. She remains one of the most active and prolific feminist activists, whose courage and candour in exposing the hypocrisies of the Islamic Republic's administration have won her a great following amongst Iranian youth both inside and outside the country.

Shiva Rahbaran: The main purpose of this project is to determine how the 1979 revolution influenced Iranian cinema according to those film-makers who live and work in Iran. For instance, neither Amir Naderi nor Ebrahim Golestan have been interviewed for this project because they have been absent from Iranian post-revolutionary society for so many years. My project approaches the subject from a socio-historical angle and does not attempt to evaluate the interviewees' films from an aesthetic point of view.

My first question is this: to what extent has the 1979 revolution influenced Iranian cinema and, in turn, what role has cinema played in the development of society in post-revolutionary Iran? I'm asking this question from the point of view of cinema as a 'popular' artform that can communicate with people regardless of class or level of education, in contrast to poetry or literature, which require a certain level of literacy and education.

Tahmineh Milani: Please allow me to begin this discussion by saying that, in my opinion, artists, regardless of which field or artform they are active in, are among the most sensitive and brightest people in society. What I mean is that the artist's awareness and his or her ability to 'foresee' the future surpasses even that of the most experienced politician. This is because of the artist's sensitive antennae and natural intelligence. The artist senses danger very quickly and can react to social issues rapidly. In comparison to other artists, the most important difficulty that film-makers face is the financing of their art. Painters, for example, work on their own. They need a canvas, some paint and a few brushes – or a poet has a pen and a piece of paper. But cinema is a group project and it can only be realized through complex and at times quite costly cooperation. This is especially the case in Iran. Here the film-maker not only needs to get funding but must also wait for a number of permits before filming starts, which can take up valuable time. Naturally the combination of these things affects your work. Apart from that, the number of viewers – that is, the number of tickets sold – affects your work, and cinema, being a group project, is dependent on many people. In cinema you face an audience of a million people. In Iran, a book sells about 2,000, 3,000, 5,000 copies – 30,000 if it is very popular. But a film can 'communicate' with one million people at the same time. For example, my film *Atash Bas* [*Cease Fire*, 2006] has been watched by millions to date. Thus, in my opinion, cinema is much more publicized and politicized than other artforms and this puts film-makers under a lot of pressure.

SR: So, from your point of view, cinema has a greater influence on society than books and paintings?

TM: Indeed. However, we should bear in mind that this influence is not always positive. It may also be very destructive. Some of the films produced in Iran have changed the culture of language as well as the behavioural standards of society. I think in this domain cinema is even more influential than television. Television demands less concentration and thus affects the audience's subconscious less than cinema does. In cinema, you have one big screen in a dark place and you have no choice but to watch (of course, you could always fall asleep!) I believe strongly in the power of the subconscious. In my films I plan such things in detail. For example, I believe that all members of society should read regardless of their income and class. So, in a scene that takes place inside the house of a poor family I place a bookcase. It's a simple and cheap book-case but it serves its purpose. Also, I like people to eat at the table and not on the floor, so in my films I never let my characters sit on the floor and eat with their hands. If they are poor, I have them sitting on cheap dining chairs. I believe you can influence people through images subconsciously. I'll give you another example from my film *Cease Fire* [2006]. In it there are scenes in which a married couple quarrels. A quarrel usually involves some rude words and verbal abuse, but if you watch this film you won't find one rude word in it.

SR: Isn't this self-censorship?

TM: Not at all! It has nothing to do with censorship. We'll discuss censorship separately. In Iran we have as many different theories and opinions about censorship as film directors. I do not censor myself. Let me tell you that I could show a fight with no verbal abuse and at the same time convey the most extreme anger and violence between the parties involved. I do this because I believe in preserving good manners. Using the right, 'meaningful' words might even emphasize the drama of the situation. Many would take the easiest route – I mean, they'd use verbal abuse to dramatize the situation – but I don't do that. And it has nothing to do with the Ministry of Culture and Islamic Guidance [the Ershad] and their censorship guidelines. As for censorship, again in the film *Cease Fire* I wanted to show some physical struggle between the couple. But I couldn't because, as you are aware, men and women are not allowed to touch each other in Iranian films. So I had to introduce into the scene a large bag in which the woman carries her divorce papers. Given that the husband is not allowed to touch his wife and throw her onto the sofa, he has to grab the bag from her and throw that onto the sofa! This was definitely done because of censorship.

SR: I personally find a physical struggle between a man and a woman just as bad as verbal abuse. Anyway, could it be said that because of the limitations imposed on you by censorship, you've been able to create a more expressive scene?

TM: No. In my opinion that scene would have been much better without the bag.

SR: So you do not believe that censorship can encourage creativity?

TM: No, I don't believe that at all. It is true that you are constantly thinking about how to communicate something forbidden to the audience, but that doesn't mean that such a limitation makes you more creative. Even without censorship I still might not have filmed any sex scenes. I dislike sex scenes as much as verbal abuse. But I could have made better films had it not been for censorship. Sometimes showing love scenes is important. Let's assume we want to show a woman's love somewhere in the film. It would be far more appealing if we were able to show how she caresses or kisses her beloved. But this is not possible under this regime, so we have to choose an alternative. Anyway, I hope you do understand that censorship and morality are two different issues.

SR: Another form of censorship that had a big effect on post-revolutionary cinema was the ban on Hollywood and other Western films in Iran. Didn't this ban help open the way for the development of Iranian cinema? From then on Iranians had little choice but to watch Iranian rather than Western films. Hollywood films pose, as is widely known, a great challenge for 'native' films all over the world. Don't you think that this policy helped the transformation of Film Farsi into what became known as New Iranian Cinema – a world-class cinema, celebrated in all major film festivals around the world?

TM: Let me explain how and when Iranian cinema came into full bloom. Before the revolution we had many intellectual film directors, but because Iranian cinema was firmly in the hands of the few Film Farsi producers, it was hard for intellectual film-makers to establish themselves. However, among this group was a minority that called themselves 'pioneer film-makers' – Kimiai, Kiarostami, Kimiavi, Farmanara, Mehrjui and others. Most intellectual directors had given up cinema (for the reasons I mentioned above) and now worked in television. Under Reza Ghotbi's management this was especially the case.[1] Ghotbi was an educated and reasonable man who believed that everyone working in television should be well educated because, in his eyes, television was vital for the education of the masses. He would send his staff to study abroad – even the secretaries were given some form of training in the West. These people had great potential to make feature films for the cinema, but, because Film Farsi dominated the scene, there were no job opportunities for them. This group included Rakhshan Bani-Etemad, Mohammad Bozorgnia and Pouran Derakhshandeh. They had all been educated both here and abroad before the revolution but weren't given the opportunity to work in their own country.

After the revolution, Film Farsi was pushed out of cinema and, perhaps more importantly, a ban was placed on the import of Hollywood films into Iran. This did not happen because the new Islamic government was especially modern or art-loving! It just wanted Islamic film-makers to make films – preferably films that propagated Islamic values and 'exported' the revolution. However, you cannot produce 'Islamic' film-makers overnight! It took time for people such as Makhmalbaf, Hatamikia and Majidi to enter the scene. Thus, a sort of a gap was created. The market was now open to those who had not had the opportunity to make films during the shah's time – people such as Amir Naderi and Bahram Beyzaie. Again, that did not mean that the regime wanted such film-makers, but it could not stop their progress either.

Let me give you an example. In the rest of the world there is the impression that the work climate and censorship policies of the Islamic Republic of Iran are vital for the emergence of Iranian female directors. I, as a female director, can tell you that this is not true at all. The Islamic Republic of Iran was not keen on Iranian female directors; they emerged because historical conditions demanded it. The regime did not ban American films in order to create the necessary space for intellectual film-makers to thrive. I don't know whether you are able to separate these two things from each other. I mean, it was not the government's plan for Iranian women to become film-makers. It was that, by then, women were ready to push their way into cinema. A few years after the revolution – I was only 23 – I knew that I wanted to become a film-maker. The Ershad had this rule that if someone worked twice as a directorial assistant, then he or she was allowed to make a short film. I had done that by the time I was 23 but they still wouldn't let me make a film. When I turned 27 and tried a second time to make my first film, again, they would not give me permission and help to do so. They just said, 'Go and make your film. Either it will work or it won't work. We don't care.' The government would not help me at all – the same government that had given permission and funding to film-makers such as Ebrahim Hatamikia, who was at the same level as I was. I really want these words to be printed. I think they are important. If you want to review the history of post-revolutionary Iranian cinema, these things must go on record.

SR: They certainly will.

TM: Directors such as Hatamikia, Darvish, Ghasemi-Jami and Raeissian were all at the same level as I was and they all made their first films with the help of government funding. The only person who got no funding was me.

SR: Was it because you were a woman?

TM: No. It was because I didn't think like them. So, their aim was to stop bright, intellectual film-makers from working by refusing them financial help and by not giving them permission to film at certain locations. Back then they didn't care about gender, really. It is possible that someone like Mohammad Beheshti, the former head of the Farabi Cinema Foundation, welcomed the idea of supporting intellectual film-makers, but I don't think that the Islamic system as a whole wanted us on the scene. We fought for it. I believe that if you really want something with all your heart, you will find a way to get it. Among film-makers, I was the only

186 IRANIAN CINEMA UNCENSORED

one who had studied architecture and not drama and film. But I really wanted to become a film-maker and I did. I made a film called *Children of Divorce* [1989], which was shown at 40 or 50 international film festivals, although it was not a typical 'festival film'. By 'festival film' I mean a film that is about poverty and misery and such things – especially when it comes to Iran. *Children of Divorce* is a film about Jungian philosophy, about 'anima' and 'animus' and so on. When I finished making the film, the Ershad said, 'Who do you think you are making a philosophical film? Get a life!'

Despite all that humiliation, though, I made the film. Not only did it do really well at the box office but was also praised by the critics. So, you see, the fact that good films were made after the revolution does not mean that the government helped bring them about.

SR: So, in a way, the period of gestation was over and the time came for the birth of world-class Iranian female film-making.

TM: The time came for a women's movement.

SR: Indeed, some experts say that Iran is one of the few places with real potential for a feminist 'revolution' – a real revolution that would finally topple the entire system. On the other hand, they are shocked when they see women in black walking behind angry men, shouting and burning flags. Isn't there a contradiction between these images and what you've just said, namely, that the time has come for a women's liberation movement in Iran?

TM: You are making a mistake here. Many of those women in black are my fans. For example, when *Two Women* [1999] and *The Hidden Half* [2001] came out, 99 per cent of women in the audience absolutely loved them. It did not matter whether they were Islamic fundamentalists or Westernized intellectuals from the middle or upper classes. Such things don't matter at all. What matters is how women communicate with a film. When I was arrested and imprisoned in 2001 – when *The Hidden Half* was suddenly regarded as un-Islamic – my warden at the women's prison used to say, 'God is punishing me!' She told me that she loved my films. So, when you are discussing women's issues, it doesn't matter what background you come from. As a woman, especially in Iran, you are under pressure. Do you think that just because I live among the intellectual and the wealthy that men around me treat me better? No! In their minds, too, I am the second-class gender – exactly as in Simone de Beauvoir's sense of the word! So women's issues are the same regardless of class. I give birth in the same way as a female worker; I am in pain and no one takes notice; I bring up my child and no one sees it.

A working-class woman is in the same situation. We both provide our services for free! I mean, no one appreciates us for having babies, cleaning the house or cooking. In the eyes of society it is our duty, regardless of our cultural or economic background. So when people talk about a women's revolution, they should realize that all women participate in this movement – whether on the right or on the left. It is true that at the beginning of the revolution women were used only as 'foot soldiers', but later on these same women started to demand their rights. Our issues, regardless of education, money and class, are almost identical. In this country, if a female Muslim fundamentalist went to court and asked to have custody of her child in a divorce case, under Sharia law she would be denied it – unless her husband were a psychopath or a drug addict. The same thing would happen to me, a well-off, modern intellectual. So when I make a film about child custody or women's education, I might even be communicating to a greater extent with the woman who is a Muslim fundamentalist.

SR: What upset me a little in your celebrated film *Two Women* [1999] was that it portrayed children as shackles on the mother's feet. I have children and yet I'm able to create free space for myself and do other things besides childcare. You too are a mother, but you're working as a successful director. Why couldn't you make a film about women such as yourself, who don't give up their freedom entirely despite motherhood?

TM: Be patient! First of all – and unfortunately – in our society having children means giving up much of your free space. Second, you should remember that art is born out of suffering. Art is not created by fortune and happiness. Show me one book or film that's all about happiness. Heroes always suffer and struggle, but no one hears them cry and complain.

SR: What about you? Why shouldn't you be the first to make a film about a woman who achieves happiness?

TM: No! Why should I? Happiness is not dramatic. What does happiness mean? Is it saying, 'Darling, tonight I'll wash the dishes!', followed by your husband saying, 'No, my sweet! Let me do them.'

SR: No. Happiness is when you are a successful female director who, despite all difficulties, still manages to make films.

TM: There's nothing to show there! It's just one sentence and then it's over. Bear in mind that happiness cannot be shown. All beautiful stories in the world are about women who suffer in one way or another. It is suffering that creates beauty in art.

SR: Don't you think that, through your films, you open the way for happiness and freedom?

TM: I have never killed hope in my films.

SR: That's true.

TM: When I make a film such as *Two Women* or *The Hidden Half* I'm saying, 'Look here, naive society! This energetic, bright, educated and "decent" girl wants to improve her family's situation. She wants to help her family. Let her finish her education. Don't trap her in the mesh of Sharia law! Do not intimidate and frighten her!' Do you understand what I am saying? The film should be like a mirror that shows the ugly reality. It should raise questions as to why we do such stupid things. Although I admit that I get 'punished' for raising such questions, my films do have their intended effect on society. Or in *Fifth Reaction* [2003], I tell fathers and husbands who make their children suffer by taking them away from their mothers after a divorce: the choice for these mothers is either to die of sadness or to run away. Well, both options are bad. For the sake of peace, give the child to the mother! Why do you insist on making a mother suffer so much? What sort of law is this?

SR: In Panahi's *The Circle* [2000] women are always on the losing side.

TM: *The Circle* is different from my films. *The Circle*, as the title suggests, is closed. I never shut all doors. I mean, *The Circle* is not my idea of a film about women.

SR: I understand, but what I'm trying to say is that both of you depict poor, weak and unlucky women. For example, in your film *Two Women* there is a scene of one of the women walking among sunflowers and tasting freedom. Why couldn't that be the ending of your film?

TM: Because such feelings are over within seconds.

SR: That's your choice as a director that it lasts for only a minute.

TM: So what do you suggest? You show me a good film in line with your taste – just one.

SR: I think the sunflower scene in *Two Women* could be extended to produce a hopeful film for women – a film with a happy ending.

TM: But that would be a fantasy. I'm realistic. I want to tell society, 'Look! This woman runs away and gets caught.' Reality dictates that to me. Of course there are women who succeed in running away. Maybe some day reality will bid me make a film about a woman who does not get caught while fleeing with her child from a court of 'justice', or, better still, does not have to flee with her child at all, because maybe one day we will have proper courts of justice.

SR: Exactly. Why do you not start today?

TM: No, I cannot do that. That would be like telling women: take your children and run away. Even if someone succeeded, that would still be the worst way out, because only a few who take such risks make it. Many lose their lives and risk the lives of their children when they try to escape.

SR: But that's the risk a woman will take.

TM: As a film-maker you're responsible for the message you put across. For example, we all know that it's every girl's right to go to parties. *I* think it is. So I could make a film that says, 'Girls! Stand up to your parents and go to parties despite repression in Iran.' But no! I make a film that says to parents, 'Your children become corrupt because of all those bans and the strict upbringing you impose on them. So, come on and change your behaviour towards your children.'

SR: So you look at yourself as an artist committed to society and not as an artist committed only to aesthetics?

TM: Yes, very much so. I don't believe in the 'art for art's sake' philosophy at all. Big American producers send me lots of scripts to tempt me to go over there and make films, but I don't want to. I can see that it makes no difference whether it's me, John Doe or Jane Doe who makes that film. It'll be a film like the rest of American films. I tell them that I will come to the US and make a film, but it will be *my* film. Accept my ideas. Let me make a film in the US as *I* want to. In Iran, too, when producers send me scripts and offer me huge amounts of money, I say, 'Anyone could make this. Why should I? This is not in line with my way of thinking.' I can only turn my own thoughts into a film and I have been lucky that so far the audience has been appreciative of my way of doing things.

SR: How much does this commitment isolate you? Are you in internal exile like Forough Farrokhzad or Sadegh Hedayat?

TM: You do not become an artist by being in exile. Exile is not necessary for art. The committed artist, however, is often alone. If you think of me as a committed artist, then let me tell you about my own personal experience. I don't get government funding as others do. I don't get good equipment. The interesting thing is that they don't even show my films at the most important Iranian film festival – the Fajr Film Festival. The Women's Film Festival does not show any of my films either and, funnily enough, it was they who labelled me a 'feminist'. This is how the regime tries to take your civil rights away from you. You are left alone or you look around you with a feeling of being separate from the rest. A pioneering artist such as Forough was way ahead of her time. In my eyes, she is ahead of her time even now. Her last book is not comprehensible to most intellectuals in Iran today. It's natural for her to be misjudged and treated cruelly. It's natural for them to make fun of her or write harsh reviews of her work. The same thing happens to me. In my opinion these are people of a traditionalist mindset who cannot tolerate new ideas. New ideas mess up their mental system. Thus a person like me should be prepared to be humiliated and to be made fun of. I accept that the committed artist suffers some form of alienation in his or her society, but it is not necessarily exile.

SR: But don't you live in an inner exile?

TM: No, I don't think so. Remember that Iranian society is constantly changing. If you are in some kind of exile, then you can't keep up to date with new developments. For example, I read the newspapers every day. I might just read the headlines, but that's enough for me to know what's going on. There is something new happening every day: a new phenomenon, a new thought, a new crime, a new style. So, if a person has been away from his or her society for 20, 30 years, he or she cannot share the same roots as the people who have stayed behind. I don't know about Ebrahim Golestan,[2] for example, who left Iran more than 35 years ago, before the revolution, but that's what I'd say about people such as Parviz Sayyad.[3] While in Iran he was wonderfully creative, but in his 30 years of exile he has not produced anything worthwhile. He's just repeating himself.

SR: Do you feel attached to Iranian society?

TM: Yes, I'd say so. I could easily live and work in the USA but I know that I would be one out of a million there. Here I am one out of a thousand or even a hundred!

SR: Many have labelled you and other film-makers 'festival directors'. They say that your success derives from Western festivals where the people in charge are interested in films that show the backwardness of Iran and other Third World countries.

TM: No. They don't label me in that way. I'm different from that lot.

SR: But you've been able to find a compromise between festivals and audiences in Iran. You and Majid Majidi, for instance, are popular in this country and take part in overseas festivals too.

TM: Louis Kahn, one of the most famous architects in the world, said something I really believe in: 'Only an art which is native can become universal.' He says this in relation to architecture.[4] For example, because the Sheikh Lotfollah Mosque in Isfahan has its roots in its environment and is not 'copying' anything else, it is considered unique and beautiful universally. Kahn's concept of nativeness or indigenousness is originality. My film *Two Women* is a good example of Kahn's idea of indigenousness. It successfully bridged the gap between my country and the rest of the world. It was very Iranian with a very Iranian subject and yet foreigners could relate to it. It was the best-selling film of its year in Iran and won many awards at international festivals. Many women, regardless of their nationality, said, 'This is the story of my life. That's me, with a few cultural differences.' People were able to connect to *Two Women* (without even seeing it) as a universal film. The same thing happened with Majidi's *The Colour of Paradise* [1999], which was recognized as a universal film and not as one from a Third World country.

SR: But even before this, Iranian experimental and 'artistic' films, such as those of Kiarostami and Beyzaie, were universally praised.

TM: Experimental and artistic films don't go far. I respect them, but I don't believe in them. They have never affected me deeply. They do not raise emotions in me.

SR: You just quoted Louis Kahn on the necessity of art being 'native' in order to become universal. Cinema, however, is a modern, imported art in our country. It comes from Europe. In the eyes of many experts, poetry is the purest form of Iranian art. Why do you think that our cinema has found its place in the world whereas our contemporary poetry, which rests on a firm 1,000-year-old foundation, has been unable to do so and still remains relatively unknown in the rest of the world?

TM: Only the tools of our cinema are from the West, not the content. The content is Iranian. If you talk about tools, then you could say that the West invented the fountain pen. The point here is how the pen is used. Also, the canvases and the pallets of Kamal-ol-Molk,[5] Michelangelo and Da Vinci have all been similar. What matters is what they put on their canvases with their paint. So when I talk about the importance of being native, I do not have the tools of art in mind; it is the attitude of the artist that is reflected in his or her work. Art has to have its roots in a specific culture in order to become universal. People in the world get to know each other through watching films. Personally, I have been a judge in quite a few festivals. For instance, I was a judge in Tunisia once. After watching 23–30 films from Africa and Arabia, I started to understand what kind of a country Kenya is or what is going on in South Africa. It is through films that I gain this insight. Literature doesn't work like cinema. Also, it isn't possible to say with confidence that Iranian film is a permanent fixture in world cinema. You should not forget that, despite its presence in film festivals, Iranian cinema faces a big challenge in the world market.

SR: Even so, Iranian film-makers have been accepted in the world of cinema. They have been able to create a universal artform based on their cultural and historical background. Persian literature has the same, if not an even older and stronger background, yet our modern literature has not been able to find its place in the world. From an international perspective, our contemporary literature seems to start with Hedayat and finish more or less with Forough. Of course, contemporary novelists and poets are being translated and published, but none can measure up to Hedayat or Forough. Our film-makers, on the other hand, have been able to move with the times. While researching my last book, *Iranian Writers Uncensored,* I spoke to many novelists and poets working in Iran and most of them said, 'You should pass our message on to the world'; that people like me should make their works more accessible to the world, but when I talk to film-makers they never request anything similar.

TM: Yes that's true. I have also written a novel – and of course never had it published – and can agree with you on that. A novel is the world of one person and is not dependent on a group. In cinema it only takes one bad cameraman, sound engineer or actor to ruin your whole project. What I mean is that in my opinion film-making is even harder. On the other hand, cinema is a completely different medium. You can communicate with millions of people within seconds – seeing an image is much easier than reading a book or a poem. Also, our writers face the language problem. Persian is not a universal language.

SR: That's true, but Persian can be translated. For example, Orhan Pamuk writes in Turkish and all his novels have been translated into all the major languages of the world and he also won the Nobel Prize.

TM: As I'm not an expert, I can't really comment, but I can say that

our contemporary architects, for example, are not internationally successful either. The same goes for our painters. Being native
does not mean building the Sheikh Lotfollah Mosque again and
again; this mosque was modern for its own time and very different from earlier mosques; it was unique, it used to be a landmark;
today, though, you should make something different. If you make
the same mosque today then you're going backwards.

SR: All these tower blocks that we see in Tehran and other large
cities of Iran were supposed to be European and modern.

TM: Yes, but the architects have just copied the Americans and the
Europeans. They have nothing new to say; they have gone backwards. In the case of modern literature, maybe there hasn't been
a proper and serious investment. Maybe it's because our governments have always been scared of intellectuals, and our intellectuals have always been active in the field of literature and their
hands have been tied by censorship, and so on. I don't know why
they are having such a hard time becoming successful internationally, but I can say that in cinema our hands are also tied – maybe
even more than in literature. For example, a lot of things you can
get away with in novels, such as eroticism, are not allowed in films.
We should really think about why Iranian cinema is more successful than contemporary Persian novels and poetry, yet I am positive
that our contemporary novels will soon get noticed by the rest of
the world. Some of the novels of Iranian female authors are really
beautiful. I have also read interesting things by our writers in exile
who represent life in a foreign country very well; their experiences and memories are very interesting to me. I think we should
be patient until the same thing happens in our literature. The old
generation of writers has come to an end. The time of Dolatabadi
and his colleagues is over. The generation of post-revolutionary
writers will surface soon.

SR: It seems that Iranian cinema and literature are not as inter-
connected as they are in Europe. Except for some of Kiarostami's
films, such as *Where is the Friend's Home?* and *The Wind Will Carry*

Us, which draw on the poetry of Forough and Sohrab Sepehri, or Farmanara's *Prince Ehtejab*, which is based on a novel by Golshiri, we hardly have any films adapted from our literature.

TM: The Europeans and the Americans sometimes invest huge amounts of money in adapting novels into films.

SR: Setting aside the financial aspect, does making a film based on a novel or poem seem appealing to you?

TM: Yes it does, but in cinema we are usually ahead of our literature. It is much easier for me to write about social issues and turn that writing into a film. Cinema progresses much faster than literature. But you are right; you could take just one minute of classic Iranian literature and make a film out of it.

SR: What about modern novels? For instance, why don't you make one of Simin Daneshvar's novels into a film?

TM: No! The subjects of her books are finished. They are behind our time.

SR: Even the *Sargardāni* [*Wandering*] trilogy,[6] which came out between 1992 and 2002 and depicted the early years after the revolution?

TM: Those books were not good at all. I've read them. Reading is my first and last love. Although good novels are being written in Iran, on the whole cinema is ahead of literature. It doesn't need the Persian novel; it is much more up to date. Literature may have deeper roots, but that makes its progress and adaptability slower.

SR: How do you evaluate your role in presenting Iranian identity to the world, especially the West? Considering that the world's media is filled with negative images of Iran, film-makers like you present a different image – an image that is less politically charged and less black and white, an image that is more human.

TM: Of course, immediately after the revolution the climate was highly politicized. For example, at one point it became common for film-makers to lie and say, 'We are an oppressed nation and you must give us your attention and awards for all our sufferings. Look how well we show filth and backwardness.' Some of those things were absolute lies and there were some films I was ashamed to say were from my own country. Personally, I make films about the middle class and about women's issues – issues that exist all over the world. I really try to stay faithful to reality. I might disregard some elements of reality because of censorship but I would never undermine a system with lies only so that Westerners like my films more! Once, when I was in Sweden, I saw a film by an Iranian director about a family of Iranian immigrants. It really upset me to watch it. Why would someone make such a film and look at the immigrant issue from that point of view? Why should he tell so many lies about Iranian immigrants? I remember an Iranian family in Sweden telling me that for many years they'd been trying really hard to communicate with Swedish families and have them come round for tea. Yet in this film there's a scene in which the child of the family urinates in the teapot and serves it to the guests. I guess Swedish people would never drink Iranian tea after that! Whoever makes such a film should bear in mind what effects it will have. Fortunately, in the arts the global climate is no longer as politicized as it was in the early years of the revolution and we are able to present reality much better.

SR: My final question concerns the eight-year war between Iran and Iraq and its representation in cinema. Considering the massive effect of the war on the economy, politics and society of this country, it is rather surprising that, except for a handful of film-makers such as Hatamikia, neither directors nor audiences are interested in war films. Why is war so underrepresented in Iran?

TM: War has been exploited by the regime and its propaganda machinery. That's why the average citizen is not interested in seeing films about our war. As a film subject it has been abused by Islamic extremists for propaganda purposes, and whatever you abuse cannot thrive; it deteriorates. During the war, everyone was ready to go and fight to stop the enemy from entering our land – men and women. Even I wanted to go to war but the authorities said, 'You cannot go to war and fight. You are not one of us.' The story began as simply as that. Even when I as an architect went to help reconstruct the war zones, they put up with me for a month and then fired me because I didn't dress like them and I was not the same as them. So that's how the war died as an art subject. Some beautiful films have been made about the war by the few who were allowed to make them, but, having been used mainly for propaganda purposes, the war and its significance have been lost on our society. The war was one of courage and sacrifice. Behind the scenes, behind the front line, war was very beautiful. What women and children did for the soldiers and the country was beautiful.

The war has not been represented through the eyes of a woman yet. I did write a script but it was rejected. They refused to let me tell the story of the war through the eyes of a woman. I think that it was only Rakhshan Bani-Etemad who made the anti-war *Gilane* from a woman's point of view. The film is about a mother who faces the wounds of war. However, it doesn't show the war directly; there are no actual war scenes. What it shows really well are the consequences of the war for a mother who has to cope with the pain and shame of having an invalid return to her from the front. Society shuns her and forgets the sacrifices that soldiers made for their country.

SR: Beyzaie's *Bashu, the Little Stranger* also depicts the war both from a little boy's point of view and that of a rural woman.

TM: *Bashu* is one of the very few films that I really like, but it was not shot from a woman's perspective. It was *about* a woman but not made *by* a female director. *Gilane*, on the other hand, was made *by* a woman. However, it only concentrates on the sufferings that a woman has to put up with as a mother – not as a woman who is in the war zone. Unfortunately the system restricts us greatly and expects us to make propaganda films about the war. That's why it never became a popular subject. As a committed film-maker you must say that war is bad; you must say that we have to defend ourselves when attacked, but that nevertheless war is a bad thing. However, because the regime didn't allow us to say such things, interest in the subject just vanished.

10

EBRAHIM HATAMIKIA

Cinema, War and Peace

MY INTERVIEW WITH EBRAHIM HATAMIKIA centred mainly on the disastrous eight-year war between Iran and Iraq (1980–88). No single event in the three decades since the revolution affected all aspects of life in Iran – the political, the financial, the social or the cultural – as deeply as this war. Yet all film-makers interviewed in this book agree that, given its importance and influence, the war has not been addressed in cinema as much as it deserves to be. Hatamikia is one of the few Iranian film-makers admired both in Iran and abroad by people of every political persuasion. His latest film, *Che* (2014), is perhaps his most radical film about war and revolution, both of which are central to his perception of contemporary Iranian identity and culture. The film depicts the last 48 hours in the life of Mustafa Chamran, Iran's first post-revolutionary defence minister, who was a militant Islamist (before the term had become part of everyday vocabulary) and a founding member of the Hezbollah movement Amal in southern Lebanon. Chamran was 'martyred' during an operation not against the Iraqi aggressors but against the separatist Kurdish Komoleh Party. During this interview Hatamikia repeatedly insists on the necessity of military force against rebels and separatist movements in post-revolutionary Iran and is full of admiration for the Revolutionary Guards, who, he believes, have always protected the spirit of the revolution and the sovereignty of Iran.

On the whole, Hatamikia has a 'romantic' view of war. He does not see it exclusively as a destructive phenomenon, ridden with pain, blood and deprivation. For him war also lights a fire that can cleanse the soldiers' souls of all pollution, making them as pure and clear as a mirror. Hatamikia was himself a member of the Sepah-e Pasdaran – the Army of the Guardians of the Islamic Revolution (also known as the Revolutionary Guards) – and served at the front as a maker of propaganda films and educational war documentaries. His first short film *Torbat* (*The Tomb*) reflected his own experience of the war, and his firsthand experience at the front is palpable in all his ensuing feature films.

In this interview Hatamikia talks extensively about the Iran–Iraq War, which was often described as a *jihad* by the Islamists of Iran. He talks about how in its last days the war was transformed from a religious conflict (the Revolutionary Guards and the para-militaries made praying stones out of Iraqi earth because it was the earth in which many Shi'a holy figures lie) into a nationalist and patriotic conflict, when the exiled Iranian group Mojahedin-e Khalq (MEK),[1] based in Saddam's Iraq, attacked Iran shoulder to shoulder with Iraqi soldiers.

Hatamikia criticizes society's forgetfulness about the war and its victims and sees the 'expropriation' of the war by the apparatus of government propaganda and nepotism as a main reason for this. When I tell him that the same reason has made intellectual Iranian film-makers also wary of choosing the war as their subject, he disa-grees and says that the so-called intellectuals are only interested in producing films that appeal to Western film festivals. He uses Kiarostami as the archetypal 'Westernized' film-maker and ques-tions his interest in Iranian identity and the history of emancipa-tion. Hatamikia's clash with Kiarostami took a new turn during the screening of *Che* in 2014. In numerous interviews Hatamikia openly criticized Kiarostami for his lack of interest in the revolution and the war and accused him of being the 'darling of foreign film festi-vals'. In an interview with the *Etemaad* newspaper (9 October 2014) Kiarostami retorted that Hatamikia's war movies were formulaic rehashes of Hollywood themes,[2] while denying that he in any way doubted the heroism of those who died fighting Iraqi forces.[3]

The confrontation between the two once again highlights Hatamikia's conviction that the revolution and its aftermath were vitally important for the evolution and development of New Iranian Cinema and its success worldwide. The revolution, Hatamikia believes, opened the eyes of film-makers to the reality around them. Although he is critical of the way in which the regime treated the war as a propaganda opportunity, he finds post-revolutionary censorship policies all in all positive. He believes that these restrictions provided fertile ground for homegrown art films and he is especially appreciative of cultural institutions such as the Farabi Cinema Foundation, under whose auspices many outstanding films have been made.

Shiva Rahbaran: The main purpose of my research is to examine the influence of the 1979 revolution on Iranian cinema and, in turn, the influence of this cinema on post-revolutionary Iranian society from the viewpoint of those film-makers who are now living and working in Iran. I wish to examine Iranian cinema from a sociological angle rather than an aesthetic one.

Bearing in mind that cinema is considered a popular artform that can communicate with people from all backgrounds, regardless of their level of education – as opposed to literature, for example, for which people need a certain minimum of literacy – how do you see the influence of cinema on society?

Ebrahim Hatamikia: I was about 18 years old at the time of the revolution. Although I attended courses in cinema throughout those years, I mainly learned my craft during the war. My films come from the heart of the Iran–Iraq War.

SR: Yes, you, together with Kianoush Ayari,[4] are one of the few Iranian film-makers whose films are almost exclusively about the Iran–Iraq War and its aftermath. You are regarded by the majority of critics and film-makers – regardless of their political position –

as an authority in this field. But most of your colleagues have either made shallow propaganda films about the war or tried to avoid the subject altogether. Why is that?

EH: During the first years following the revolution, I thought I should help the war effort. I was 'contaminated' by the Islamic ideology of the war. One of the ways of serving was to join Jahad-e Sazandegi,[5] an organization that would send young volunteers to villages to help farmers and their families. We would go as teachers, farm-workers, nurses, builders – you name it. When the war broke out, our duties began to change. War meant chaos! The battlefields were chaotic and everything was a mess. I was only 18 and full of ideals. For me it was only natural to go to the battlefields and help out. Right from the start I did not like guns and missiles, yet I wanted to serve. So I returned to my passion – film-making.

SR: When did you start making films in the first place?

EH: Before going to war I attended some film courses and made a few short films. At the time there was an institute for amateur film-makers called Azad Cinema – 'Free Cinema'. I studied there. I knew a bit about cinema and had some elementary knowledge of filming, but it was the war and its special circumstances that turned me into a film-maker. I went to the battlefield with a Super 8 camera and made a series of documentaries, which did not have much of a theme – I mainly recorded random events and scenes of the war.

The turning point in my life as a film-maker was 1982. I had just turned 22 and decided to join the Sepah-e Pasdaran – the Army of the Guardians of the Islamic Revolution. I started work as a cameraman for the Propaganda Department. One day the operation we were due to film got cancelled and I was left with a camera and some film stock. With the permission of my commander, I moved further back from the frontline and started to make my first feature film there and then, using real people and real locations. This is how my first film about the war was born. I called it *Torbat*

[*The Tomb*, 1984]. It was a narrative of the war and even now I think of it as my strongest film. The visual elements and the technique are very basic but the subject is really strong. I got the idea for the film from what I had seen on the battlefield – you know, the guys who fought there thought Iraq's earth was sacred; they made *torbat* out of it.[6]

SR: Do you mean that the soldiers' point of view was Islamic rather than Iranian?

EH: Absolutely! We had two kinds of soldier: one was from the pre-revolutionary army, who had a very professional approach and a more nationalistic attitude to the motherland; the other was from the Revolutionary Guards [Sepahi], or the soldier from the para-military group, Basij – people like me, really. We took a religious attitude to the war; we regarded the earth of Iraq as sacred, to be protected from the enemy. We regarded Saddam Hussein as the infidel who had occupied the sacred [Shi'a] soil of Iraq and wanted to occupy our land as well. That's why I called the film *Torbat*, which means sacred and pure earth.

SR: Didn't this anti-patriotic approach cause some hostility towards you from the Iranian people? As you know, Iranians take their Iranianness very seriously!

EH: Not at all! I did not feel any hostility from the Iranian people. The climate in the early 1980s was strongly war oriented. We moved outside intellectual circles – which many regarded as decadent and degenerate, as subservient to the West. I was really involved in shooting films on the battlefield and making advertisements to persuade people to join the Revolutionary Guards, that is, the Sepah and the paramilitary Basij. It was part of my job. Propaganda for the war was more or less the main task of the Sepah's audio-visual wing during the war and that organization was my employer, as it were. I did the same thing that John Ford and other US film-makers did in the US navy during World War II. In Iran, too, war was propaganda.

SR: People like John Ford had a patriotic attitude, but yours was Islamic, religious.

EH: That's true. However, you must bear in mind that the 'colour' of our religiosity was completely Iranian. Our approach was based on Shi'a principles, which, except for a few minorities in the Muslim world, are mainly practised in Iran. It was actually this Iranian brand of Islam that made war sacred for most soldiers. They made praying stones with earth from Iraq because they believed that if they were lucky enough to die as martyrs they'd die holding the earth that was close to the graves of the Shi'a imams. Many soldiers took handfuls of earth and praying stones as souvenirs back to their families.

SR: Did they feel that they were defending the land of Iran?

EH: They did, but they felt less like nationalists than like Shi'a ideologists. You see, they thought of Iran not necessarily as the land of Iranians, with its great pre-Islamic history and art, but as the stronghold of Shi'a Islam. Towards the end of the war nationalistic sentiment amongst the soldiers became stronger. When the Mojahedin-e Khalq – the organization that opposed the Islamic regime of Iran and operated against it from Iraq – attacked Iran alongside Iraqi soldiers in the last days of the war, the propaganda became more nationalistic. But before the war our view was much broader – more spiritual, more idealistic. It was a religious war and we fought it with all our strength – it was a *jihad*. At the end of the war, the nationalistic propaganda did not motivate us as strongly as the religious.

Of course, it was a different matter for those soldiers who had had a pre-revolutionary army background, but their numbers were not high anyway. Most of the fighters were from the Sepah or the Basij and came from a very religious background. The reality was that the former wouldn't sacrifice their lives as readily as the latter. The religious soldiers believed that they would go to Paradise after dying a martyr's death. The army of Iraq was a conventional army and, had we fought them with conventional methods, we would have lost the war right at the beginning. Our own conventional army had lost its commanders as a result of the revolution and did not have much strength. Thousands of acres of our land were invaded by the Iraqi army and we were in a very bad situation. The non-professional soldiers who joined the war would gladly sacrifice their lives to push back the enemy. Their hope was to die as martyrs – only if they died such a death would they be victorious. Well, this attitude and this tactic of resistance were completely different from what had been taught at the army academies before the revolution! The Iraqi army was very well equipped and was considered the strongest in the Middle East. Iran had nothing except the bodies of its soldiers. I remember we would say things like, 'My body against tanks!' or 'My body against the Iraqi iron!'

So, in such an atmosphere, my first short film, *Torbat*, was very well received. It was broadcast on TV, which enabled me to carry on making films. My second film was about someone who loses his legs on the frontline and is worried that if his mother sees him it will devastate her. My third project was a poetic film about war called *Togh–e Sorkh* [*The Red Collar*, 1985]. It's a short film about a pigeon whose neck has been injured in the war and is looking for a human to help it. My breakthrough came with my second feature film, *The Scout*, which was released in 1990.

SR: Did you make that film after the war was over?

EH: Yes, the war was over by then. Except for my first feature film, *Identity* [*Hoviyat*], which was made in 1986, my other 14 feature films, most of which are about the war, were made afterwards.

SR: It must have been difficult to make films about the war in the postwar climate, where everyone wanted to forget about the conflict. Weren't you ignored and dismissed?

EH: This didn't happen immediately. I'm part of a generation that comes from the heart of war; I'm one of the 'war kids'. Up until 1988 war was a reality in society. I mean, back then I had no time for cultural or intellectual circles. All I ever thought about was going to the frontline to fight. I was going to film what was happening and I am proud of what I did. Significantly, I made films for Ravayat-e Fath, an organization responsible for the strongest war documentaries. They would film on the frontline, which meant that many of our cameramen got killed or were wounded. Today the films that give us the best insight into war are their documentaries.

SR: But weren't these films more or less advertisements for the war? How could they offer insight into the war by means of advertisements?

EH: Absolutely! They were meant to excite people and persuade them to join the army, but they were real. After the end of the war in 1988, the kids who had come back from eight years of fighting felt as if urban society – the city people – didn't understand them. In my third feature film, *The Immigrant* [1990], I criticized this society and asked, 'Why have you forgotten us?' The film is about soldiers who are stuck somewhere on the frontline; their commanders have left them behind and they do not know what to do. The film has a poetic and spiritual feel about it and is told from the point of view of an aeroplane that is empty and has no passengers. My next film was *Vasl-e Nikan* [*The Joining of the Good*, 1991], which tells the story of the wedding of a soldier who has come back from the front while his hometown is under attack. Obviously no one comes to the wedding – everyone is hiding because of the bombardment. The film criticizes society and its inability to celebrate the happiness of those who are back from the war. It shows that the 'war kids' are left to their own devices and nobody appreciates their sacrifice.

My next film was *From Karkheh to Rhine* [1993]. It's about the survivors of the Iraqi chemical attacks and the effects that their situation has on those around them. It is also about reconciliation with those with whom we have lost touch, be it because of the revolution or the war, and about the Iranians of the diaspora who miss their families and country. The hero of the film has been to war and suffered a chemical attack. His sister is a member of a political group in exile and seeks asylum in Germany. They've been out of touch for many years, but now come face to face with each other and want to communicate. The brother has lost his sight and is critically injured. The reconciliation between brother and sister is the story of reconciliation between people from different parts of society with each other. Both are in some sort of exile from their society.

After *From Karkheh to Rhine* I made *The Green Ashes* [1994], which was filmed in Bosnia. I believe that this film was the first dramatic portrayal of Bosnia but unfortunately, because of the political situation there, it did not receive the recognition it deserved. Nevertheless we were the first country to make a film about Bosnia! It's the story of an Iranian photojournalist who goes to Bosnia and falls in love with a Bosnian girl. There was mixed reaction to this film in Iran. Those in the film business liked it as a romantic war film but those in politics said that it was not proper for an Iranian photojournalist to go to Bosnia and fall in love with a Bosnian girl! They said that the film was not really about war in a Muslim country but about love and flirting; the subject was even discussed in Parliament!

My next film was *The Scent of Joseph's Coat* [1995]. This is about a woman who comes back from abroad to see her brother – a former POW – after many years. The film was about the forgotten Iranian POWs and was made under very difficult conditions. Political and cultural freedom was very limited – of course, in those days we did not know that a certain Mr Ahmadinejad would make us yearn for the 1990s, but that's a different story. In order to show the dark and heavy atmosphere of those days, 95 per cent of the film takes place at night. I wanted to show the claustrophobia of prisoners, so only about five or six minutes of the film was shot during daytime.

My next film was *Borj-eh Minoo* [*Minoo's Watchtower*, 1996]. It's about those who have come back from the war, become financially successful and have turned their backs on their past. The film criticizes these people and asks why they're hiding from their past.

All the films I've mentioned so far look at things from the viewpoint of those who have come back from the war. The symbolism is all about the war and the fighters. For example, the symbolic element in *Borj-eh Minoo* was that on the battlefield you move either vertically or horizontally depending on what can screen you from the enemy's sight. A tower is being built higher and higher – there is only vertical movement – and the higher you climb the more you are within the enemy's sight and the greater the possibility that you will be killed. This is a spiritual point of view. After *Borj-eh Minoo* I made *The Glass Agency* [1999], which reflected the social unrest of the 2nd of Khordad [23 May].[7]

SR: Do you mean the demonstrations that took place on the 2nd of Khordad 1376 [23 May 1997], which resulted in Mohammad Khatami's landslide victory in the presidential elections?

EH: Yes, exactly. The film is about 'war kids' protesting against society's indifference to the fate of war invalids and veterans. The 'war kids' ask: why do people only think of their own happiness and forget those who suffered great losses in war?

My next film was *The Red Ribbon* [1999]. This took a more artistic, experimental and symbolic approach to love. It told the story of three people in a desert where the frontline used to be. These are the only characters in the film. One of them is a landmine detector and he's obviously stuck in the past. Another is a woman who's there because that's where her home used to be. The two fall in love. The third character is a man who's turned up and wants to sell the tank that has been abandoned in the ruins of a house. A love triangle is created. The story has a symbolic narrative.

SR: Your films look at the war from a distinctive viewpoint and often protest against society's indifference towards the 'war generation'. A lot of serious film-makers told me that they did not use war as a subject because the regime had exploited it for propaganda reasons. Do you agree with this?

EH: I preserved my own point of view. None of my films advertise war. For instance, in *The Scout* there is no war propaganda – even though I worked as a war propaganda film-maker! It's about a person who is captured by the Iraqis and is caught in a dilemma: if he gets a message to his comrades to bombard the enemy position, he will die as well; if he tries to save his own life, the Iraqis will go ahead and kill many Iranian soldiers. It was a sad and upsetting film. On the whole, my films take a more or less nostalgic look at a generation who fought in the war at some point, have memories of it and will always carry the experience with them. This point of view is different from that of Mrs Bani-Etemad, for example, who lives her life in the city and sees the war from that angle. Her experience, however, is not firsthand. I come from the frontline *to* the city whereas she looks at the frontline *from* the city and these two perspectives are very different.

The unfortunate fact remains, as you mentioned, that, considering that we had eight years of war, we have very few artistic films about the war. I might be one of the few who insisted on making war films. This is not because I am fascinated by war. If there had been no war, I would have made other films instead. I am a social film-maker and have always insisted on not being regarded as a war film-maker per se. As there happened to be a war, I try to deal with social issues from the viewpoint of the war generation.

SR: But why is such an important event so rarely reflected in cinema? The war might be the most important event in our post-revolutionary history, yet why is its artistic representation so scant, whether in literature or in cinema?

EH: Something quite unfortunate happened to our cinema – our art as a whole – in the aftermath of war. In the first years after the revolution the climate was completely different from what we know now – there was a martial spirit about. Just the other day I was reading some letters that I had written to a friend of mine during the war years. We had grown up together; I stayed whereas he left for Germany to study. Our letters are really weird. We were living in a peculiar environment. You can only understand it if you have lived in that time and are aware of it. The atmosphere in those early post-revolutionary years, when many political parties were actively against the Islamic Republic, plus the sudden invasion of the country by Saddam, was frighteningly explosive. For the new Islamic state the positive side of the war was that it united the people and forced the anti-regime parties to practically give in. Those who didn't give in were pushed to the periphery of people's consciousness, as the main issue now was the war. Do you remember that within a month of the revolution our garrisons in Kurdistan were under attack? The Kurds were asking for autonomy! At the other end of the country, the Turkmens were also asking for autonomy. Sistan, Baluchistan and Azerbaijan all had active and popular separatist parties calling for independence. Well, Iran is and has always been a multiethnic country. And now there was so much tension, so much chaos, that the whole country could have fallen to pieces. The old Iranian nationalist ideology was considered subversive and there was no time for peace talks about Swiss-style federations! Thus the central government's reaction had to be harsh.

It really was a very bad atmosphere in which the concept of freedom was too complicated to describe. I mean, if anyone wanted to describe freedom, it would have been mixed up with separatism. I believe that the regime shrewdly silenced the protests, but it was a Herculean task. The opposition parties practically backed off – they were decimated. This happened to all parties whose ideology was not in line with that of the system; the pre-revolutionary nationalistic ideologies suffered especially heavily. Now we were not even supposed to see ourselves as a nation, but as the Faithful – the Shi'a people, as it were. The national anthem 'Ey Iran' was banned for over ten years after the revolution. We heard it for the first time – and perhaps the last time – on the radio in 1989 during the offensive of the opposition group Mojahedin-e Khalq, who operated against the regime from Iraqi soil and under Saddam Hussein's protection. The operation was called *Mersad* and it was the only time that the nationalist ideology, which until then had been considered subversive and anti-revolutionary, was used for war propaganda. Now the regime no longer said, 'Oh, Shi'a faithful stand up' but, 'Oh, nation of Iran stand up.' It might interest you to know that during this operation many young people on the Iranian side who had entered the war for the first time were killed. These young men did not die for religious, Shi'a values; they did not want to become martyrs. They joined and died for the old, pre-revolutionary idea of motherland. It was a strange situation. I cannot express the sense of tragedy to you. I wish, I wish, I wish that we could talk and make films about it. It was one of the most tragic events in human history. We were fighting against Iranians – it's like fighting against your own brother! We spoke Persian on both sides of the frontline, but we were standing against each other – we were shooting each other.

SR: So the regime first appealed to Iranians' religious sentiments and eventually to their nationalistic sentiments to survive. That might have made quite a subject for cinema!

EH: Oh, you cannot imagine what opportunities have been missed! But what happened? Amir Naderi, a film-maker from before the revolution, a film-maker who came from the south and whose home, Khoramshahr and Abadan, became the symbols of cities ravaged by war, made two deeply sad and critical films, *Jostejoo-ye 1* and *Jostejoo-ye 2* [*The Search 1* and *The Search 2*, released in 1980 and 1981 respectively]. They were funded by the Kanoon [Institute for the Intellectual Development of Children and Young Adults]. He was treated quite harshly by the regime at the time, which I think was justifiable to some extent. In such a tense atmosphere, when someone turns up and says, 'Why are you fighting?', this can be very demoralizing for the troops. So the films kicked up a lot of dust. You see, the films were good, but it wasn't right to make them at such a time. When the war was over, some people assumed that now was the time for everyone to come out and say what they really thought about the war. The reality was that things did not happen as they should have done. I was one of the few who went to the south of Iran and the Persian Gulf – the battle grounds – to make my films; great masters, though, like Mr Kiarostami, went in the exact opposite direction, to the north, the idyllic region of the Caspian Sea! So the war divided us into two kinds of film-maker: the one who goes south and the one who goes north.

SR: Did you regard the latter sort as escapists? Many Iranian films at the time were either made in picturesque villages or dealt with the idylls of childhood. In your opinion, was this a kind of escape from reality?

EH: Yes, yes. When you don't see the bigger picture right under your nose you are in a state of denial. This, from my point of view, has a political meaning. For example, Kianoush Ayari, who comes from Ahvaz, a city that still bears the scars of the war, made a film called *Ansouyeh Atash* [*The Other Side of Fire*, 1990] right after the war. The film is about two brothers who fight over an inheritance, while their city, Ahvaz, is under an Iraqi missile attack. He says in his memoirs that the film was symbolic: Iranians and Iraqis were symbolized by the brothers fighting over something that belonged to both of them – in this case oil and the passage to the Persian Gulf. Mr Ayari's other film, *Abadani-ha* [*The Abadanis*, 1994], was based on Vittorio De Sica's *Bicycle Thieves* [1948]. De Sica's film is set in the immediate aftermath of World War II in Italy, where there is so much poverty that the livelihood of a family depends entirely on a bicycle. When it is stolen, they suffer terrible hardship. The film was made in the docu-fiction or *cinéma vérité* style. In Ayari's version the bicycle becomes a car in postwar Abadan in the south of Iran. He was actually making a political statement and obviously faced many restrictions and problems.

These difficulties produced a second type of war film-maker, who was preoccupied with the war but did not want to deal with the difficulties that beset people like Mr Ayari. So these film-makers, such as Mr Kiarostami, went up north. They were actually social film-makers and had a social point of view but knew that going south meant that they would face many restrictions and constraints. So what they did was to play an Iranian, Oriental trick. Instead of going south, they would go north! They would choose a spot in the exact opposite direction of where they should have gone if they'd wanted to make a war film. In this way they could make their war film at a safe distance and avoid the regime's propaganda directives! That's what Kiarostami and Beyzaie did. Beyzaie made his masterpiece about the war – *Bashu, the Little Stranger* – during the worst years of the war [1985–86]. It was a very strong and beautiful film that spoke right from within the heart of the war without being set *in* the war as such. So, to cut a long story short, you see that in reality the regime was not in the least interested in having intellectual film-makers enter the arena of war films. The regime wanted the war to be seen and to be shown in line with official propaganda.

SR: Is not the Iranian audience fed up with the war and war films?

EH: Maybe, but their reality is still determined by war. The memories of war are still there. The streets are still named after martyrs. The families of martyrs are still around.

SR: Yet it seems that no one has time for the victims of war; no one has time for the soldiers and their war stories.

EH: Perhaps that's natural. Any society under the cloud of an eight-year war would react in the same way. The children that grew up then have bad memories from those days. When we rushed to carry them downstairs to the basement during Saddam's missile attacks and our lives were only saved because a house two blocks away got hit instead of ours, well, I think such experiences must have been traumatizing for children. German and British people had the same reaction towards their wars. This is the nature of any society, but the question here is, why didn't our film-makers really get into the subject of war? The same thing could be asked about our contemporary literature. The answer is that you were either an insider and complied with the regime's rules on how to make a film about the war or you were an outsider and there was nothing for you in that subject. In my opinion, this attitude has deprived the Iranian nation of important works of art. Now, some might say that Hatamikia could have made his films 'from the inside' because he was trusted by the regime. They might say that the system has handed me *carte blanche* and I can say whatever I want. As a matter of fact, if you look closely you'll see that, because I've been at the heart of the war – as a soldier, as a member of the Revolutionary Guards – I've always said exactly what I've thought. Of course, as a member of the Sepah who fought under the influence of Islamic ideology, many of the things I had to say were not that incompatible with the regime's propaganda. So they couldn't give me any hassle then. But later on, when I started to become more critical of their politics, they started to throw obstacles in my way. For instance, I made *The Glass Agency* with great difficulty. You see, they could not exclude me or refuse to let me make my films – although they would have very much liked to do so – because of my position as a real 'war kid' – as a real Sepahi. I was one of those who had made sacrifices for the Islamic ideology underpinning the war. So, when I began to be more critical, they could not simply shut me up.

SR: You were one of them.

EH: I am seen as one of them, but that doesn't mean that I have *carte blanche* and can do as I please. Right now the Ministry for Information has stopped my film *Beh Rang-e Arghavan* [*In Purple*, 2004][8] and confiscated all copies – though originally I had been given permission to make it! And everyone thinks that I make films for the Ministry of Culture and Islamic Guidance! When the film was finished they just stopped it – just before the Fajr Film Festival. During Mr Khatami's presidency, the obstacles were gradually lifted. In literature some good works came out on the subject of war, but this was rare. If you look at my film *From Karkheh to Rhine* you will hear dialectical conversations between sister and brother. The sister, who lives in Germany, says that war is a bad thing. The brother says that it depends on your definition of war and from which angle you look at it – sometimes peace is also a bad thing. This is true. By the way, that was the problem the intellectuals had. They did not know how to say something of the sort without sounding propagandistic. This was also a reason – besides the regime putting obstacles in their way – why they could not go south to make films about the war.

In Europe, as a reminder of wartime, they still sound the air-raid sirens once in a while. Everyone should remember the bloodshed; everyone should remember the cause of those wars and also learn that they should not be repeated. In Iran, though, such preoccupation with the war is not allowed. You see, to me, as an

Iranian who lives next to Pakistan, Afghanistan, Iraq and Israel, war and peace are both existential issues. I'm like a child from the poor part of town who, in order to survive, to be able to get some bread for himself, has to learn how to stand up to bullies on the block. Dialogue is not enough. I can't always argue with them. I have to learn some techniques and tricks and I have to react in time. Unfortunately, that is the reality in the East. In the West, the old enemies, some 70 years after World War II, have learnt to defend their interests without fighting a war among themselves.

SR: Speaking about the West, I would like to discuss a subject altogether different from that of war. What role do Western film festivals play in the success of Iranian cinema?

EH: I believe that these festivals have ruined our nature, our style and our taste, just like a destructive virus.

SR: Our films – especially after the revolution – introduced Iran to the world more than any other artform, such as painting or literature and poetry. It was mainly after the revolution that the Iranian New Wave became known around the world. Many film-makers, such as Kiarostami and Beyzaie, believe that this wave had already started before the revolution and would have progressed without it, that the revolution delayed the growth of the wave but at some point had to yield because there was no stopping it. Other film-makers, such as Majidi and Milani, believe that the revolution did play an important role in letting a whole movement grow out of a pre-revolutionary spark. All agree, however, that the revolution was a sort of advertisement for Iranian cinema in the rest of the world. Westerners saw hardly anything coming out of Iran other than chanting, burning flags and making fists, so this made them curious about feature films coming out of the country. What do you think about the globalization of our cinema?

EH: I don't believe in this globalization business at all. As the saying goes, 'Each person should look after his own camel.' Doomed is that culture that wants to change its nature through politics!

Getting permission to screen your films at festivals is a political game. Many films that had been banned from being screened in Iran by the Ministry of Culture and Islamic Guidance then got permission to be shown at foreign festivals after the intervention of the Ministry of Foreign Affairs! The Ministry of Foreign Affairs has always had this *idée fixe* that screening Iranian art-house films at festivals would be like raising the Iranian flag. When political interests are involved then the issue turns into something else.

SR: Do you mean that the Ministry of Foreign Affairs benefits from the festivals? In what way?

EH: Yes, in my opinion the Ministry of Foreign Affairs benefited most from overseas festivals. The bad thing, though, is that foreigners reaped the fruits that were meant for our own country. You know, it's like, 'we need wheat in our country but the Europeans want kiwi'. So instead of growing wheat we grow kiwi so that we can sell it to the Europeans and buy wheat from them with the money! If our society needs wheat, then let it grow its own wheat. Let our cinema deal with our own issues. Why should we make films based on other people's tastes? In my opinion the person most responsible for this trend in Iran is Mr Kiarostami, who makes films in the way *they* want them to be made. Of course, Kiarostami is completely original in his manner. I mean, he doesn't copy anyone else and he does not pretend; he really works and lives like that. He is the perfect example of a European film-maker. His intellectual and humanistic way of looking at things is the same as that of a French intellectual. And we see that these films have either a romantic look or are very sharp and radical in their realism – just as the French like it! Masoud Kimiai is another example – not as original as Kiarostami, but someone who's aware of the signs of the time and makes his films accordingly. His film *Snake Fang* [1990] was of that sort. The setting of that film is Abadan, a city riddled with prostitution and corruption after the war. The film has a very 'filthy' atmosphere about it. It was selected for the Berlin Film Festival right away and won a prize, yet in Iran it hardly got any attention at all.

SR: You cannot deny that these festivals were an opportunity for Iranian films to get noticed in the rest of the world – especially a chance for films that couldn't easily get screened in Iran.

EH: Yes, but the festivals hardly made a difference to our film-makers in Iran. I mean, international attention did not help us acquire greater freedom in our work. The forbidden films were shown at festivals, but the bans were not lifted here in Iran. But there is a positive aspect to these festivals, which is that they brought respect for the Iranian film-maker, who had been humiliated in his own country or had not been given due attention and respect. Naturally, a humiliated artist who is treated with respect abroad would continue to behave and talk in the way that brought him this respect. However, we shouldn't forget that although a foreign distributor or producer may respect the film-maker, he also thinks about his own pocket! Making a film in Iran is virtually free of the financial risk involved in making one in the US or Europe. The producers and distributors can thus have their cake and eat it – making excellent films to European tastes and hardly putting any money into them!

Now, the question is, what sort of films do they want from us? They like the primitive look of Eastern cinema – either stories from the *One Thousand and One Nights*, where you see people riding camels in the middle of Tehran, or films showing extremely poor and backward people. They want to see our women giving birth behind a bush or the misery of a family who have to share one pair of shoes between them!

SR: So, you think that many of our film-makers feed the West with such images and, in that way, condone the way in which the West views us?

EH: This is a chicken-and-egg question. Was it they who asked first or was it we who fed them first? It all began with Kiarostami's *Where is the Friend's Home?*. Amidst the deluge of Hollywood films, with all their high-tech effects and melodramatic stories, here was a film about a child who wants to return the notebook of his friend. Western viewers took great pleasure in its simplicity. It was an original film and of completely the right kind. Other Iranian film-makers thought, 'Aha! Over there they like such films! So, let's start making more!' But when I watch such films, I can't recognize my own country in them! I ask myself after every screening, 'Why are we portraying ourselves as primitive people? Is this the only depiction of Iranians that foreigners want to see?' Kiarostami often has his characters drive Renault cars – the epitome of the French automobile industry. Why? You can't hide these things.

In my opinion, Kiarostami is the pioneer of a movement which is more interested in being appreciated by a European rather than an Iranian audience. Other film-makers have begun to copy him. Unfortunately it has now got to the point where we have a type of film called the 'festival film'. It is a kind of cinema that involves no effort of any sort. The technique used is of the simplest variety. It only has to be the opposite of high-tech Hollywood films and that is enough for the 'intellectual' festival goers in the West! The first such film, even before Kiarostami, was Shahid Saless's *Still Life* [1974], a political film, as it happens, which creates an atmosphere full of numbness and malaise. It was apparently in vogue in Europe in the early 1970s! Later on, though, when fashion amongst European intellectuals had changed, Iranian film-makers started to make films according to the new taste! If you want a spiritual film, they will make a spiritual film; if you want an action film, they'll make it; if you want a romantic film, they'll make it.

SR: Either way, we see that in the last few years international interest in Iranian cinema has grown. In your opinion, has the revolution had an effect here or would this have happened anyway?

EH: The revolution has definitely had an effect on the way our cinema has developed. On the whole, Iranian cinema as an artform had come to a dead end. Around 1975–76, Iranian cinema had nothing to say. Of course, there were some interesting films, such as those of Kiarostami and Mehrjui, but they were a flash in the pan. In reality, our cinema was completely overshadowed by Hollywood and Europe. After the revolution, and with the establishment of the Farabi Cinema Foundation under the leadership of Mohammad Beheshti, who, in my view, is the most important architect of our new cinema, our film industry was able to grow into an important movement. Our film-makers were now free to say what they had to say.

SR: Some people in the film business think of the Farabi as an extension of the Ministry of Culture and Islamic Guidance which implemented censorship policies merely in a more civilized and gentle manner! Some disagree and say that the Farabi was a mediator between film-makers and those fanatics who were against cinema altogether. As Beheshti himself puts it, the Farabi was like a gardener who tried to protect the young buds of Iranian cinema from both the storms of Islamist censorship and the overpowering influence of Hollywood and Film Farsi. How do you see the Farabi's role?

EH: Now, after 20-odd years, this issue can be discussed without it becoming politicized. From my point of view, Mr Beheshti was largely responsible for our success as film-makers. He managed to show the government that they could have cinema without thinking of it as an anti-Islamic threat. Although the government faced many political and financial problems in those days, they trusted us enough to provide us with the material means necessary for film-making. Mr Beheshti was able to convince the government to give us a chance to develop in a relatively calm environment – and that in the middle of war and unrest. Anybody who denies the influence of the Farabi and that of Mr Beheshti should remember the degenerate, decadent situation in pre-revolutionary Iran, where intellectual film-makers were given no space to thrive. They could hardly progress, because the shah's system had its own agenda, based on its own capitalist rules.

Of course, capitalism is more or less back on the agenda and determines increasingly what our film-makers do. Our cinema is becoming more and more like that of the West, where supply and demand rules. It is now the fundraisers who decide what kind of film should be made. We are now at a point where the Dutch embassy, for example, funds Iranian films and in that way has a say in how they should be made. This is the most tragic situation possible. Those Iranian film-makers whose projects are funded by foreigners don't care about the development of our cinema. They know that their films won't get screened in Iran anyway. Kiarostami complains that his films are not screened in Iran, yet outside Iran he's respected and they make such a fuss over him!

Now, next to film-makers such as Kiarostami, we have those whose films receive little attention outside Iran but are very important for our country and society. Their films look at Iranian identity within Iran and seek a dialogue with the Iranian audience. This I call the 'national cinema' – it's those of us who insist on protecting the specifically Iranian elements of our cinema and, yet, we are the most vulnerable people in the business today.

SR: You have said much in defence of the Farabi Cinema Foundation. Let's not forget that it was the Farabi that was very active in getting our films shown at Western festivals. Would you not say that the Farabi is slightly responsible for the vulnerability of what you call the 'national cinema' and the success of what you call 'festival films'?

EH: This is indeed the case. However, the attention given to festivals was not supposed to take over our cinema completely – they were supposed to help us introduce ourselves to the world. But somehow things got out of hand. It is analogous to farming. To increase fertility you use chemical fertilizers and pesticides. But these have certain side effects; they can make your land barren if you overuse them. I am not denying for a second that the Farabi under Mr Beheshti initiated the globalization of our cinema, but those who succeeded him should have controlled this process better. As a film-maker I've been to a few festivals but there, on the red carpet, where they asked me to be someone I didn't want to be, I refused to participate. I felt that I didn't fit in. Yet I have seen many Iranian film-makers who couldn't wait to be approached by foreign producers and companies. I once saw one of our very fine film-makers, who has decided to leave Iran for good –

SR: Do you mean Mr Makhmalbaf?

EH: No, and I don't want to mention any names, if you don't mind. He's always been a very dedicated film-maker and made a point of refusing to cut any shots from his films – no matter how minor the change might have been – if those changes had been demanded by the Ershad. Yet, at the same time, he'd send the first 'rough cut' of his film to the head of the Cannes Film Festival and ask whether it was all right! If they asked him to intensify the drama, for example, he'd see to it that their demands were met! Out of respect for this artist I won't name him, but I believe there are dirty dealings going on behind the closed doors of these festivals.

SR: Do you mean that just as the Ershad imposes censorship on films, the festivals do the very same thing and so we end up with two kinds of censorship?

EH: Yes. That is exactly what I'm saying. The image of me in the Western media is that of a terrorist. This is the mentality that has been ingrained in their minds. Now, if an Iranian film-maker decides to talk about the human condition or says that his subject matter is philosophy – you know, like Theo Angelopoulos[9] would do – they'd look at him or her with raised eyebrows.

SR: So, Iran is either a romantically backward country, with poor, happy kids in an untouched countryside sharing a single pair of shoes, as in Majidi's Oscar-nominated film, *Children of Heaven*, or it's a place where urban life is horrible, with city-dwellers suffering from poverty, corruption and violence and having no chance to escape, as in Panahi's *The Circle* – which was actually produced by the French company MK2.

EH: Exactly.

SR: Do you think that the West is really interested in our suffering – in the unofficial truth – or do they just want to confirm that they are superior to us in all ways?

EH: It could be both. There's our underground film-making tradition, which only serves the interests of the West. Those films are not made for an Iranian audience. Our dear Mr Ghobadi shoots an underground film about rap singers in Iran and then makes a huge fuss about how he had to smuggle it out of the country. The Western festivals like films that have been smuggled out! The Makhmalbafs are another example. The Kurds live in Iran, Syria, Turkey and Iraq and have often fought the central government and demanded independence. Now, how is it that Samira Makhmalbaf makes a film about Kurdistan, Mr Makhmalbaf makes a film about Kurdistan, Mr Kiarostami makes a film about Kurdistan, and Mr Ghobadi, who is actually the only Kurdish person among them, makes a film about Kurdistan? What I'm trying to say is how come Kurdistan suddenly becomes the subject of our films? Could all this be a coincidence? We are aware that Kurdistan is an issue in Europe and that Europeans want to provoke the poor Kurds into starting trouble in this region. Well, my question to Mr Kiarostami is, what are you doing in Kurdistan? Why don't you go south? We had a war down south for eight years. Why did you go to Kurdistan at that time? I can't just say that it was a coincidence and Kiarostami just happened to decide to make a film about Kurdistan. There's definitely a market for it – a market that unfortunately smells of politics and many other things. In my opinion, such matters compromise the artist's integrity.

SR: So, you agree with Mr Beheshti that having the freedom to seek out foreign investors does not make Iranian film-makers freer but actually makes them vulnerable to exploitation?

EH: This exploitation results from the media, politics and the market acting jointly. Every time I see one of these Iranian films I became furious. I don't want to name any of them, except Jafar Panahi's *The Circle*, which utterly enraged me.

SR: Yes.

EH: Some people had been pushing me to do something about this. What could I do? How could I protest against such films? Would anyone want to listen to me? If showing images of Iran like those in Panahi's *The Circle* puts us on the international scene, I'd much prefer not to have that international attention! Why doesn't this happen to Western-made films? Less than a year ago a man in Austria who had locked his own daughter in his basement and raped her and had children by her was imprisoned for life. Why don't the Austrians make a film about that?

SR: Knowing the Austrians, they would definitely make a film about it. If they do, however, it wouldn't be such a big deal, really. They don't feel that that monstrous man is typical of Austria.

EH: That is not true. A friend of mine asked an Austrian film-maker why they don't make a film about this subject. The Austrian said, 'Should I make a film that shows the Austrians in such a bad light?' Why do Austrians feel this way and we don't? Think of Samira Makhmalbaf's *The Apple* [1998], where a man imprisons his two kids in a house in order to protect them from the evil world outside. Why should someone make such a film? Doesn't she realize that her country is mocked because of films like this?

SR: The point is, if an Austrian makes a film on that subject, it will be one among hundreds of other films. It won't necessarily be seen as indicative of Austrian society.

EH: No it won't. No one will ever say that all Austrians are like that.

SR: That's right. That film will become a film among thousands of others. Our problem, though, is of a different nature. When our films go to festivals, they reflect our own identity. So the issue for us is much more critical and sensitive. However, some say that it's the government's fault. They say that the Iranian government's policies have created such a bad image of our people and our country that the West cannot think of us differently.

EH: It has nothing to do with the government. The problem is that we have forgotten our own culture and literature. Mr Beheshti rightly points to the codes of behaviour that have been handed down to us through the centuries. The guilds of butchers and bakers all have their own codes on how to treat people, what hierarchy to respect, and so on. How come we don't have such a code in cinema? Why don't we have a code by which we learn how to respect ourselves. Why do we not learn how not to accept funding from another country that likes to dictate to us what films to make?

SR: To a large extent the situation is like that because of the government's policies. One of these policies concerns the depiction of women in our cinema. Representing women – their sexuality, their eroticism – is very difficult in Iran. It means that you cannot see half of Iranian society unless they're wearing a *hijab*. On the other hand, there are those such as Mr Beheshti who regard this kind of censorship as a good thing. They say that before the revolution roles for women in films were extremely limited: they'd be either lascivious sex bombs or tearful weaklings. Once censorship was imposed on our cinema, film-makers were forced to depict alternative dimensions of women. So, in order to access these other dimensions, we had to sacrifice the sexual and erotic dimensions of being a woman.

Yet, most of our film-makers – and most of those I've interviewed – don't agree with this interpretation. They say that they are unable to depict romantic and erotic love as they happen in this country every day! For them this is a great loss and means that an important part of life *as it is* has be sacrificed in the name of Islam.

EH: I don't know what exactly you mean by eroticism. Are you talking about pure lust?

SR: Partly. Eroticism can relate to pure lust but it can also relate to love. For instance, if you want to portray non-Platonic love between a man and a woman, you as a film-maker cannot even show them holding hands! You could only show them pass a glass to each other, for example, even if they're supposed to be married in the story – and, as a matter of fact, even if the actor and actress are married in real life, you could still not show any physical contact between them on screen!

EH: We're talking about two different things here. One is sex, which attracts large audiences. Well, the depiction of sex was banned in films so that the audience could concentrate on other important aspects of human interaction! But let me tell you, many films about love *have* been made in Iran. Of course we have problems in this area. One is the issue of the *hijab*, which, to be honest, can only be dealt with by the highest assembly of our clergy in the holy city of Qum! As long as this country is called an Islamic Republic, the *hijab* issue can only be resolved in that city, I'm afraid! And, as we all know, they will refuse to rescind the law requiring the wearing of the *hijab* – both in real life and in film. At the same time, we do portray women tossing and turning in bed – they toss in bed with their *hijab* on! Now, does that not count as erotic? In a film such as *Nar o Ney* [*The Pomegranate and the Cane*, 1989] by Saeed Ebrahimifar, lovemaking and marriage are all visualized symbolically. We have many such films that say what they want to say through symbolism and implication, which have become a sort of language in themselves. During Mr Khatami's presidency, cinema opened up and suddenly there was a flood of these romantic films.

SR: Is censorship a good thing, in that it forces the artist to be creative in order to bypass restrictions?

EH: I don't know about that. When you ask me whether censorship is good or bad, it's like asking me whether oxygen is good or bad. How could I say oxygen is bad? Oxygen is required for breathing, but too much of it could burn your lungs.

SR: Censorship can hardly be compared to oxygen. I would think it has more in common with carbon dioxide or carbon monoxide!

EH: Censorship in itself is a bad thing. If someone imposes limitations on me and forces me to do things I don't like, naturally it's not a good thing. I am a grown up, right? No one likes restrictions, be it for financial, political, religious or cultural reasons. The fact is that we owe everyone respect. When we respect people, we should respect their culture as well. The *hijab* is part of our culture. If someone says that our cinema's problem is the *hijab*, they're wrong. Nowadays, if someone wears a pile of fabric on her head instead of a scarf, we don't even notice! We've learned to disregard the *hijab* in our films; we have learnt not to reduce the woman underneath the scarf to that piece of cloth on her head. Automatically our eyes don't see. Someone abroad might think, why is this woman wearing a *hijab* in this scene even though she's alone with her husband? But we in Iran don't register that. I've no issues with the *hijab*. It's different in the West, but the *hijab* is everywhere in the Middle East. That's the way it is. Such religious restrictions exist and breaking them will lead to a strong reaction because the government is a religious government. We are still in the transitory stage – we are still torn between tradition and modernity. Even in Europe the issue of women's rights was tackled step by step. In Sweden women didn't have the right to vote till 30 years ago.

SR: You mean Switzerland.

EH: Sorry, yes, Switzerland. What I'm trying to say is that such developments should progress piecemeal – whether we like it or not. We live in a traditional country. When we want to get married we go to a mullah to perform the ceremony. You can't eliminate a tradition and set it aside overnight. Please don't get me wrong, though: I am not a defender of censorship at all.

SR: Now, the question is whether censorship is good for art – whether it 'fertilizes' creativity.

EH: Censorship usually does make the artist become creative and inventive. He or she has to look for new ways of doing things. Symbolism is one way. Incidentally, we have an abundance of symbols and metaphors in the East and that's how we talk among ourselves. We are very complicated in this regard. But this is what makes our art and literature beautiful. Take a moment to look at

our architecture, for example, and then go and look at the architecture of Canada, a newly built country. You go four steps and
reach the entrance door, five steps and reach the bedroom and
you think, 'Wow! What a simple and straightforward people!' But
our history and civilization span many millennia; our country has
had to absorb many languages and cultures from all corners of
the world and our people have had to endure numerous invasions.
Well, obviously, in such a country architecture is very different
from that of Canada. Our traditional houses are full of corridors
and hallways and courtyards and private and public areas. Each
has its private parts – yes, almost as in a human body – and not
everyone is allowed everywhere. Now, someone with no knowledge
of our traditions would wonder why such a house is so complex.
I'll give you an example of our mentality: if you ask a person from
Isfahan how much his house cost, he'll answer, 'Why do you ask?'
and make jokes typical of an Isfahani. But if you ask an American
the same question, he'll give you a straightforward answer and tell
you about his mortgage details, his salary, and so on. Yes, but there
are reasons for our complexity and their straightforwardness.

SR: Might this complexity not slow us down on our path towards
modernity, democracy and new forms of thought and art?

EH: I don't know. I'm not much of an expert on this subject, but I
believe that when the time is right, the fruit will ripen. Everything
happens in time.

SR: What is our artistic background in cinema? There's this
complexity in our traditional literature and art, as you've just
mentioned. However, cinema is a modern artform imported
from the West. What is surprising is that in Iran this imported
art has found very fertile ground and is very successful, whereas
our contemporary poetry and other forms of literature are almost
unknown abroad. Why is that?

EH: It's difficult to answer this question. The USA, with its
200-year history, is much further ahead of us in all arts, and yet

we have thousands of years of history and civilization behind us. I think that we have 'contracted' some kind of forgetfulness; we suffer from being in awe of the West, and, despite our 'anti-West' revolution, feel deeply inferior to them and want to be like them. We have forgotten our own achievements. I believe that this sense of awe originated in the Safavid era – in the 1500s CE – when we were introduced to the West. We can see the same sense of awe in the reign of Nasser al-Din Shah Qajar [1848–96], who brought the cinematograph and the camera from Europe to Iran. We were both puzzled and dazzled like children! I believe that we can only achieve our own Iranian modernity if we shake ourselves out of this starry-eyed awe. I am hopeful.

SR: Let's go back to the question I asked earlier. Why is our cinema so much more successful than our contemporary literature? Is this only because the medium of cinema – the moving image – is easier to consume than books?

EH: I don't know much about literature, but what you are saying rings very true. Yes, we have been able to use a modern medium of art and develop it.

SR: Surely your success cannot simply be attributed to the medium?

EH: I can only speak for myself. I wouldn't make a film if I didn't have something to say – if I did not have a message. Being where I am now means that I've got something to say. Of course you can only say something meaningful if you carry emotional baggage. You know, a film-maker's heart must be filled with emotions – he or she can only be free from this sea of emotion by making art. Artistic expression is an act of liberation. Unfortunately Iranian cinema today has become a race where finance and the market determine lots of things.

SR: Do you think that you can influence the audience by your works?

EH: A long time ago, in an interview about my film *The Scout*, I said, 'Even if only two people come to see my film, I'm happy. I have a debt to history which I hope to repay at least partly with this film. The rest is not important to me.' Today I don't think like that. I can only make a film if I am sure that at least two million people will come to see it! The rules of the game are different now. I have to stay in the race if I want to survive at all as a film-maker. I need as many tickets sold as possible – something that I absolutely did not care about while Mr Beheshti managed the Farabi Cinema Foundation. In those days I made my film and did not worry about whether the audience would attend or not. Now the situation is such that I don't want any money from the government because their funding agencies want *me* to say what *they* want to say! So, I need private funding, but this follows the rules of the market and I need to be careful. In order to keep my artistic and social integrity and at the same time create something attractive to the audience I have to be very skilful. Times are very tough. When I made *Invitation* [2008], some of my younger and more idealistic fans were really angry because of the presence of quite a few stars in the film. In an online poll they said that they would never have expected Hatamikia to use stars in order to lure people to the cinema! Fortunately when the film was screened, it was clear to everyone that I wasn't looking to film stars as a selling point and that the stars who acted in it were able to convey my message very well. It was clear that I didn't want to show them off and make a blockbuster. Anyway, times are tough now for committed film-makers.

SR: Couldn't this tough situation push you into an internal exile or even into the Iranian diaspora? Many of our artist, writers and film-makers had no choice, or at least felt they had no choice, but to leave the country – Hedayat, Golestan and Naderi are prominent examples. Have you ever felt that you were in a similar situation?

EH: To be honest, when I came back to Tehran from the battlefield, I felt like a total stranger – and so did my comrades. I objected to the hypocrisy in the city. And in my films I try to convey this feeling.

SR: Do you mean that Tehran was your exile?

EH: Well, it felt like a sort of exile. We had been at war for eight years and whenever we came back to the city we felt alienated. We felt as if our views and ways didn't fit in. On the battlefield, for example, money didn't mean anything to us. But our relationship to each other was very strong – we were all friends and each one of us knew that we could die at any moment. In such situations people naturally have strong feelings for their friends and companions. But in the city, the first issue we faced when getting off the train was money – we had to pay for a taxi ride! We thought everyone was greedy and it made us mad. We actually longed to get back to the battlefield. This feeling is common all over the world. I was watching Spielberg's *Saving Private Ryan* [1998] and it showed exactly the same phenomenon – American soldiers feel the same way as Iranian soldiers when they return to the city from the battlefield! Life in the city is very complicated, but at the front everything is simple and you know with brutal clarity that you can die any minute; you live intensely in the present. So a soldier has to be completely honest and straightforward with himself if he wants to bear the heat of war. He won't last there a second if he has complex feelings and thoughts! Don't forget that many soldiers have fond memories of the war. You might ask how is it possible for someone to be in the middle of bloodshed and have fond memories of it! But when you have breathed in the air of the battlefield, when you've felt it in your own flesh and soul, you deal differently with your feelings and with yourself. You are more honest with yourself. There, when someone says, 'I love you', he means it. He says it not expecting anything in return. He is not manipulating anyone. His heart is as pure as a mirror, as the saying goes.

SR: Besides feeling alienated in the city and in face of its complexities, do you feel in exile in Iran as such?

EH: Of course I don't. As time goes by, my Iranianness, so to speak, becomes more and more important to me. I now have a family. I have three children, I have a son in-law and I will soon have grandchildren. My life is changing and so are my thoughts. I look at things differently. I mean, I can no longer go backpacking wherever I want. Soon I will turn 50 and will want to settle down. I've travelled abroad many times. It was quite nice, but I want to live in Iran. Living abroad doesn't suit my nature.

11

MOHSEN MAKHMALBAF
An Interview That Never Was

I MET MOHSEN MAKHMALBAF FOR THE FIRST AND ONLY TIME at the
Munich International Film Festival in June 2006. At the time, I
had completed an outline of my project and had a few ideas about
how to approach the film-makers I intended to interview in Iran
(some of whom are notorious for their lack of trust in 'outsiders').
Winning Makhmalbaf over, I thought – quite naively, with hind-
sight – could prove crucial to the realization of my project. A few
minutes before his talk began, I approached him and introduced
myself. He seemed polite and attentive when I told him about the
project I had in mind. I explained that it would be extremely kind
and helpful of him if he agreed to be the first person to be interviewed, because his participation would make it easier for me to
gain access to the other Iranian film-makers living in Iran. He and
his colleagues are notoriously suspicious of 'interviewers' who more
often than not turn their interviewees' words round and exploit
them for their own political ends, whether within Iran or abroad.
However, if he consented to talk to me, the others would trust my
intentions.

He asked me about the aim of the project, whether I had
already started 'networking', and which film-makers I had in mind.
I answered that the project was concerned with the role that film-

makers living and working in Iran play in Iranian cinema and how their work has influenced society after the revolution, and vice versa. I had already started networking, I added, and was pretty sure that Mohammad Beheshti, the former head of the Farabi Cinema Foundation, and Jafar Panahi, who had made a name for himself by making documentary-style neo-realist films such as *Offside* (2006), would see me. I also showed him the Persian edition of my book *Iranian Writers Uncensored* and explained that the format and structure of the new project would be similar to that book. As I described the project and its aims, I noticed that Makhmalbaf's initial interest and openness began to vanish. When he heard the names of the film-makers I planned to interview, he looked somewhat disconcerted and annoyed. He talked less and less, but at the end of our conversation said that he would talk to me later, after the press conference.

The press conference was the most interesting episode of the entire meeting. It seemed as if Makhmalbaf had directed the *mise-en-scène*. The whole event seemed almost ritualized, like something out of an Iranian religious 'passion' play (known as *Ta'zieh*). The Makhmalbaf family, whose members are all involved in filmmaking and collaborate with each other to such an extent that it is often impossible to tell who has made this film or that, was called out by the presenter. The family, all dressed in black, consisting of the master himself, his two daughters, Samira and Hanna, his son, Meysam, and his wife, Marzieh Meshkini (who also happens to be the sister of his former wife, Fatemeh Meshkini, who died in a tragic accident), made their entrance from both sides of the stage and, after a short bow, took their seats. It struck me that, except for Mohsen Makhmalbaf, who stood erect, showing off a well-built frame (except for a small potbelly, perhaps), and exuded an air of authority and superiority, the rest of the family were extremely thin and stooped and looked shyly at their shoes and at each other. I could not help feeling that I was watching a sect rather than a group of directors, whose charismatic leader sat on a throne amidst his humble, adoring followers.

After quite a lengthy laudatory introduction, the presenter announced that he would pose some essential questions to the

Makhmalbaf family and that afterwards the audience would be able to ask whatever questions they had. However, owing to the tight schedule, there would be time for only three questions. The presenter went on to portray the Makhmalbaf family as a creative lot who, thanks to their 'alternative education', had a unique view of reality; this, in turn, enabled them to make their films in their celebrated neo-realist trademark manner. The presenter laid great emphasis on the role of the 'informal' education that Makhmalbaf had given his children, niece, nephews and even friends in all possible subjects. Makhmalbaf had taken his children out of school at a young age and constantly encouraged his friends to do the same. The main achievement of this 'instruction' was that it had made the children question the country's education system as a whole and thus forced them to use their own judgement in every situation. Through his approach to schooling, the presenter went on to say, Makhmalbaf had declared war on the state's brainwashing methods.

What caught my attention during this glowing introduction was the emphasis given to the issue of education and to Makhmalbaf's seemingly unlimited pedagogic abilities. The presenter also mentioned that in 1974, the 17-year-old Makhmalbaf, still at school at the time, was arrested for shooting a police officer and sentenced to five years in prison.[1] He was freed after the victory of the Islamic Revolution in 1979 and, at the young age of 22, became almost at once an 'Islamic film-maker' with missionary tendencies.[2] However, it was not mentioned where and how he had acquired all his knowledge of art, literature, history, chemistry, mathematics and biology.

The second thing that caught my attention was the absolute devotion of the family to the father, not at all typical of a 'normal' family but rather of a sectarian or religious group in which absolute obedience and devotion to the master is expected. Throughout the press conference, whenever the children and the wife were addressed, they would look at the father rather than the audience while answering the questions. Perhaps it was out of shyness; however, for a family so used to the international platform, this seemed unlikely.

All in all, the greater part of the introduction was devoted to the importance of self-education in the Makhmalbaf family, thanks to the breadth of the father's wisdom and knowledge. The presenter also reminded the audience what they already knew, namely, that all family members are film-makers and that for them, film-making is a family project. This is why they all deal with the same subjects – for example, the repressed people of Afghanistan, Tajikistan and Kurdistan. All films are made and edited under the supervision of the father, Mohsen Makhmalbaf. It was also mentioned that Hanna Makhmalbaf, the youngest film-making member of the family, made her first film at the age of 14. The audience seemed impressed by this family of autodidacts.

After the presenter had finished his introduction, it was Mohsen Makhmalbaf's turn to tell the audience of his family's projects. He spoke in Persian, with his son Meysam translating into English. Mohsen Makhmalbaf started his talk with a long list of complaints about Western governments and their strict immigration policies. He stated that he was deeply disheartened and disappointed by the indifference of the West towards his family's difficult situation. Arguing in a manner reminiscent of Émile Zola's 'J'accuse',[3] he asked how a country like France, the spearhead of nations that championed art and freedom, could refuse to grant a residence permit to a family that had collectively won more international awards than any other. It looked as if the Makhmalbafs were truly offended by the way in which the Western authorities had treated them.

In the course of my subsequent research on Makhmalbaf, I learnt that a couple of years after this press conference the family did succeed in acquiring a French residence permit and now live in Paris. I also learnt that Makhmalbaf had become politically active in exile, campaigning and serving as a spokesperson for the 'reformist' presidential candidate Mir-Hossein Mousavi, who lost against Mahmoud Ahmadinejad in the questionable, perhaps fraudulent, presidential election of 2009.[4] Makhmalbaf's opposition to the regime and its then Leader, Ayatollah Khamenei, was particularly interesting considering that, after his release from prison at the outbreak of the 1979 revolution, he had become a fiercely Islamic ideologist who, in accordance with Ayatollah Khomeini's guide-lines, believed strongly that cinema ought to serve the educative and missionary purposes of Shi'a Islam.[5] His early films, such as *Boycott* (1985), *The Street Vendor* (1986), *The Cyclist* (1987), *Dastforoush* (*The Peddler,* 1989) and *Arousi–ye Khouban* (*The Marriage of the Blessed,* 1989), testify to his Islamic, missionary zeal.

Despite my efforts, as I shall explain below, I did not manage to interview one of the most important figures in post-revolutionary Iranian cinema, so instead I met some of his colleagues, critics and fellow film-makers in Iran to get a better picture of him. Some of the people I met are interviewed in this book. However, everyone who talked to me about Makhmalbaf asked to remain anonymous. All without exception pointed to Makhmalbaf's aesthetic intel-ligence (some went so far as to call him a 'genius'), courage and unwavering determination. Interestingly, most interviewees saw him as someone who had come from 'below' and was determined to conquer those 'above'. When I told them about the family being educated at home, most interviewees said that Makhmalbaf's lack of academic education is a vital clue to understanding his rebellious spirit. Some even went so far as to say that over the years his lack of formal education grew into a sort of 'complex' and determined his development from a critical film-maker into an 'outsider'. His imprisonment as a young man during the shah's reign was a turn-ing point in his life, they said.

One of the interviewees told me that in the beginning of his career all Makhmalbaf needed was a camera and an Islamic subject. Together with fellow film-makers such as Majid Majidi and Habib Sadeghi, Makhmalbaf started working in the newly founded Hozeh-ye Honari-ye Sazman-e Tablighat-e Eslami (abbreviated as 'Hozeh Honari'), whose aim was to Islamize art and literature in Iran.[6] Their task was to make films that propagated Islamic values and condemned the decadence of life in Iran before the 1979 revolution. At the Hozeh Honari, where formal education was not as important as the 'right kind' of ideological fervour, new doors were suddenly opened to the young Makhmalbaf. However, some of the interviewees in this book thought that it was exactly this lack of formal education that made Makhmalbaf's films interesting.

He looked at everything like a child – the technique was perhaps clumsy and unlearned (if not crude), but there was a freshness to his films. Later on in his career, he would improve the technique but maintain that early freshness.

I put this view to one of the interviewees critical of Makhmalbaf, and he replied that, although this might be true, he felt that Makhmalbaf always attributed his lack of success in the early years of his career to a lack of formal education. Makhmalbaf typically sought to blame those early disappointments on critics, fellow film-makers and 'ignorant' viewers, instead of taking responsibility for the weaknesses of his work. This attitude led him to conceive of himself as a rebel, as someone always in opposition, despite his later worldwide success with films such as *Gabbeh* (1996) and *Kandahar* (2001). He seemed to be constantly under the belief that he is either misunderstood or not properly understood by the ignorant masses. Some of the interviewees thought that this attitude fostered Makhmalbaf's courage and experimentalism – his determination to push the boundaries. One of his fellow film-makers said that Makhmalbaf was the first member to rise against the rigid restrictions and policies of the Hozeh Honari. In his view *The Peddler* and *The Marriage of the Blessed*, which were made during Makhmalbaf's time at the Hozeh Honari, were turning points in his career. These films, which were a kind of manifesto against the rigid ideology of the Hozeh Honari, helped him escape the tight confines of that institution – a rebellion that was much more radical than Majidi's, for example, who went on to receive an Oscar nomination for his film *Children of Heaven* (1997). After the break with the Hozeh Honari, Makhmalbaf, who had started his career as a promoter of Islamic ideology, did not fit in with any of the cultural institutions in post-revolutionary Iran. Gradually this drove him into inner and eventually physical exile, at which point he felt forced to leave the country.

On the other hand, some of the interviewees thought that Makhmalbaf's exile had nothing to do with his resistance to the regime but to the simple fact that he had fallen foul of the disease that affects many 'illiterate' artists and intellectuals who 'read' a lot of books without a guiding hand. Because of that, he saw himself

as a 'misunderstood' and 'oppressed' artist. His international fame
only exacerbated these feelings within him. One of the interviewees
said that Makhmalbaf, once he had acquired national and international recognition, was unable to cope with the fame that came
with it. He did not know how to handle fame and took applause
for granted, like a child-actor caught in the limelight. He did
not possess the patience and depth that come with 'real' education, experience and, of course, failure, without which an artist
cannot survive the ups and downs of praise and criticism. Thirsty
for praise, he left Iranian subjects and moved on to Afghanistan,
Tajikistan and other countries. It was at that point, these interviewees believe, that his films became trivial. Some even went so far
as to call him an 'opportunist' who bends any way the wind blows
for the sake of praise: *Kandahar*, his 'Bush-friendly' film, as critics
call it, was lauded in the White House and used for propaganda
purposes during the invasion of Afghanistan in 2002 and 2003.
By then Makhmalbaf had gone through a change typical of many
ideologues – from ardent Islamic propagandist to a favourite of
the arch-enemy of the Islamic Revolution, namely, the 'crusaders'
under George W. Bush. When I reminded my interviewees of his
open support for the Green Movement, they dismissed it as a show
put on for the sake of the West. They saw their scepticism regarding his activism confirmed by his participation in the Jerusalem
Film Festival in 2013 which was, in their eyes, at best an attention-
seeker's attempt at taboo-breaking and at worst an opportunist's
attempt at 'bootlicking' the most important ally of the imperialist
West in the Middle East. They all thought that since his departure
from Iran, Makhmalbaf has not produced a single worthwhile film.

Admittedly, the views of various interviewees on Makhmalbaf
were often not only contradictory but occasionally quite exag-
gerated.[7] I had the impression that some of them felt personally
affronted by him. Nevertheless, they all agreed on two things:
one was Makhmalbaf's lack of formal education and the other
was his rebellious nature. The 2006 Munich Film Festival was
indeed an opportunity for me to experience both these aspects of
Makhmalbaf's personality at first hand. After the end of the press
conference, I went up to him, as had been agreed beforehand, to

fix a date for the interview. I told him that I was truly lucky to have
him as my first interviewee because that would definitely open the
doors to other notoriously distrustful artists who live and work
under the Islamic regime in Iran. Makhmalbaf and his daughter Samira gave me a friendly, unassuming smile and asked me
to call them at 10 o'clock the following day so that they could fix
the time and place for the interview. For that purpose, I was given
the mobile number of a young Iranian student at the Munich Film
Academy who acted as a sort of personal assistant to the family. I
skipped happily towards the underground station – my project was
about to take off.

The next day I called the young student, as agreed. Sahar, as
she was called (I took that as a good omen, as my daughter has
the same name), affably and politely forwarded me to the *Ustad* –
the 'Master'. After a few seconds Makhmalbaf came to the phone
and in a very aggressive and impolite manner, skipping the typical
flowery Persian greetings, said:

'Madam, I am not going to take part in your project because I
do not even see myself as part of New Iranian Cinema.'

I, as if a bucket of cold water had been poured over my head,
replied in a trembling voice: 'But Sir, how can you not see yourself
as part of this school?'

Makhmalbaf answered: 'I left Iran for good over a year ago.'

Unconvinced, I persisted: 'But, Mr Makhmalbaf, you have made
almost all your films in Iran.'

'That is not true,' he retorted. 'My latest films were made in
Afghanistan and Tajikstan.'

'It is true that you have spent the last year outside of Iran,' I
conceded, 'but the films that established you as a world-class
director were all made while you were living in your home country.
You only left a year ago, Sir.'

Makhmalbaf would have none of that: 'No, madam. I repeat, I
do not consider myself part of the Iranian cinema and will not take
part in your project under any circumstances.'

I gasped. He rang off. After a while, I thought I would try to
convince him through his daughter Samira, and, anyway, an interview with her, a young Iranian artist who had attracted a lot of

positive attention, would be very interesting in itself. I tried again.
Sahar was not as warm and friendly as before but she did pass me
on to Samira, who was polite and obliging. I asked her:

'Ms Makhmalbaf, does not such a project interest you?'

She answered: 'I find it very interesting and worthwhile. I do
hope that you will carry it through. However, it wouldn't be nice of
me to be in a book which "Baba" refuses to be in.'

I persisted: 'But, madam, you are a world-class film-maker in
your own right. Why can't you take part in it even though it interests you?'

She merely repeated: 'I cannot do it without "Baba".'

NOTES

Introduction: New Iranian Cinema in its Cultural, Historical and Political Context

1. From Baran Kosari's open letter to the Ministry of Culture and Islamic Guidance after it ordered the closure of the House of Cinema in 2012. Baran Kosari is an award-winning Iranian actress and the daughter of the director Rakhshan Bani-Etemad, who is also interviewed in this book.

2. Hamid Naficy, 'Islamizing Film Culture in Iran: A Post-Khatami Update', in Richard Tapper (ed), *The New Iranian Cinema: Politics, Representation and Identity* (London: I.B.Tauris, 2002), p. 27.

3. *Tehran Times*, 28 December 2011, vol. 11331.

4. The re-election of Mahmoud Ahmadinejad in 2009 gave rise to one of the largest protests in Iran since the Islamic Revolution. The elections were considered engineered and fraudulent by many voters, who took to the streets for weeks afterwards. The protests were brutally repressed by the Revolutionary Guards; reports about the killing and torturing of protestors reached the world thanks to Facebook and Twitter and released a wave of sympathy for the agitators. This movement became known as the 'Green Wave' or 'Green Movement'. The parallels between this uprising, the crushed hopes and the resulting despair amongst Iranians were pointed out by

many observers during the so-called 'Arabellion' that followed only a year later. Ali Ansari's *Crisis of Authority: Iran's 2009 Presidential Election* (London: Chatham House, 2010) gives a good account of the events that led to the fiasco of the 2009 presidential election and their aftermath, which is still felt in Iran today.

5.   Simin Behbahani and Amir Hassan Cheheltan were interviewed in my previous book, *Iranian Writers Uncensored: Freedom, Democracy and the Word in Contemporary Iran* (London: Dalkey Archive Press, 2012), pp. 3–14, 181–200.

6.   This institute was founded in 1983 as a semi-governmental 'mediator' between the Ministry of Culture and Islamic Guidance and film-makers. It helped film-makers to finance their films to a certain extent and played an important part in distributing and promoting them abroad. For details see Hamid Dabashi, *Close Up: Iranian Cinema, Past, Present, and Future* (London: Verso, 2001); Richard Tapper (ed), *The New Iranian Cinema*; Hamid Reza Sadr, *Iranian Cinema: A Political History* (London: I.B.Tauris, 2006).

7.   The Revolutionary Guards were originally a paramilitary organization that tried to impose the Islamic ideology of revolution by force. Their missionary activities expanded during the Iran–Iraq War, in which thousands of them zealously fought for the cause of the Islamic Revolution and its export to neighbouring Iraq. Today they are a gigantic, formidably armed organization and not only control the export trade but also have immense influence on Iran's foreign policy and its hegemonic ambitions in the region. Many observers sarcastically remark that, given that 80 per cent of the export and import of satellite dishes is either directly or indirectly in the hands of the Revolutionary Guards, dismantling them is yet another way in which this mafia-like organization can maximize its profit by forcing people to buy new dishes on the black market after having had their old ones dismantled for free, as it were. For a more detailed account of the Revolutionary Guards and their activities see Ali Alfoneh, 'The Revolutionary Guards' Looting of Iran's Economy', *AEI Online*, 23 June 2010 (http://www.aei.org/article/foreign-and-defense-policy/regional/middle-east-and-north-africa/the-revolutionary-guards-looting-of-irans-economy).

8.   Mehrjui's *Gaav* was made in 1969 – ten years before the Islamic Revolution – and was banned from being screened in Iran. It had to

be smuggled out of the country in 1971 in order to take part in the Venice Film Festival (see John Wakeman, *World Film Directors*, vol. 2 (New York: The H.W. Wilson Company, 1988), pp. 663–9). The fate of this film shows that censorship is not an exclusively 'Islamic', post-revolutionary phenomenon in Iran, but that it existed under the shah's totalitarian regime as well.

9. Nine months after the monarchy was toppled in Iran, a group of Islamist students and paramilitary Revolutionary Guards occupied the American embassy in Tehran and held 52 Americans hostage for 444 days from 4 November 1979 to 20 January 1981. The crisis was heightened by the failed attempt of two US helicopters to rescue the hostages, who were freed only after Iraq invaded Iran in September 1980 and Iran agreed to enter negotiations with the US through Algeria's mediation. This was the darkest chapter in the history of Iranian–American relations and to this day remains a source of distrust between the two countries.

10. The reader should note that the term 'West' is sometimes used synonymously with the word 'world'. The author is aware of the problems inherent in this but relies on the works of the philosopher Dariush Shayegan to justify the usage. Shayegan sees little sense in using words that are popular in post-colonial societies for describing the present geopolitical situation. Terms such as 'the usurping West' or 'the exploited Third World' are obsolete in his eyes. In Shayegan's view, the only terms that can 'classify' countries are 'modern' and 'not-modern' and 'anti-modern'. Modern values are universal and can be acquired by all nations regardless of race, religion and geography. The scope of this book does not allow an extended treatment of the term 'modernity' and what it means geopolitically in the West or East. What we can observe, however, is that those parts of the world that generated modernity in the last two centuries are generally called 'the West'. Furthermore in Shayegan's eyes, those countries that lag behind in modernization are excluded from this 'world' and are thus not global actors. Shayegan's attitude to this part of the world is very radical. He goes so far as to view 'non-modern' countries as geographical entities (Shayegan calls these countries 'grey' entities) of which the rest of the world cannot be conscious. In his view, these countries are, therefore, not part of the world. See Dariush Shayegan, *Afsoonzadegi-e jadid: hoviat-e chehel tekkeh va tafa-*

kor-e sayar (Tehran: Nashr-e Farzan, 2001), pp. 29–33.

11. Said Amir Arjomand (ed), *Authority and Political Culture in Shi'ism* (Suny Series in Near Eastern Studies, 1988).

12. Naz Massouni, 'Iran: A Cinema Born out of Poetry and Resistance', *Socialist Review*, September 2005 (http://www.socialistreview.org.uk).

13. Ruhollah Khomeini, *Islam and Revolution: Writings and Declarations of Imam Khomeini*, trans. Hamid Algar (Berkeley: Mizan Press, 1981), p. 258.

14. Wakeman, *World Film Directors*, vol. 2, pp. 663–9.

15. This phenomenon can be seen in all totalitarian and isolated countries, such as Cuba or North Korea. All states that have cut off their society from the influence of the 'West' and its socio-economic system suffer the same fate: they are cut off from the time and space of the rest of the world.

16. Ansari, *Crisis of Authority*; Abbas Milani, 'Cracks in the Regime', *Journal of Democracy*, vol. 20(4), October 2009.

17. Julian Borger, 'Iran nuclear deal: world powers reach historic agreement to lift sanctions', *Guardian*, 14 July 2015 (http://www.theguardian.com/world/2015/jul/14/iran-nuclear-programme-world-powers-historic-deal-lift-sanctions).

18. His latest film *Taxi* won the Golden Bear for best film at the Berlin Film Festival in 2015. The prize was collected by his ten-year-old niece, as he is still banned from travelling abroad. See Ben Beaumont-Thomas, 'Jafar Panahi asks for Golden Bear winner *Taxi* to be shown in Iran', *Guardian*, 17 February 2015 (http://www.theguardian.com/film/2015/feb/17/jafar-panahi-golden-bear-taxi-iran).

Chapter 1. Mohammad Beheshti: The Role of Post-Revolutionary Institutions in the Development of Iranian Cinema

1. 'Film Farsi' is a term commonly used for pre-revolutionary Persian B-movies of little substance that rely on violence and the sex appeal of the main actors and actresses. Thanks to their mixture of bare flesh, dance, music and simple plot, these films were (and still are via underground distributors and satellite TV) very popular among the masses in Iran, although considered sinful by the clergy and looked down upon by the Iranian intelligentsia.

2. Since 2002, the Film Museum of Iran has been housed in Bagh-e Ferdows (Paradise Garden), a historical palace in north Tehran, built during Nasser al-Din Shah Qajar's reign (1848–96) for his daughter. The museum exhibits documents, images, equipment and other memorabilia and holds seminars and conferences on Iranian cinema.

3. Sadegh Hedayat (1903–51) is arguably the most renowned modern Persian writer. His *The Blind Owl* (1937) is considered a masterpiece of modern Persian literature. He was also a renowned scholar of Indo-Iranian languages and Iranian history. Although he had many enemies, owing to his European lifestyle and writing, his suicide in Paris in 1951 came as a shock to the literary world of the time.

   Forough Farrokhzad (1935–67) was the most influential female poet of twentieth-century Iran, not only because of her poetry but also her bohemian, unorthodox lifestyle. In 1962 she also made the celebrated documentary *The House is Black* about a leper colony in Iran. She left her husband and son in an age when women's emancipation was not part of the Persian vocabulary and wrote openly about female lust and love in a country where this subject was taboo. She lived in an open relationship with the famous avant-garde film-maker Ebrahim Golestan until her untimely death in a car crash in Tehran at the age of 32. To this day, it is still not clear whether it was an accident, suicide or even murder. Her writings were censored and partly banned both before and after the Islamic Revolution. See 'Farrokzad, Forug-Zaman (b. Tehran, 1935; d. Tehran, 1967), usually known as Forug, Persian poet', *Encyclopaedia Iranica* (http://www.iranicaonline.org/articles/farrokzad-forug-zaman).

4. Along with Forough Farrokhzad, Nima Youshij (1896–1960) and Ahmad Shamlu (1925–2000) are doyens of modern Persian poetry. They belonged to a generation of Persian poets that broke radically with the classical forms of poetry and advocated liberating verse from the shackles of thousand-year-old rhymes and rhythms.

5. On 30 September 2005 the Danish newspaper *Jyllands-Posten* published 12 cartoons depicting the Prophet Mohammad. This led to a huge controversy regarding the boundaries of respect for religious values and of freedom of speech in the press. In some Muslim countries, such as Pakistan, the controversy led to violent riots.

6. A Hebrew term for the Holocaust.

7. Mohammad Ali Fardin (1930–2000) was an extremely popular Iranian actor who starred in numerous films in the 1950s, 1960s and 1970s. He tried to shake off the image of the leading actor of shallow 1970s films by taking on more serious roles, but never really succeeded in doing so.

8. A drink similar to *raki*.

9. This interview took place about a year before the 2009 uprisings (also known as the Green Movement), which were caused by the fraudulent re-election of President Ahmadinejad. The uprisings were brutally suppressed and the restrictions became even harsher. The censorship policies of the regime soon followed suit. A telling example of this development is the fate of the film-maker Panahi, who has also been interviewed in this collection. To date, Panahi's *Offside* has not obtained permission to be screened. Panahi himself was imprisoned on charges of being an 'enemy of the state' and of 'disseminating unsuitable art' a few years after this interview was conducted.

10. Saadi Shirazi (Saadi of Shiraz) was one of the most important Persian poets of the medieval period, whose fame extended beyond the Persian-speaking world. Worldwide he is now considered a great master in the classical literary tradition. His most famous works are *Bostan* (*The Orchard*) and *Gulistan* (*The Rose Garden*), written in 1257 and 1258 respectively.

11. In 1974 Bahman Farmanara filmed Houshang Golshiri's novel *Shazdeh Ehtejab* (*Prince Ehtejab*, published in 1968), for which he won the Grand Prix for best film at the Tehran International Film Festival in 1976. *Dash Akol* (*Brother Akol*) is one of the stories in Sadegh Hedayat's collection of short stories *Seh Ghatreh Khoon* (*Three Drops of Blood*) published in 1932. The story was filmed by Masoud Kimiai in 1971. See Hamid Naficy, *A Social History of Iranian Cinema, Volume 2: The Industrializing Years, 1941–1978* (Durham, NC: Duke University Press, 2011).

12. Sohrab Sepehri (1928–80) was one of Iran's foremost modernist poets and painters. He was a traveller who tried to convey a universal spirituality and ecological awareness in his works. See 'Sepehri, Sohrab (1928–80). Notable Iranian poet and painter', *Encyclopaedia Iranica* (http://www.iranicaonline.org/articles/sepehri-sohrab).

13. The Safavid dynasty ruled mainly in Iran and parts of Mesopotamia,

the Caucasus, Central Asia and the Indian subcontinent from 1502 to 1736. Their capital was moved twice, first from Tabriz to Qazvin and then from Qazvin to Isfahan. Isfahan was the capital of the dynasty for the greater part of their reign. See 'Safavid Dynasty', *Encyclopaedia Britannica* (http://www.britannica.com/EBchecked/topic/516019/Safavid-Dynasty).

Under the reign of the Qajar dynasty (1794–1925) the diplomatic contacts, trade and cultural exchanges between Iran and the West intensified (the camera was introduced to Iran during the reign of Nasser al-Din Shah Qajar, who ruled from 1848 to 1896). The consequence of this development was an increase in rivalry between the Russian and European powers over Iran and its territories, which led to many wars and unrest in the region. The Qajars moved their capital to Tehran, which has remained the capital of Iran to this day. See 'Qajar Dynasty', *Encyclopaedia Britannica* (http://www.britannica.com/EBchecked/topic/485405/Qajar-Dynasty).

14. After the revolution the Islamic Moral Police was founded as a means to enforce 'Islamic' behaviour and way of life on the population. They would warn or even arrest young people for holding hands, kissing or wearing provocative clothes in public. The target of the Moral Police, however, is mainly young girls who do not wear their *hijab* properly.

Chapter 2. Bahram Beyzaie: The Myth of Revolutionary Cinema

1. Beyzaie is referring to the woman-protagonist (played by Susan Taslimi) who 'adopts' a little boy fleeing from the Iran–Iraq War in the south to the relatively peaceful Caspian Sea in the north.
2. Shortly after this interview was conducted in 2010, Beyzaie left Iran for San Francisco in December of that year to hold discussions and workshops on Iranian cinema at a number of universities such as Stanford, UCLA and UC Berkeley. He denies all rumours about emigrating to the USA and insists that his stay there is solely for teaching and research purposes.
3. This film was made in 1969 and was banned for one year before being released in 1970.
4. As Beyzaie mentions these scripts were never made into films. The English titles of the scripts are my translations.

5. Abul-Qasem Ferdowsi (940–1019 or 1029) was the renowned poet of the national epic of Iran, *Shahnameh* (*Book of Kings*). See 'Ferdowsi, Abul-Qasem', *Encyclopaedia Iranica* (http://www.iranicaonline.org/articles/ferdowsi-index).

6. *Dibachehye Novin–e Shahnameh* was published in 1993. However, Beyzaie was not allowed to make it into a play or a film. The English title is my translation.

7. *Avesta* is the holy book of the Zoroastrians. This religion emerged in the second millennium BCE among the Aryans that populated the Iranian plateau and the Punjab. The majority of Iranians were Zoroastrians before the Arab invasion of the Persian Empire in seventh century CE. See 'Zoroastrianism: Historical Review', *Encyclopaedia Iranica* (http://www.iranicaonline.org/articles/zoroastrianism-i-historical-review).

    Khodaynameh or *Khwaday-Namag* was a Middle Persian history text written during the Sassanid period (224–651 CE). It is believed that Ferdowsi used this text as a source for his masterpiece *Shahnameh* (*Book of Kings*) written in the tenth century CE.

    Hezar Afsan (*Thousand Tales*) is a collection of Indo-Iranian stories that was translated from Middle Persian into Arabic in the fourth century CE. In the eighteenth century, the Arabic translation, *ALF LAYLA WA LAYLA*, became known in the English-speaking world as *The Arabian Nights*. See 'ALF LAYLA WA LAYLA "One thousand nights and one night," Arabic title of the world-famous collection of tales known in English as *The Arabian Nights*', *Encyclopaedia Iranica* (http://www.iranicaonline.org/articles/alf-layla-wa-layla).

8. Rudaki (858–941) is considered a founder of classical Persian literature; Ferdowsi (940–1020) is the writer of the Persian epic *Shahnameh* (*Book of Kings*); Rumi (1207–73) is a Persian mystic poet and Sufi, whose popularity has been growing rapidly in the West in recent years; Saadi (1210–91) and Hafez (1325–89) are Persian poets, whose tombs in Shiraz, southern Iran, are visited by thousands of pilgrims each year.

9. Amir Naderi (1945–) was an important film-maker of New Iranian Cinema in the 1970s and 1980s, but was forced into exile in the early 1990s after the regime made it virtually impossible for him to work in Iran. His most important film was *The Runner* (1984), which gave a poignant and undogmatic portrayal of a boy's life in war-ridden

Abadan, in southern Iran. The film was eventually banned as it did not comply with the regime's propagandistic views about the Iran–Iraq War. Naderi now lives and works in the USA.

Chapter 3. Abbas Kiarostami: Where is the Revolution?

1. Alberto Elena, *The Cinema of Abbas Kiarostami* (Saqi Books, 2005).
2. It is important to bear in mind that this interview with Kiarostami took place 18 months before his film *Copie Conforme* (*Certified Copy*) was made in 2010. After making *Like Someone in Love* in Japan (2012) it became obvious that making films outside his 'natural surroundings' was becoming routine – especially considering that both films were received very positively by critics and viewers.
3. Catherine Deneuve kissed Kiarostami while presenting him with the *Palme d'Or* trophy. The press in the Islamic Republic reacted violently to this, as the Sharia strictly forbids all physical contact between unrelated men and women.
4. Kiarostami is also a well-known poet; his poetry, which draws on both traditional Persian verse and Japanese haiku, has been translated into several languages. The English translations include the collections *Walking with the Wind,* translated by Ahmad Karimi-Hakkak and Michael Beard (Harvard University Film Archive, 2002) and *A Wolf Lying in Wait* (Tehran: Nashr-e Sokhan, 2005), translated by Karim Emami and Michael Beard to great acclaim. As a poet he sees himself as a 'modern nonconformist' who is all the same acutely aware of the millennium-old tradition and heritage of Persian poetry. In his two books *Hafez According to Kiarostami* (Tehran: Nashr-e Farzan, 2006) and *Saadi According to Kiarostami* (Tehran: Nilufar, 2008) he shows an imaginatively modern understanding of the works of these masters of Persian poetry by framing a selection of their lyrics in a form based on haikus and thus presenting them in a new light. His latest poetic work, which was published after this interview took place, is *Atash (The Fire). Selection of Shams Sonnets by Abbas Kiarostami* (Tehran: Chap va Pakhsh-e Nazar, 2011).
5. It should be noted once again that the situation has changed in the past two years even for Kiarostami (thanks to the anti-government Green Movement in 2009). He made his latest films, *Copie Conforme* and *Like Someone in Love,* in France and Japan respectively.

NOTES TO PAGES 65–99

6. The film was banned for one year and had to be smuggled out of the country in order to be shown at the Venice Film Festival in 1971. See 'Dariush Mehrjui. Filmmaker, producer, and scriptwriter', *Iran Chamber Society* (http://www.iranchamber.com/cinema/dMehrjui/dariush_Mehrjui.php).

7. Gilles Jacob began managing the Cannes Film Festival in 1977. He became the festival's president in 2001. Jacob is one of the most influential men in world cinema.

8. Film critics often refer to Golestan's speech at the 1969 Shiraz Festival in which he did not hide his contempt for both Iranian viewers and Iranian cultural institutions.

9. Flowers, such as violets, daffodils, hyacinths and tulips, are planted in Iran during the Noruz festivities on 20 or 21 March (equinox), at which people celebrate the New Year and welcome the spring.

10. *Casablanca* was produced by Warner Bros and released in 1943. It is important to bear in mind that as an American production it was not made amidst the war in Europe but in the US, which, with the exception of Pearl Harbor, did not suffer attacks or invasions. This difference makes Kiarostami's comparison a little problematic: Iran didn't merely participate in a geographically distant war as the US did. The lives of Iranian civilians were directly affected by warfare and therefore the social context for making war films was different from that in the US in the 1940s.

Chapter 4. Dariush Mehrjui: Islamic Ideology and Post-revolutionary Intellectual Films

1. Esmail Fasih (1935–2009) died a few months after this interview was conducted. He is considered one of the greatest contemporary novelists in Iran. His *Zemestan-e 62* (*Winter of '62*) is seen by many as a masterpiece. His novels have been banned and it is now extremely difficult to get hold of them.

2. Hamid Naficy, *The New Iranian Cinema, Politics, and Identity*, ed Richard Tarper (London: I.B.Tauris, 2002), p. 50.

3. This film was screened only once in Iran and has had limited screenings in Europe and North America. It is still banned in Iran.

4. Mohsen Makhmalbaf, who is also included in this book, was a very pro-revolutionary Islamic director in the first years of his career.

The chapter in this book gives a good insight into his transformation
from a pro-regime film-maker into a dissident artist in exile.

Chapter 5. Bahman Farmanara: Exporting New Iranian Cinema

1. During the religious anti-shah uprisings of 1963, which led to the
    imprisonment and forced exile of Ayatollah Khomeini (who later
    became Leader of the Islamic Republic after the 1979 revolution),
    the government tried to quell the protests by giving the religious
    currents in society enough scope to grow. The Hosseiniyeh Ershad
    was a centre for the propagation of Islamic values and culture,
    founded in Tehran in 1967 by a number of clergy and Bazaari
    merchants. It aimed at re-educating the youth and eradicating
    the secularization of the school system. The centre was eventually
    closed in 1972 after a number of prominent members of the opposi-
    tion, such as Ali Shariati (who died under mysterious circumstances
    in Southampton, UK, in 1977), delivered fiery speeches against the
    shah there. See Baqer Moin, *Khomeini: Life of the Ayatollah* (London:
    I.B.Tauris, 1999).
2. Seyyed Mir-Hossein Mousavi was one of the reformist candidates
    who ran, and lost, against Ahmadinejad in the fraudulent presiden-
    tial elections of 2009. The elections gave rise to the greatest upris-
    ings against the regime since 1979, which were brutally oppressed by
    Ahmadinejad's supporters. Mousavi and a number of his colleagues
    have been under house arrest ever since.
3. See Note 1 above.
4. Mahmoud Dolatabadi (1940–) is one of the most famous and best-
    loved Persian writers living in Iran today. He is revered as a real-
    ist novelist with a lyrical style. His epic novel *Klidar* is considered a
    milestone in contemporary Persian literature and *The Colonel* was
    listed for the Man Asian Literary Prize in 2011. His work has recently
    been translated into English, German, French and other languages.

    Simin Daneshvar (1921–2012) was the *grande dame* of modern
    Iranian novel-writing. Her masterpiece *Savushun* (1969) was the
    first novel to have been written by a woman in Iran and went on to
    become a best-seller despite having been repeatedly banned.
5. A radical shift towards fundamentalist Islam in the early 1970s led
    to the closure of all film theatres in Saudi Arabia. They reopened in

2009, soon after this interview was conducted (see 'Saudis in Riyadh enjoy first taste of film-going in three decades', *Guardian*, 9 June 2009).

6.   Mahvash and Foroozan were pre-revolutionary actresses, popular for their lascivious dances in B-movies.

7.   Googoosh (real name Faegheh Atashin, 1950–) is an Iranian actress and singer, whose popularity in the 1960s and 1970s exceeded that of all her contemporaries. She was an icon of popular culture before the revolution not only in Iran but also among other Persian-speaking peoples, such as the Afghans and Tadjiks. After having been banned from singing and acting for over 20 years, she left the country in 2000 and continues her artistic activities within the Iranian diaspora – mainly in Los Angeles. Thanks to satellite TV, the number of her fans in Iran has been growing continuously.

8.   Ebi (1949–) and Dariush (1951–) are popular Iranian singers who were forced to leave the country after the revolution. They now live in Los Angeles and, thanks to satellite TV and the internet, enjoy great popularity among Iranians today. Akbar Golpayegani (1933–) is a famous singer of traditional and classical Persian music, who also experiments with Persian pop fusions.

9.   Masaki Kobayashi (1916–66), Yasujirō Ozu (1903–63) and Akira Kurosawa (1919–98) were important film-makers of the Japanese New Wave. This movement started in the 1950s and reached its peak in the 1960s and 1970s.

10. Kiarostami did eventually give up film-making in Iran after the government became increasingly aggressive towards film-makers in the second period of Ahmadinejad's presidency. See the interview with Kiarostami in this book.

Chapter 6. Rakhshan Bani-Etemad: Cinema as a Mirror of the Urban Image

1.   This interview took place a year and a half before Saudi Arabia's first – and only cinema – was opened (see 'Saudis in Riyadh enjoy first taste of film-going in three decades', *Guardian*, 9 June 2009). Whereas over the last two decades the percentage of female film-makers has been consistently higher than in most other Asian countries, the first film to be made by a Saudi woman, Haifa Al-Mansour,

was only released in 2012 (see 'Wadjda: Saudi Arabia, Cinema and Women's Rights', *Film International*, 23 March 2013).

2. Baran Kosari, the main character of *Mainline* and daughter of Bani-Etemad, was banned from acting and appearing on screen in 2012. Consequently, *Mainline* was also banned from screening. See 'Cinema under the Sword of Suppression', *Iran Human Rights Voice*, 16 December 2012 (http://www.ihrv.org/inf/?p=5189).

3. During the Iran–Iraq War many child-soldiers (some as young as 12) were brainwashed and told that by going to the front and dying in battle against the Iraqi infidel, they would be looked upon by Allah as martyrs and go to heaven. Many of these young warriors carried symbolic keys around their necks.

Chapter 7. Majid Majidi: The Revolution and the Cleansing of Film Farsi

1. In 1998 Majidi's film *Children of Heaven* was the first Iranian film to be nominated for an Oscar and so helped to put Iranian film on the agenda of American commercial cinemas and consolidate its place on the 'radar' of the Academy. His compatriot Asghar Farhadi took this development a step further by actually winning the Oscar for best foreign film in 2012 for *A Separation*.

2. The production costs of this film (said to be over $35 million) were unprecedented in the history of Iranian cinema. The master cinematographer Vittorio Storaro, who had worked with directors such as Bertolucci and Coppola and whose works include *1900*, *Last Tango in Paris*, *The Last Emperor*, *Apocalypse Now* and *The Sheltering Sky*, is said to have brought his own crew from Italy to shoot scenes in Iran, Morocco and South Africa. Oscar-winning Scott E. Anderson was responsible for the visual effects in the film. See Saeed Kamali Dehghan, 'Iranian film on Prophet Muhammad set for premiere', *Guardian*, 30 January 2015 (http://www.theguardian.com/world/2015/jan/30/iranian-film-prophet-muhammad-premiere).

3. See Dehghan, 'Iranian film on Prophet Muhammad set for premiere'.

4. See 'Saudi furious over Iranian film about Prophet Muhammad', *Arab News*, 6 September 2015 (http://www.albawaba.com/entertainment/saudi-furious-over-iranian-film-about-prophet-muhammad-739980); Benn Child, 'Indian clerics issue fatwa against makers of Muhammad: The Messenger of God', *Guardian*, 14 September

2015 (http://www.theguardian.com/film/2015/sep/14/fatwa-muhammad-the-messenger-of-god-majid-majidi-ar-rahman).

5.   Mohammad Beheshti was the most famous head of the Farabi Cinema Foundation, from 1983 to 1994. Under his management Iranian cinema witnessed a great surge of success. He is the only interviewee in this book who is not a film-maker.

Mohammad Khatami was president of Iran for two terms from 1997 to 2005. His landslide victory in 1997 over Ali Akbar Nateq-Nouri, the candidate favoured by the right-wing conservatives, was compared by many to the 'Velvet Revolution' and the end of political tyranny in Eastern Europe. Despite all this, the assassination of intellectuals, artists and dissidents both inside and outside Iran, which became known as the 'Chain Murders' and had started in 1988 under President Rafsanjani, continued well into the Khatami era. Khatami's opening towards the West (called the 'dialogue among civilizations') did loosen to some extent the grip of censorship on artists, film-makers and writers.

Mir-Hossein Mousavi was prime minister of Iran during the Iran–Iraq War from 1981 to 1988. He was also Mohammad Khatami's political advisor during his presidency from 1997 to 2005. He was a candidate in 2009 against Ahmadinejad for the office of presidency. After his defeat, his followers claimed that the elections had been fraudulent and took to the streets. Their wave of protest became known as the Green Movement. Since then Mousavi has been under house arrest. With the election of Hassan Rouhani in 2013, the hopes of the Reformist politicians for his release are rising.

6.   *Dar Emtedad–e Shab* (*Throughout the Night*, 1978) is a drama starring the Iranian singer Googoosh. See Chapter 5, note 7.

7.   Mohsen Makhmalbaf's *Kandahar* (2001) was one of the few Iranian films to be shown at the White House. Makhmalbaf was accused of providing the Bush administration with propaganda material for America's war against the Taliban in Afghanistan in 2003. See 'The film Bush asked to see', *Guardian*, 26 October 2001.

Chapter 8. Jafar Panahi: Cinema and Resistance

1.   Ben Beaumont-Thomas, 'Jafar Panahi asks for Golden Bear winner *Taxi* to be shown in Iran', *Guardian*, 17 February 2015 (http://www.

theguardian.com/film/2015/feb/17/jafar-panahi-golden-bear-taxi-iran).

2. This interview took place before Dalkey Archive Press published the English version of this book in 2012.

Chapter 9. Tahmineh Milani: New Iranian Cinema and the Education of the Masses

1. In 1971 National Iranian Radio and Television (NIRT), founded in 1966, became incorporated as a public broadcasting monopoly and was run independently. The shah appointed Reza Ghotbi (1940–) as its first director-general. Ghotbi remained director-general until 1979, when the NIRT was abolished by the revolutionaries and renamed Islamic Republic of Iran Broadcasting (IRIB). Ghotbi left Iran after the revolution and is currently living in the USA. See http://en.wikipedia.org/wiki/National_Iranian_Radio_%26_ Television.

2. Ebrahim Golestan (1922–) is a pioneering Iranian film-maker of art films. He is also known for having had a 'scandalous' relationship with the poet Forough Farrokhzad. He had a very hard time making films in Iran under the shah and left for the UK in 1975, having become disenchanted with the government and with society.

3. Parviz Sayyad (1939–) is an Iranian satirist, film-maker and actor who became hugely famous in Iran for his feature films about a naive peasant, Samad, who is eternally wooing his sweetheart, Leila. He also acted in many comedies in both film and theatre. He was forced to leave Iran for the USA after the revolution, where he is still active today.

4. Despite extensive research I have been unable to confirm the quote attributed to Louis Kahn by Ms Milani.

5. Kamal-ol-Molk (1847–1940) was an Iranian painter who revolutionized and modernized the artform in Iran by applying European painting techniques and skills to traditional subjects. He was a 'realist' whose subjects came from everyday life and he 'freed' Iranian painting by taking his canvas and tools from the atelier out into the open.

6. The trilogy is made up of *Wandering Island* (some have translated it as *Island of Wandering*; *Jazire-ye Sargardāni*, 1992); *Wandering Cameleer*

(*Sāreban-e Sargardān*, 2001); *Wandering Mountain* (*Kuh-e Sargardān*, never published).

Chapter 10. Ebrahim Hatamikia: Cinema, War and Peace

1. The Mojahedin-e Khalq (MEK) is a militant dissident group that was originally allied with Khomeini against the shah, but fell into disgrace in the early 1980s – two years after the revolution. Its members were brutally oppressed, tortured and executed by their former allies – the Islamic Republic. Their remaining members left Iran in the 1980s and formed a self-governing entity in Iraq, from where they conducted anti-regime propaganda as well as military attacks against Iran. They were considered a terrorist group by the EU and the US until recently. See Ervand Abrahamian, *The Iranian Mojahedin* (London and New Haven: Yale University Press, 1992) and Anne Singleton and Massoud Khodabandeh, *The Life of Camp Ashraf: Mojahedin-e Khalq – Victims of Many Masters* (Leeds: Iran Interlink, 2011).
2. Both the title and the poster of Hatamikia's *Che* are strongly reminiscent of Steven Soderbergh's film *Che* released in 2008 about the Argentine Marxist revolutionary and guerrilla fighter Che Guevara.
3. Ladane Nasseri, 'Filmmakers Clash as Rouhani's Agenda Leaves Iranians Divided', *Bloomberg Business*, 27 October 2014 (http://www.bloomberg.com/news/articles/2014-10-27/filmmakers-clash-in-iran-as-rouhani-agenda-leaves-nation-divided).
4. Kianoush Ayari's (1951–) war films are considered masterpieces. He was born in Ahwaz, south Iran, which was heavily bombed during the Iran–Iraq War. His film *Ansouyeh Atash* (*The Other Side of Fire*), released in 1990, is a poignant portrait of a boy reminiscing about his hometown, which was ruined and lost during the conflict.
5. Jahad-e Sazandegi, or the 'Jihad of Construction', began as a movement of volunteers to help with the 1979 harvest but soon took on a broader, more official role in the countryside. It was involved with road building, piped water, electrification, clinics, schools and irrigation canals. It also provided extension services, seeds, loans, etc. to small farmers. Finally it was merged with the Agriculture Ministry in 2001 to form the Ministry of Jihad-e Agriculture. See http://en.wikipedia.org/wiki/Organizations_of_the_Iranian_

Revolution#Jihad_of_Construction.

6. *Torbat* is the sacred earth from which faithful Muslims make the piece of clay that they use for their prayers. It is usually found near holy places. In this case, the frontline was near Karbala, the shrine of the Third Shi'a Imam, Hussein, and so the earth was considered sacred by devout soldiers.

7. This is the date of the presidential elections of 1997, which led to the landslide victory of the liberal, reformist clergyman Mohammad Khatami against the more conservative candidates favoured by the Leader Khamenei. Many compared Khatami to the Soviet reformer Mikhail Gorbachev, but were greatly disappointed by Khatami's weakness in face of the conservative establishment.

8. After extensive modification, the film finally came out in 2010.

9. Theo Angelopoulos (1935–2012) was a world-class Greek director whose films, such as *Eternity and a Day* (winner of the *Palme d'Or* in 1998) and *Ulysses Gaze* (1995), have become canonical in European cinema.

Chapter 11. Mohsen Makhmalbaf: An Interview That Never Was

1. Hamid Dabashi, 'Dead Certainties: The Early Makhmalbaf', in Tapper (ed), *The New Iranian Cinema*, p. 123. Makhmalbaf reflected on this event, which was a turning point in his life, in his autobiographical film *Nun o Goldun* (*A Moment of Innocence*, 1996). More details on Makhmalbaf's life and work can be found on his website, http://www.makhmalbaf.com.

2. *Ibid.*, pp. 123, 117–53.

3. 'J'accuse' is the title of an Émile Zola letter in which he protested against the conviction of Alfred Dreyfus for treason. The political and intellectual crisis that was caused by this conviction became known as the 'Dreyfus Affair'. The controversy centred on the question of the guilt or innocence of army captain Alfred Dreyfus, who had been convicted of treason for allegedly selling military secrets to the Germans in December 1894. See 'Dreyfus Affair', *Encyclopaedia Britannica*, http://www.britannica.com/EBchecked/topic/171538/Dreyfus-affair.

4. Ian Black, 'Iran should face smarter sanctions, says Mohsen Makhmalbaf', *Guardian*, 25 November 2009.

5. Hamid Dabashi, *Makhmalbaf at Large: The Making of a Rebel Filmmaker* (London: I.B.Tauris, 2008).

6. On its website, the Hozeh Honari describes its history and aims as follows: 'In the very first years of the 1980s, "Hozeh Honari" joined the "Islamic Development Organization" or, as we pronounce it in Farsi, "Sazman-e- Tablighat-e- Islami" and since then it has acted as one of the most important artistic and cultural institutions in Islamic Iran, casting its role as a major agent in the creation of artistic and cultural productions in line with the demands of the Islamic revolution.' See http://www.hozehonari.com/Default.aspx?page=17449.

    In his book *The Politics of Iranian Cinema: Film and Society in the Islamic Republic* (Oxford and New York: Routledge, 2010), pp. 38–9, Saeed Zeidabadi-Nejat speaks of this organization as a 'parallel organization to the Ministry of Culture and Islamic Guidance' with its own sources of funding: '*Howzeh-ye Honari* was created to produce propaganda for the Islamic regime. Since the head of the organization was directly appointed by the Supreme Leader [i.e. Ayatollah Khomeini], and it had its own sources of funding and later even technical equipment, the Art Centre became a powerful parallel organization to the MCIG [Ministry of Culture and Islamic Guidance].' He goes on to say that the young Makhmalbaf, one of the founding members of the Centre, was a very active Islamic filmmaker at that time. 'The Centre was also the place where many of the ideologically committed film-makers such as Makhmalbaf and Majidi learned film-making.'

7. Since he left Iran for good a decade ago, Makhmalbaf's artistic career has not reached the heights of his outstanding achievements during his years in Iran. The films that he made in Iran, both his opponents and admirers agree, greatly contributed to putting New Iranian Cinema on the map; few films could compete with the elegance, humanity and wit of *Gabbeh*, *Salaam Cinema* or *The Bread and Alley*. However, contrary to his opponents' prophecy about Makhmalbaf's artistic death in exile, his career as a diasporic film-maker is emerging steadily. The warm welcome and good reviews that he received for his film *The President* at the 2014 Venice Film Festival testify to this. See Peter Bradshaw, 'The President review: satire, suspense and gusto – Venice film festival', *Guardian*, 27 August 2014 (http://www. theguardian.com/film/2014/aug/27/the-president-review-satire-venice-film-festival).

INDEX